My Father, His Daughter

My Father, His Daughter

YAËL DAYAN

Farrar, Straus & Giroux

NEW YORK

Library of Congress Cataloging in Publication Data
Dayan, Yaël.
My father, his daughter.
1. Dayan, Moshe, 1915-1981. 2. Dayan, Yaël.
—Biography. 3. Statesmen—Israel—
Biography. 4. Israel—Armed Forces—Biography.
5. Authors, Israeli—Biography. I. Title.
DS126.6.D3D38 1985 956.94'05'0922 [B] 85-15995

For my mother,
who loved, understood, and
tolerated us both

F O R E W O R D

This is a book I had to write. George Weidenfeld, my British publisher and friend, believed it should be published, and read as well. I thank him affectionately for his unfailing confidence.

Dov Sion, my husband, objects to and abhors any self-induced exposure. With gentleness and understanding, he deviated from this principle and gave me his full support during the long and often painful writing of this book. David Rieff, senior editor at Farrar, Straus and Giroux, was my first objective reader. I am indebted to him not only for editing the manuscript for publication but for easing my anxieties and enabling me to work with the right perspective on the final version.

My friends Shimshon Arad, Kay Cohen, Bess Simon, Betty Epstein, Marianne Griessman, and Ira Bermak were kind enough to read the book in manuscript form. For their comments, encouragement, and support, I am profoundly grateful.

I must mention with thanks Pamela Levy, who managed the impossible and turned the undecipherable handwritten manuscript, with attention and care, into a typed readable one.

My mother's contribution to this book was invaluable. She made available to me her amazing memory and the hundreds of letters my father wrote her. She let me touch exposed sensitive nerve ends and bravely removed protective fences in order to help me learn and understand.

My brothers' role in my life and my father's is reduced to a minimum in this book. That does not reflect reality but their wish, which I wholeheartedly respect. They may want to tell their own stories one day, and it should be their prerogative when and how to do it.

My father wrote me when I was working on my first book: "As you are writing a book, you should put all your efforts into making it a good one, and when I say 'good,' I mean 'honest.' I see no harm in full exposure of inner statements, providing you don't compromise on honesty." It comforts me to think that, were he alive and read this book, he would have been satisfied that no such compromise was made.

Y.D.

CONTENTS

My Father, His Daughter

Memories are not history. They are fragments of things and feelings that were, tinted and sifted through varying prisms of present time and disposition. This book, then, is not the story of Moshe Dayan, or my own life story, but an attempt to depict a relationship of four decades between a father and a daughter, from birth to a mature emotional and spiritual connection—one that to some extent has survived death and still continues to inspire and have meaning.

I have not aimed for objectivity of any kind. That would be absurd and pretentious, since I was and am a participant rather than an observer. What truth I can offer is neither historic nor scientific; my own subjective, intense, one-sided, emotionally loaded truth. If my portrait of my father clashes with the memories or observations of others, that does not mean I doubt their truth or mean to impugn their Moshe Dayan. My father had a number of significant relationships in his life. In this book, I will consider them subjectively from the vantage point of my own involvement. My mother, my brothers, my father's friends, and his second wife may see that their perceptions of some of the episodes in my father's life or of elements of his character are different from mine, but then, their memories are not history, either.

PART

One

ONE ❧ A LONG

FRIDAY

I am compelled to begin with the end, with the image of my father as a dead man, devoid of heartbeat and blood pressure, feeble and small in the intensive-care unit. A body still connected to tubes and electrodes, its maimed face turning yellow; gray fingers; a deep scar for an eye; a meaningless green line on an EKG screen.

I have seen many dead faces. Tranquil or accepting, amazed or tortured, childish or wrinkled. My father's conveyed angry frustration, as if he didn't mean it to happen quite then, and for the first time ever was caught unaware, deprived of the last word. Those things unsaid and unaccomplished hovered there, almost palpable. This furious aura has haunted me ever since.

Early on Friday, October 16, the phone woke me long before the alarm clock, set for six-thirty, went off. This was not in itself unusual. My father's wife, Rahel, was on the other end of the line, assuring me there was no cause for alarm. He had been in the hospital for a few hours, having had pains the night before. He had refused to be carried to the ambulance and insisted on walking, had been conscious and stable when admitted, and was refusing to see any visitors. There were no tears in Rahel's voice, nor was there a false effort at cheerfulness. Rahel simply didn't know more than she communicated, and I hung up with an enormous sense of anxiety.

The morning news on the radio contained the brief statement that Moshe Dayan had been hospitalized due to a heart problem and that, according to the doctors, his condition was stable. I packed my children off to school and drove to Tel Hashomer Hospital in the heavy morning traffic, turning the radio on loud to block thought. It was not the first time I had driven in haste to Tel Hashomer to be at my father's bedside. There had been the time when, while he was excavating for antiquities, a hillside had caved in on him and almost crushed him to death; then there was the year he was operated on for cancer of the colon; and there had been other, more minor occasions. My father had suffered from heart disease for a long time. He was an undisciplined patient. But he had taught me to think logically, and I strove not to give way to premonitions or emotionalism as I drove to the hospital. I shifted gears automatically, stopped when the traffic lights turned red, drove by the maternity ward where both my children had been born; I parked and walked to the intensive-care unit of the cardiology department. The attending doctor greeted me unsmiling and refused to go further than to describe the situation as stable. Rahel was there, looking tired and pale but not desperate or hysterical. He was in a small room, lying on a narrow bed. Although sedated, my father was awake and irritable, and he didn't want to see me. She said she was sorry, since she knew how I felt, but there was no persuading him. She told me my father had ordered everybody out, and promised to call me later and tell me when to come.

Mumbling something about calling my brothers, I turned to listen as the young cardiologist explained to me in detail my father's heart-muscle malfunction. I remember looking at the small screen which was transmitting electronic signals from his heart. The lines went up and down—pretty green lines. Although my father wouldn't see me, I stood at the edge of his room, watching him through the half-drawn curtain. His good eye was weakening, tragically so, and he couldn't have seen me even if he'd been able to keep it open, which he didn't. His face had the intensity of an angry fighter unable to grasp the dreadful thing that was happening to him. It was then I realized I had arrived too late. My belief in his love for me wasn't shattered, for I knew he couldn't face me. Had I walked in, he would have realized how near he was to his death.

And perhaps I, too, couldn't face it. There was an accumulation of unsettled accounts between us that he was too weak to confront in his pain. Within moments, my father had ordered the nurse out, summoning Rahel and the doctor. As she entered his room, she promised to call me as soon as she could. Her sympathy was genuine, and I walked out, inhaling fresh air and swaying lightly.

Friday in Tel Aviv is always a short, crowded day. Traffic is heavy, the lines in the shops are long, and the school day is over early. Our family is totally secular, but the Sabbath still holds a special meaning of family communion for us: a cake in the oven, household chores, fresh flowers in the living room. As I hurried home, I tried to keep my mind on the trivial duties I had to take care of before lunchtime. But, back in the apartment, the phone was ringing. Rahel, apologizing for the morning's "unsuccessful visit," had called to suggest I come in the early evening. She said my father couldn't eat the hospital food, and asked me to prepare some chopped liver. His condition, she said, was still stable. I called my brothers. Udi, three years younger than I, happened to be visiting Tel Aviv from Nahalal, the Dayan family farm, where he lived and worked. Assi, the youngest, lived in Tel Aviv, and I got through to him without difficulty. Neither of them wanted to go to the hospital alone and we decided to meet there at six that evening. They asked the obvious question: was our father dying? I had no answer, but I remember that, unlike previous illnesses of his, for once we didn't indulge in morbid jokes.

Next was the chopped chicken liver, into which I poured all my hopelessness, as if preparing a life-saving remedy. I called my husband, Dov, at Army HQ, and his driver was duly dispatched to help with the delivery of the clay dish. The ability to repress feelings, to ignore warnings, to create preoccupations is God's gift to the human psyche. I remember that I ironed a load of shirts, scrubbed greasy pans, polished the shining silver, and all the while my father's lungs were filling with liquid and his body was growing heavy. At one point in the afternoon, I called the doctor and found comfort in his clichés. For a moment at least, I could believe the radio bulletins and go on baking cakes.

My mother had been living in Washington, D.C., for several years, and I didn't feel the need to get in touch with her immediately. Fleeting through my mind, piercing my heart through, was a pathetic prayer for time to stand still. We weren't ready yet, I wanted to whisper; whatever was between my father and myself—the love and the hurt and the desperate longing for balance—wasn't yet settled.

I sent my daughter, Raheli, ten then, to sleep over at a friend's house, promising her she could visit her grandfather the next day. My son, Dan, almost thirteen and a man, remained at home while Dov and I went to the hospital. As always, we didn't need to exchange words to produce an identity of feeling, and we drove through the empty streets in silence. At Tel Hashomer, we met my brothers (who had come together), and as we walked, it was almost necessary for each of us to prod the others forward. Rahel and two young doctors were waiting in a central ward from which the staff control—visually and electronically—the individual units that open onto it. A drawn curtain hid our father's bed from us, as we walked to the doctor's small office for a briefing. Udi was more silent than ever; Assi's expression was a mixture of disbelief and confusion. Rahel seemed to be clinging to the doctor's words, as if being attentive could postpone evil; and Dov's eyes had doom in them.

When the doctor was through. leaving us suspended and baffled, Rahel went in and came back to say we could enter. Our father would see us. Not joyfully, not with a longing to be surrounded by loved ones in his moment of pain and, if he suspected, moment of farewell, but reluctantly. It had to be done.

We stood around his bed. There was our father, lonely and dependent, yet not stripped of the powers he always had over us, unquestionable authority, a soliloquy which seldom developed into a dialogue. He talked—rather, delivered a statement. He was very ill. He wasn't sure whether he'd get out of the hospital alive. If he did, he had decided to undergo an operation which was very risky, but he'd rather take the risk than live a half-life. He was tired, he said. "End of meeting," it sounded. He looked and felt exhausted; I wanted to touch him, hold his hand, tell him I loved him. Instead, I angered an angry man. I mumbled something about being strong. I was bullshitting and couldn't help it. I had to cut the deadly silence as if talking held the countdown.

Stupidly, I managed to irritate him. He stared at me with his one eye, not sadly, not lovingly, a stare of discontent: I don't need your philosophies right now, I don't care what the doctors told you or what you think of it. I told you how I feel. He shut his eye, shutting us away totally. He had a manner of doing it whereby he didn't isolate himself, but rather imprisoned the others. We left the room. He had nothing else to tell us, to ask of us, to communicate to his own children. What he didn't say then, we found out a few days later, was already written in his will, in a personal letter and in a poem addressed to us.

Back in the doctor's room, we weren't sure what to do. I turned to Dov, who seemed to be the only mature person around. The look on his face meant my father's death. He knew this was the last time we would see my father alive, hear his voice, note the expression in his eye. Assi talked to the doctor. We are not babies, he said. Please tell us the truth. Is he dying? Should we stay here? Would he live through the night? All the young doctor could do was shrug. He couldn't promise, he couldn't predict, he didn't know.

My brothers decided to leave and be in touch later. One thing was obvious: the man inside, fighting for his life, would not summon us. Dov, who knew—better than the doctors, better than my father —said we should stay. The nurse came rushing in, and Rahel and the doctor followed her. I was left alone in the room with Dov. We exchanged looks and hurried to the central unit. The curtain was drawn and Rahel, her face white as marble, was watching the screen.

He lost consciousness, as he had earlier that day when alone with her. Nurses were wheeling oxygen canisters into the room; two more doctors hurried by and entered. None dared look at us. We had a plea in our eyes they had no way of answering; we didn't utter a word. At precisely this moment, the television announcer read a bulletin, assuring the viewers that "Dayan survived a massive heart attack, followed by complications, and is resting now, his condition stable." We talked in whispers. Rahel was recounting the events of the day and last night. He had had a couple of good hours in which he dictated two letters to the press and made sure they reached the editors in time. He was cold and tired and angry but totally in control of his thoughts and words.

The blood left my body. My fingers and toes were frozen and I felt lightheaded. I watched the irregularity of the green line on the screen and held tight to the nurse's counter, unable to ask for the glass of water I desperately needed.

Then we heard the pounding. The doctors were manually pounding on his chest, an act of desperation when all medical knowledge failed, when all the rest proved ineffective, or when, I didn't dare think it, the man was no longer alive. I could vaguely see Dr. Goldman, my father's personal physician, coming out of the room, dazed and not quite believing what had just happened. He shrugged, and though he stared at the three of us the way people look at orphaned children, he still didn't have the heart or the courage to pronounce the words of finality. He spread his hands sideways. "It's the end," he whispered. Rahel looked at him and at us. He didn't say he was dead. He is not dead? she asked, knowing the answer.

We walked in, as the nurses and doctors hurried out, expressions of failure on their faces, heads bent. I knelt by the bed, held the dead man's hand, touched his face, and could no longer control the flood of tears and agony that had been welling up for so long, maybe for much much longer. Dov looked on. If he wiped a tear, I don't know. He stroked my hair and knew to leave me alone.

I wasn't crying, I was sobbing. I was crying "Aba" once more, as I had when I was small and hurt, or an adult and in pain, as when screaming from far away lest the sound shake him back to life. Rahel was across the bed from me, holding his other hand, very composed and collected compared to my near-hysteria. She never consciously stood between us, and when I imagined she did, I found ways to bypass that, but as he lay there between us, still attached to tubes, his heart stopped and his eye shut to me, she was a stranger I knew I should call my mother, but I couldn't bring myself to move.

The mind is odd. I thought of figs. I thought he would never bring me big baskets of figs, as he had done every season. I looked at the hand I held, fingers twisted and scarred from wounds, hands that held me as a baby, slapped me as a naughty teenager, tickled my children into happy laughter, picked forbidden fruit for me—the lush, stupid image of figs again, food of the earth . . . Across the bed, Rahel held his other hand up and said something about his wrist-watch. My mind wasn't functioning as I felt his hand growing cold in mine. I covered it, hoping to warm it up. The doctor was with us now, and I urged him to detach the tubes and electrodes. He led Rahel out of the room. I still couldn't move. Dov left the room; someone offered me a glass of water; I was weeping uncontrollably. Please let my mother and brothers know, I asked, then realized I should be the one to do it. The nurses were busy with the body, which had to remain there for a while before being wheeled out, and I got to the telephone. I called Ezer Weizman and his wife, Reumah, my aunt. Father is dead. (There, I said it, I said the words I thought would never cross my lips.) Please call Mother and let her know. Suddenly I had a horror of not being left alone, the fear of a "situation" I couldn't find the strength to cope with. The funeral will be on Sunday, I said. Perhaps she shouldn't hurry back right away, it might be embarrassing for her. I regretted the words the minute I said them. Too late. My aunt didn't spare my mother this unkind suggestion. Dov went to call Prime Minister Begin and Arik Sharon, and a journalist who was present went to break the news to the public.

I desperately needed my brothers. Assi's phone had a recording machine on it, and I was, with a tremendous sense of humiliation and anger, made to dictate to a tape a tearful message saying our father was dead (I said it again now, still not believing) and to please come to Zahala.

Back in the little room, it was peaceful now. He lay there, covered to his neck with a sheet, as if asleep. In a short while, they would take him away. I knew, and I will never . . . never . . . never a million things . . . The ring of the word sufficed to send a painful shiver through my body. Every minute of the hours and days that followed froze with the word "never," and that served as a full stop to every thought and feeling.

The garden in Zahala was lit, as on many festive occasions, and people began to gather. Whether out of respect or frustration, they left me alone, as I couldn't stop crying and every handshake or hug produced a new stream of tears. I touched the pillars and stones in the garden, the plants, the tree trunks, searching for support. My brothers arrived, handsome and young and lovable. In all the years, I never felt as close to them as I did that evening. I was the oldest, they were my kid brothers, and here I drew from them strength and courage and a gentle guideline to reality. I couldn't talk to my children but had to. My son knew already; he was answering phone calls, composed and distant. As for my daughter, the sweet dear child my father loved, I tried to spare her till morning.

Faces floated around me; hands touched me; women cried with me; they were wise to offer no comfort, and I sought none. My growing sense of loss could not be shared. My mother would arrive tomorrow, I was told, and the funeral would take place in Nahalal on Sunday. Jews don't have burials on the Sabbath.

T W O ✄ F I R S T

K A D D I S H

Saturday morning, I went to Zahala with my daughter, who was torn between her own sadness and a desperate desire to console me. I returned there for eight days, clinging to something that wasn't there, pretending it was home. Did I expect to see my father, dressed in shabby khaki clothes, reconstructing a broken jar? There were Rahel, her daughters and her grandchildren, her friends, and a few people who were discussing funeral arrangements. I walked in the garden with the strange sensation of being watched, constantly, almost suspiciously. I was quite unapproachable, and between me and the group around the garden table there was a curtain of tears, distorting and impenetrable.

As if trespassing, I entered my father's room. It used to be mine, then mine and the children's when they were born. When he married Rahel, the kitchen was enlarged—incorporating my parents' bedroom—and he moved to my room, Rahel using my brother's room as her own separate bedroom.

I was still being watched through the open door, but I sat on the bed. Above his desk was a large oil portrait of me, painted a few years back. It was moved, appropriately so, to his room from the living room when Rahel moved in. A photo of my grandmother—his mother, Dvorah—another of his sister Aviva, and a colored one of Rahel were on other walls. Surrounded by women, as befitted him.

Rahel was standing next to me. She had tears in her voice when she talked. He wanted you to have the painting. He was so proud of the fact you needed nothing and were independent, but he told me to make sure you had the painting. In my state of mind, nothing sank in. I should have realized there and then what was to come, and run away, never to come back. If there was ever embarrassment, it was contained in that sentence. But I froze, irritated by the sound of Rahel's grandchild hopping around, repeating, "Moshe is dead, Moshe is dead . . ."

The phone was ringing constantly. People were coming and going, and a good number were still due from abroad. The cables were piling up, and time-consuming activities helped push away reality. For a second, with people coming in with food and cakes, it seemed as if we were preparing for some festive event. Who will go in which car, were the ambassadors notified, will there be room in the helicopter for a close friend of Rahel's? Where in Nahalal can people gather before going to the cemetery, even what to wear. I promised Moshe never to wear black, said Rahel. Some big national party in which my father will be the honored guest. He is in Tel Hashomer mortuary, I kept saying to myself. He is being washed and cleaned and covered in white shrouds. He will not know if we wear black or red, and all the promises and vows and even memories are one-sided now, acts without a partner, a broken link dwindling into limbo.

Back in our own apartment, we found the atmosphere not much different. Friends who felt uncomfortable in Zahala and chose to come to us; my brothers; some groupies who rotated between Zahala and Ramat Aviv to make sure they didn't miss anything, reporting in each house what they saw in the other. But my mother was here, warm and large-hearted and embracing. She let me cry with her while holding me. In a sense she had already mourned the loss of him. The love she felt for my father had never diminished, but she was stronger for having courageously faced her own period of mourning. Hers was over, while mine was beginning. Mother was almost cheerful, or carried away with stories of her last voyage. I was amazed at this remarkable woman. She preserved the image of my father at his best, while we were left with shreds and a sense of deterioration from which we had to reerect our hero.

Had my children ever seen me cry before? I was touched by their helplessness as they watched me. Suddenly I was their size, a daughter, a child rather than the all-able mother, and they were delighted my mother was staying with us, someone who could cope. If only I could stop crying. Someone was kind enough to give me a sedative. It was a warm night, but I was shivering when Dov covered me and Raheli cuddled next to me, holding me very gently.

I woke up drained and dehydrated Sunday morning, into reality. Not one second of—maybe it's all a dream, just a big bland hangover, as if this very moment a new era, a new count began. We were going to Nahalal to bury my father. From this moment, as I heard my mother in the kitchen, everything had a dual quality, like a broken lens or a cracked mirror where the scene is twice reflected, doubled into two different entities. It was, strange to say, comic.

A large black car, supplied by the Foreign Ministry, waited for my mother and Raheli and me. Rahel and others went in a helicopter. Dov and Dan joined the helicopter to be split again in Nahalal. My mother went to my brother's house, where oldtimers gathered, village people, old war comrades, my cousins and family. Rahel went to the village "club"; there was the coffin, draped with the blue-and-white flag of Israel. With her were close friends and her family, as well as government officials and dignitaries. Between these two centers, for several hours, moved thousands of people who gathered from all over the country to pay their last respects. City people and farmers, soldiers and civilians, Arab and Druse, priests and rabbis, some in black formal clothes, others in working outfits and sandals; old ones supported by others, and children sitting high on parents' shoulders.

I found no place for myself. I went from the house to the club and back, meeting the same people, shaking hands or embracing, listening to banalities or to touching words, feeling near collapse when I noticed how lonely the coffin was, separated from the crowd by a police rope, a barrier, away from the club, up on a small black stage not yet close to the earth. And I sat by it on the dry grass, weeping and alone, half touching the flag, which was just a cloth then, forcing myself to accept.

Nahalal is shaped like a circle. The houses are its perimeter, the public buildings in its midst, and the farmland stretches behind each house to form yet a larger circle. The procession moved along the circular road, passing in front of Udi's house, stopping there and moving on with people joining from each house. Behind the command car carrying the coffin walked Rahel and her daughters, supported by an elegantly dressed man—a leader in the Jewish community in Spain—her local friends and others behind her. Government people followed, and the Dayans, like a strong solid wave, together. My cousins from Nahalal, my mother and brothers, a few older people who had known my father when as a child he had run barefoot in the muddy circle, our own children, his grandchildren.

I couldn't bring myself to walk in the procession. I kept to the edges of the road, choosing my own path, walking my own Nahalal circle, stopping in front of my grandparents' house and looking at the cypresses piercing the cloudless skies, not quite remembering being there at another time and age, in slow motion. The circle seemed to be pouring itself out into a dark line, emptying itself and being pulled upward along the narrow road to the cemetery hill where the good brown end-of-summer dry earth was awaiting my father, the way it engulfed his parents, his brother and sister, the way it awaited us all.

The cemetery of Nahalal was not designed for state funerals, so it was necessary to limit the number of people who could enter it. The thousands who walked past the coffin in the village stayed behind or along the road, and only a few hundred drove up to where the empty, newly dug grave held a promise of inevitable rest.

The coffin was carried on the shoulders of six generals in uniform, along the earth path. Preceding it walked an officer holding medals and insignia in an open black velvet box. The cantor chanted something, and the wooden box, still covered with the flag, was carefully lowered into its cradle. I didn't walk but was propelled, Raheli holding my hand tightly, Dov just behind me. We stood in a tight circle as the horribly cruel sound of dry gravel on wood overwhelmed the soft murmurs and tearful sighs. Spades resolutely dug in the unyielding soil, small clouds of gray dust, dust unto dust, and in seconds the earth was heaped and piled up.

A white wooden marker bearing my father's name and date of death was quickly set in it when the Chief Chaplain of the Army read the customary psalm. It all happened with amazing speed. It takes longer to plant a tree, or tuck a child in for an hour's sleep. As if covering up a crime, as if ashamed. Almost for the first time now, I looked around, bewildered but focusing. Now the earth had sealed my father in. Rahel was standing, composed and erect, dark glasses and dark silk two-piece suit, held by her daughters, dust covering her open sandals. Next to her stood Assi and his daughter. Udi wiped his forehead and face, sweat or tears—I didn't know. The Prime Minister, who even on happy occasions looked slightly funereal, and the President and his pretty, overdressed wife were next to my mother. My mother didn't wear dark glasses; tears came easily to her, and her eyes were shining. She looked at the valley below with acceptance and serenity. Assi's first wife, Udi's first wife and children, Rahel's mother—a beautiful, gentle lady who loved my father —my own grandparents, well into their eighties; my uncle and aunt, cousins, Arik Sharon—wet-eyed and emotional, a gallery of loving and loved. Udi was given a piece of paper to read from and was made to approach the microphone. He pushed it aside. He was going to say Kaddish, a first Kaddish, and this was between him and his father, not for the world to hear. He whispered it, almost inaudible. "Yitgadal veyitkadash shmei Raba . . . Magnified and sanctified be his great name in the world . . ."

Kaddish is a doxology, read in Aramaic. A mourner's Kaddish is read by the son or next of kin, and the crowd recites with him and says Amen. The words held no meaning whatsoever for Udi or myself. They were a symbol of duty rather than love, a declaration of tradition, of belonging and continuity. Udi was whispering his first Kaddish, the words artificially muttered, but there was tenderness in his voice. My father's parents' tombs were a few yards away, barren, almost deserted. So were my father's brother's and sister's. Not a flower, not a visitor, dull stones scorched by the summer sun and eroded by winter torrents.

Udi's Kaddish, barely heard, was meant for them, too. This was our hill, our village and valley. My feet felt rooted as I looked at my brother's hands and watched his lips moving.

The cantor took over and sang "El Maleh Rachamaim, God is full of mercy," a beautiful chant, but from another world, another faith. The prayers and the lamentations had to do with God, his mercy, his glory, his benevolence, and his forgiveness. We were not lucky enough to find peace and comfort in God's glory or to be consoled by his mercy. We understood rainfall and drought, birth and blossom, hatred, love, and envy, and when the end came, there was earth and pine roots and worms, and soon the first rain would wash away the dust and give life to seeds and dormant bulbs, and next spring the hill would be covered with anemone and cyclamen and young lovers would seek privacy among the pines. This was our faith, not the Aramaic litanies and the Amens. My father had not said Kaddish each year over his parents' graves.

Wreaths were being placed now, by young soldiers saluting the fresh grave, accompanied by the various dignitaries. "The wreath of the Knesset," the announcer proclaimed . . . "Of the Israeli Army" . . . "Ministry of Defense" . . . "American ambassador" . . . German, French . . . Prime Minister, President . . . There was no room, and the flowers were placed in layers, colorful and bright, until the soil could not be seen and even the wooden marker was almost hidden.

The ceremony was over. Rahel bent down, picked a flower from one of the wreaths, and turned away. My mother was surrounded by friends. Udi disappeared the minute he could, and I couldn't move for many long moments.

We flew back home in the helicopter. My eyes were swollen and red and I felt numb. Through the window I could see the valley, a tapestry of fall colors. White cotton and green corn, evergreen orchards and red-tiled roofs. The circle of Nahalal was empty but for a single tractor, and buses were leaving from the parking lot at the foot of the hill. We flew over the slopes of Mount Carmel and along the waterfront, where the huge body of water touched the fertile coastline. In the airport, and later back at home, I sensed a shameful new feeling. Not quite clear or dominant, barely present perhaps, but still there. A feeling of relief. As one feels when a tragic event is anticipated, finally erupts, and is over. I lay awake and regained an ability I seemed to have lost for three days, that of disassociating myself from what was happening to me. Slightly schizophrenic, but very useful, ruinous or constructive, depending on the circumstances.

I was anxious to comprehend this uncomfortable new feeling. Relief? Not quite, more the disappearance of a dreadful fear, as if for a few years, certainly the last few months, I had carried a clue to the unknown yet bound to happen, and now that it had come to pass, all options were closed. I was tossed from a suspended board, and finally fell and hurt, and as bad as the pain was, I was on solid ground, not on the top of an abyss. I have always derived security from the certain and known. I also noticed I'd stopped crying. The rabbis in their learned books say: "Three days for weeping, and seven days for lamenting . . ." They must have known the limits of the tear glands to produce, and excessive grief was forbidden by them, being considered indulgence and God's exclusive privilege.

PART

Two

THREE ❧ BEFORE

MEMORY

Four generations of Dayans found eternal rest in the Nahalal cemetery. My great-grandparents, my grandparents Shmuel and Dvorah, my father, his brother and sister, and my cousin Nurit. Of the four, only my generation could look across the valley from the graveyard and, on a bright day, see the Hill of Moreh, where the maternity ward of the central hospital is still located. There I was born, on the eve of the Second World War.

My grandparents came to Palestine from the Ukraine, soon after the turn of the century, and settled in another valley, where the Jordan River flows south out of Lake Tiberias. There they founded Deganya, the first kibbutz, where my father, Moshe, was born, less than a year after the First World War began. Most people on this globe are born, live, and die within a few miles' diameter. The roots are where the home is, where the grave is, where some of the children are to live and be buried. The human cycle of permanence and stability. I was born on the Hill of Moreh, lived in Nahalal, and will be returned to Shimron—overlooking it. My father was born in Deganya, grew up in Nahalal, and despite the long, complex, eventful, and rich route his life followed, he was returned, as he wished, to rest near where the roots are. The reclaimed land, the fertile valley, the Bedouin herds, the droughts were his home territory. The real miracle was the story of his parents. From the Dnieper and the

Black Sea to the Jordan and the Sea of Galilee was more than a journey, and my father and I, who were born into the Zionist struggle, could never quite stop admiring, without ever fully grasping, the strength and determination that sparked and motivated their move to the malaria-ridden, Ottoman-governed valley.

Shmuel came from a poor family. His father was a peddler of cheap merchandise, moving with horse and cart from village to village. Dvorah's background was affluent. Her father was a lumber merchant. She herself had been a student in Odessa, well versed in Russian literature and deeply impressed by the 1905 revolution. The world was aflame with war when these two good-looking youngsters stood under the canopy and were married on the bank of the Jordan River.

My grandmother's intellectual aspirations made it difficult for her to integrate into the commune. It was not the scorching heat at 650 feet below sea level, or the locust or malaria, or the trachoma my father contracted, that made them leave Deganya with their child, but the new idea of a moshav—a cooperative settlement, where some privacy could be retained without compromising the ideals of Jewish farming, mutual aid, and equality. In the fall of 1921, the small family arrived on foot in the Valley of Jezreel and settled with a few others in a tent encampment. The marsh had to be drained, the undrinkable water was infested with malaria and typhoid, and the winter rains turned the valley into a quagmire of black, sticky mud.

The layout of Nahalal was a large circle, the communal buildings in its midst and the individual farm plots its larger perimeter. The reclaimed land was plowed and the wheat and barley crops had to be protected from the herds of the neighboring Bedouin tribe. The tent was replaced by a wooden shack, where my father was given a tiny room of his own when his sister Aviva was born. Shmuel was active in public life, traveling, lecturing, organizing, and the burden of the farm fell on the thin shoulders of my grandmother, never a healthy woman, and my father, who often had to take charge of the farm work while attending primary school.

School existed thanks to an extraordinary teacher who assembled the children, ignoring the variety of age, outdoors or in a small cabin, infecting them with curiosity and a zeal for knowledge. Dvorah introduced Russian literature to my father's life, and more often than this poor family could afford, he was lost in the intricate romances of Dostoevsky's characters rather than in farm chores.

The British Mandate replaced the Ottoman Empire after World War I, and the dream of a sovereign national life was not only a subject for discussions in Zionist congresses but a military challenge as well. At fourteen, my father joined the Haganah, the national underground, and was allowed to learn to use his father's old carbine. Self-defense consisted of protecting the fields from Bedouin raids, attacks which probably had no political meaning and did not damage the pattern of friendship that existed between my father and the Bedouin youngsters.

In 1934, my mother arrived in Nahalal to attend the agriculture school. Her parents lived in Jerusalem: Zvi, a well-established lawyer, and my grandmother, Rachel Shwarz, active in education. Both were university graduates, spoke several languages, and were part of the Jerusalem social elite, which was politically socialist. They did not prevent and indeed rather encouraged my mother's joining the Labor youth movement and planning her future as a member of a commune.

The Dayan dwelling was small, my father's room tiny, but my mother, Ruth, soon moved in and became part of the family, helping on the farm, helping my father with his English, and, a short while later, getting married under the nut tree in the back yard. The village rabbi presided at the ceremony, the Mazarib Bedouins danced, the guests from Jerusalem enjoyed the grapes and corn my father picked that morning, and even Shmuel overcame his suspicions of the bourgeoisie introduced to his family. My mother went to milk the cows after the ceremony, and at the age of twenty my father was an enthusiastic, loving husband with no immediate plans but with a growing involvement with Haganah duties as the tensions mounted toward the outbreak of acts of terror in 1936.

The Arab violence interrupted my parents' honeymoon in England, and had more effect than Shmuel's letters complaining about the easy, good time the young couple chose to have rather than till the land. They returned home to join a group of Nahalal young people who attempted to establish a kibbutz of their own, on the Shimron Hill.

My parents were the only married couple in Shimron and were allotted a dwelling of their own, but obviously my father was not cut out for kibbutz life. He was unable to form his life according to committee regulations; he sought individual challenges and did not find comfort or security in the fact that decisions were shared and tasks performed in unison. He found a suitable escape, in joining a British local police-training course, from which he graduated a sergeant. My mother wanted to have six children but soon found that my father was less than enthusiastic. He loved her, he loved being married, he couldn't see his life without sharing a home with her, but home should be mobile, and children, he thought then, "would tie him up to the family tap." Running water was still a novelty, and the source of running water also meant the end of nomadic life roaming from well to well.

My mother's backaches brought her to a specialist, who suggested pregnancy as a remedy. My father accepted the verdict, though it wasn't for two more years that he was actually faced with the screaming being that claimed his fatherhood. Events were moving fast, and so were my parents' plans. They wanted to leave Shimron, to settle in Nahalal, or perhaps to study abroad, or go to sea, or even join a kibbutz in the north, where the challenges were greater. Meanwhile, my father participated in several Haganah training courses, from which he wrote my mother: "I miss you so much and I am miserable and I do so much want a home of our own and for you to be happy. I don't believe in groups or communes, and at this point I almost think we should go back to Nahalal. Even though it's awful there, and the farm is bad, and it's bad to be with my father and mother and the work is terribly hard for you—I can't think of anything better. I feel strongly that I must have my own house and I must take care of you. All I want is quiet, and all there is is terror which we must fight, what will be the end?" And with his usual humorous twist at the end, referring to the boxer bitch they had then: "And we will love Laba too. It's not her fault that she is so fat . . ." Laba vomited when taken on buses, and my mother rode her bicycle for hours with the dog across its rear to visit my father in camp.

My father was now training with Captain Orde Wingate, the odd, idealistic British officer who developed the special night squads. In him, he found someone to admire, and Wingate rewarded my father with encouragement and respect. Rather than dull training based on textbooks or on old-fashioned rules, Wingate's was unconventional, his military thinking based on an amazing knowledge of the Bible, of the terrain of Palestine, and of the enemy. The combination of cool professional approach and the unexpected and unorthodox attracted my father and encouraged his own originality. Individuality and inventiveness were not necessarily disadvantages, not even when one faced challenges that required teamwork.

The Shimron commune dissolved, and at the same time my mother found that she was pregnant. This put an end to my father's strong opposition to the communal way of raising children. Some of the Shimron members established a new kibbutz near the Lebanese border, Hanita, and my parents joined them as helping guests, my mother in her pregnancy developing a craving for olives and pickles which was easily satisfied in the commune's kitchen.

A small cabin was available for rent in Nahalal, and compared to what they had had before, it offered my parents the great luxury of two rooms, a small kitchen, washing facilities in the back yard, and a vegetable garden. There was room for Laba, and room enough for the baby. My mother was famous for her lack of self-confidence, for what were mostly trivial reasons. She hadn't finished high school, or the Nahalal agriculture school. The Shimron experience was finally a failure, and so her kibbutz experiment had come to nothing. My grandparents in Nahalal criticized her and only much later grew loving and dependent on her. At the time, in February 1939, though nine months pregnant, she didn't manage to develop an impressive child-bearing size and was sure this small frame could not really produce a living baby.

She was standing on a ladder scrubbing the walls of the new cabin with soap and water when the first labor pains came, but she ignored them, as there was too much work still undone. There were sheets to launder and hang to dry, and two more wooden walls to wash, and even Dvorah, who naturally knew everything and better, assured her it wasn't yet time to go to the hospital. The local doctor thought otherwise, and in his small car drove my mother, frightened and in pain, to the Afula Hospital on the Hill of Moreh. The obstetrician gave her a short, angry look and told her she could go home. "You must be five months pregnant," he said. She insisted, was examined and accepted. Labor was on, and for the next two days she endured pain and misery, was certain she was dying and would never have a baby.

At six in the morning, on her third day in the hospital, a rainy February 12, I was born—healthy, small but normal-size, kicking and screaming, jaundiced and hungry, to my mother's sheer amazement at her own success, and my father's wonderment and delight. Not having prepared themselves for the birth of a real child, they hardly cared whether it was a boy or a girl, and my father took the trouble to examine the other babies in the ward to reassure my mother that I was by far the prettiest, best-formed, and, of course, the cleverest-looking of the lot.

My Grandmother Rachel arrived from Jerusalem (she had her own car, a rarity at the time, and was one of the first lady drivers in the country) and helped my father prepare the room I was to occupy. Nothing was too good for me, and the little room in the wooden cabin was turned into a palatial nursery. No child in Nahalal, to Shmuel's dismay, had luxuries like that, and if one could ignore the knee-deep mud that surrounded the cabin, and the absence of a washroom in the house, it looked like a fairy-tale picture, the huge ginger cat on the shelf above my bed not excluded.

The idyll ended as soon as I was brought home. For three whole months I cried ceaselessly, turning the family, helpful neighbors, the local doctor, and everyone else into helpless nervous wrecks. The rule was to let a crying baby cry, and a way of keeping me warm and dry in diapers was not found. Finally, with the help of a private pediatrician in Haifa and at my father's initiative, peace was achieved. I was given a bottle—my mother had to admit another minor failure, as her production of milk was insufficient; my father picked me up whenever I cried, against everybody's better judgment;

and he also devised a way to diaper me, strong and tight, and often enough. The ginger cat—in spite of horror tales about babies strangled in their sleep by the cat's weight—was allowed to cuddle in my bed and keep me warm, and my mother could relax and regain her good health. She devoted her free hours to knitting, sewing, and embroidering a layette that gained me the deserved title of the Princess of Nahalal.

I realize as I write these lines that, had world affairs been different, this could have been an opening chapter to a quiet healthy "Little House in the Valley" saga, where the big events have to do with the bitch having puppies, the raising of the first turkeys and rabbits in the village, and occasional visits from the outside world. But this was 1939, and only a few months after we had settled into our new home and I had been given the name Yaël—carefully selected by my father from an assortment of biblical symbolic names—my father was detained by the British and sentenced to a long jail term for illegal military activities. The Second World War started almost simultaneously. It was these two earth-shattering events, both in my first year of life, which affected us as a family, village, people, and nation, and tilted us to great heights and greater tragedies. On Sunday, September 3, my father was away instructing a Haganah course. He had a car now, and tried to come home as often as he could. My mother had some guests for lunch—two officers from the British Royal Dragoons, a tank unit stationed nearby. Lieutenant Makins was playing with me on the floor when the radio was switched on and the familiar voice of Neville Chamberlain announced that a state of war existed between Germany and Great Britain as of eleven that morning. Our guests left in a hurry, as if this were a private war they were expected to win that afternoon.

The three years before the war had been turbulent, and it didn't take a formal declaration of war for people to oil their guns, dig trenches in their back yards, or shudder as Hitler was mentioned. The inevitability of the coming Israeli-Arab struggle was evident; if anything, the world war only postponed it. The war against the Germans was top priority, though at the outbreak we were still ignorant of the scope of the Jewish tragedy or of Hitler's crimes. Certainly, it took the British far too long to realize who their allies were in Palestine, and for a long while they invested effort and material means into curbing and limiting Haganah military activities. Rather than train, equip, and use our budding fighting force against a mutual enemy that didn't hide its intentions to take over the Middle East, they sought out, to bring to trial, members of our underground. That is how, and why, my father—an excellent potential fighter for the British—spent the first two years of the Second World War in their prison at Acre.

October 5 was the eve of the Simchas Torah holiday. Mother received word that my father would come home for the holiday, and she didn't need more encouragement to bake half a dozen cakes, put chicken to roast, and cut fresh vegetables for his favorite salad. A vase of flowers was placed on a newly embroidered tablecloth, the cabin was scrubbed clean and myself dressed in my best smocked dress. She was too impatient to wait at home, put me in a pram, and pushing it, walked the long dirt track to the main Haifa–Nazareth road. Every passing bus, truck, and car made her pulse quicken, but as it grew darker, the traffic subsided. It was chilly and not too safe, and in frustration and anger she started pushing the pram back toward the distant village lights. She put me to bed and cried herself to sleep. The next morning, I was playing with a visiting child and Mother was taking pictures of us under a tangerine tree. My grandparents had joined us, when the picture-taking session was interrupted. Our dog—the one who was with my father at the course—trotted into the picture frame, followed by a man from another village. The man gave Mother a piece of paper which had been fastened to the dog's collar. It read: "Ruth, we have been arrested and taken to Acre on a seemingly minor charge. I hope it will end well. Kisses to you and Yaël. See you soon—your Moshe."

Forty-three young men, the entire Haganah officers' training course, most of them armed, had been picked up by the local police, loaded on trucks, and taken to the Acre fortress. The Acre prison was built by the Turks, on the foundation of a Crusaders' castle overlooking the bay, and the British used the massive stone-wall citadel as their central prison. The convicts ranged from common criminals to underground activists, and some, in both categories, met their death in the execution chamber. This was the threat used on my father when he was taken to be interrogated on the first night. "Your daughter will be orphaned and will grow up knowing her father has been hanged as a common criminal," they told him.

My father had to think fast. What went through his mind was not his infant daughter orphaned and shamed, or the prospect of being hanged. One man was interrogated before him, and they could hear, in the heavy silence of the night, the man's groans and cries. There was no point in putting them all through the routine of kicking and beating. He decided to tell what he was sure they knew anyway, rather than act the hero. As often before, cool logic and pragmatism won over false or external gestures for appearance's sake. He gave his name, his age—twenty-four—admitted he and his comrades were members of the Haganah, mentioning the fact that they often cooperated with British troops, and calmly refused to disclose their source of arms or name names of people not being detained. Attack was a good defense, and he blamed them for the atrocious conditions and behavior at a time when they were all partners in the fight against Hitler. He was taken back to the large cell, and the interrogations that followed the next day were conducted in a civilized manner.

Those who were freed, Haganah commanders, lawyers, Jewish Agency officials, all assured my mother and grandparents that there was no cause for alarm. It was, they said, a matter of a few days before the military trial would take place, and the prisoners should be released soon after. The prisoners—or rather, detainees—were allowed one visit a week, and a few censored official letters until the trial. My father wrote in his first letter: "My Ruthie, I don't think it's a good idea to bring Yaël here, though I miss her very much. Every night I wake up with a start and think of you two, my poor darlings . . . Pre-trial rights are good, the food sufficient and we are outdoors most of the day. Please bring me an undershirt, shaving cream and a sweater. You can send me two short letters a week, they must be in English . . ."

The first Saturday visit was a disaster. Each visit was limited to three to five minutes. My mother dressed me in a bright, festive dress, and held me over her head so he could see me. The conversation was conducted in shouts across the high barbed wire and consisted mostly of "How are you." The one-legged Captain Grant was famous for being severe if not outright cruel, and he ordered me quickly back when I tried to crawl toward my father, ignoring the barbed wire.

In a letter received after the visit, my father wrote: "My Ruth, if sometimes during the visit it seemed to you that I'm not enough of a family man . . . if only I could pass on to you one thousandth of the love I feel for you both every night, if only you could know what you and Yaël are to me . . . Also, if I told you not to bring the little darling here, it is only because of the filth and because I'm not sure I wouldn't start to cry if I saw her over the barbed wire. I have the strength to endure it all, I know you do too, and the day will come, and very soon, we'll be sitting having tea, you'll be knitting, I'll be reading and the darling will be crawling on the rug . . ." Soon it wasn't, and I stopped crawling and started walking and talking long before they could have tea together, or read or knit.

The trial began on October 25 and lasted five days. My Grandfather Zvi was one of the lawyers for the defense. On the morning of the thirtieth, the verdict was announced. Each name was called and each of the detainees stood up. Finally the judge declared: "You are hereby sentenced to ten years' imprisonment at hard labor." Only the buzz of flies could be heard on this hot October day in the stifling courtroom. Fists clenched; tears appeared in brave eyes; and the shocked forty-three, now officially prisoners, were shoved out of the room.

Two incongruous images went through my mother's mind—she told me later—me at the age of ten, and *Gone with the Wind*. My father and his comrades soon noticed the change in their status. They were dressed in prison uniform, brown and shapeless; their heads were shaved; and they were placed in a new, dark cell with narrow barred windows. The family regarded the verdict as a major tragedy, whereas my father thought of it as an episode one had to put up with. "A spell in prison was just that, nothing more. When it's over, I'll go out, have a good wash and start life anew. Acre is no rest home but it isn't a medieval dungeon either, nor Siberia. This is part of the struggle for a state, and I'm sorry we are in jail as a result of a luckless error and not of some special operation with a significant impact. What is particularly burdensome for all of us is being cooped up and helpless while a war in which we all desperately wish to take part is being waged."

My mother tried to appeal to Ben-Gurion, and took me with her to his office in Jerusalem. I crawled happily on the floor when in his curt and decisive manner he told her off. Nothing more could be done then, and he said only, "Ruth, my dear, you have in your life only Moshe Dayan. In my life, I have all the Jews in Palestine." She picked me up, started to cry, and walked to her parents' house.

Mother appealed to British officials, to Jewish Agency officials, and even decided to try to see the Queen of England. She felt at times encouraged but mostly humiliated and crushed, and when the sentence was reduced to five years, she directed her efforts toward smuggling letters, extra food, and obtaining permission for special visits. She had accepted the fact, and now my father's life as a prisoner had to be made easier, be it by procuring an extra bar of soap or chocolate or making it possible for him to touch his daughter on her first birthday.

My mother, to this day, believes that the benevolence, kindness, and generosity in her are shared splendidly by humanity at large. When the first official visit after the trial was set for February 12, coinciding with my birthday, she saw in it a God-sent sign and she carefully explained to the officer in charge the marvelous coincidence. The major told her to see Captain Grant, who briskly answered: "If I had to decide about bringing my own children to see me in prison, I wouldn't want them to come at all."

"This is not the point, Captain Grant. You are not in prison, my husband is."

"It's not educational to bring children to prison, and we'll start having kindergarten classes here if we let everyone's kids through the gates." He was not going to allow it.

My mother, as usual (it is not a weapon with her, but an automatic reaction), started crying while being propelled with the other visitors toward the gate. The prisoners were standing, waving, behind the wire, when suddenly the tall Sudanese policeman at the gate lifted me up from my mother's arms, on his own initiative, and opened the gate and passed me over the wire to my father for a quick hug and a kiss, to everybody's tearful delight. He then handed me back to my mother.

My father's next letter said: "I am not prepared to give Grant the satisfaction of seeing us hurt. I ask nothing of him, for he is a boor who gets a sadistic pleasure out of refusing an appeal, so why make one? A kiss for our baby, and may she enjoy other days in a different kind of world . . ." He went on to ask my mother not to bring me again, though when she didn't, on her next visit, he was sure something terrible had happened to me.

The prisoners, after a few long months, were moved to another prison—in Mazra, where they worked on an "agricultural station." Their living conditions were improved, but their patience was growing thin, mostly because of what went on outside the prison walls. The "White Paper" ordinances were announced, restricting Jewish immigration and the purchase of land in Palestine. France had fallen, and preparations for the battle over the Middle East were at a peak. The first rumors of massacres of Jews by the Nazis began to circulate while my father was making a necklace from peach pits for my mother's birthday. British authorities did accept some Palestinian Jewish volunteers, who were ultimately incorporated into the "Jewish Brigade" of the British Army. This must have seemed a paradox to the forty-three prisoners who were kept busy spreading fertilizer in a vegetable garden, reading O. Henry's short stories, studying English and Arabic, and writing letters to their loved ones.

Visits were easier in Mazra, but were still conducted in shouts across a wire fence. I was walking and running and on one occasion managed to cross the wire and hug my father. The camp sergeant looked at the prisoner in brown holding tight a little girl in a white dress, and shouted in a panic: "If you don't get that kid out, I'll shoot." It was no game. My mother took pictures of Father in prison, and taught me to say "Aba"—Father—which of course I said to all prisoners I encountered; and my small vocabulary included the word "Acre."

The war was nearing our part of the world, and Mother took a first-aid course in Tel Aviv, where she moved with me for a few weeks. I was left with a caretaker each morning while Mother went to the Hadassah hospital. One morning, Italian planes bombed Tel Aviv. The few minutes of terrifying explosions caused a lot of damage, and my mother got special permission to leave and see if I was safe. She wrote to my father: "Bodies were brought into the hospital, smashed to a pulp. I realize what it is to see small children like Yaël without legs or hands or faces . . . Only after five hours of emergency work I've asked to go home for a while and found the street we lived on closed off, as there were many casualties in the area. A bomb fell between our house and the next one, the house itself had gaping holes and no windows, and I couldn't find Yaël. Someone said my sister Reumah came for her, and I soon found them, eating yogurt on the balcony. All her clothes were torn and there was a shrapnel burn on her leg, but that was all. When she saw me she called out 'Mother.' I cried and told her that her father would come very soon and take both of us . . . How absurd it is—you in prison and us without you . . . Later I found out that Yaël was in bed, and Zipora was saved by being outside and lying down. She cried hysterically, 'The child, the child,' and people gathered to enter through the dust and smoke of the hit house and find Yaël sitting and crying, covered in cement and dust, being the only undamaged object in the room. My darling, can you grasp what a miracle befell us . . . All night I embraced her and could see maimed bodies and cut limbs, and with sunrise I decided to move with the child to Jerusalem, which seems safer. I walked with her to the bus station, where we met my parents, worried to death, and my mother, who never cries, had tears in her eyes when she saw the laughing child in my arms. Yaël was not feeling well, vomiting and complaining, and the doctor said it must have been the shock of the exploding bomb . . . I can't leave my work now, and I feel useful. Don't worry about us, did you worry? Or were you spared it by knowing nothing? Why can't we be happy together about this miracle, and kiss our child together. What a crazy world it is, my child, with endless love—yours—"

The *Palestine Post* of September 11, 1940, had the story: "An infant girl, whose mother was acting as a volunteer nurse at the time, was in a room whose wall collapsed, almost burying her in debris. She was found with one shoe missing and plaster in her hair, but otherwise unscathed . . ." I was given a new pair of shoes, the few scratches soon healed, and we were back in Nahalal for the winter, a second winter with Father away.

Their letters, smuggled out on toilet paper or with bribes, never fell into a routine, or lost the quality of my parents' deep longing for each other. This written dialogue of hundreds of pages conveys the love and trust and friendship of a married couple, together with the optimism, the dreams and plans of two people who have just met. I, their baby, was not what kept them together, not even the deep emotion they shared, but an additional gift, a product of their love, a proof of it.

For the second time, the prisoners lit Hanukkah candles in December; so did we in our poor cabin in Nahalal, a sad, melancholy Feast of Lights. The battlefront was approaching us from North Africa in the south and Vichy-occupied Syria in the north. The British military command in Palestine was in need of additional fighters, and rumors spread concerning the possibility of setting free the Acre 43.

A few days after my second birthday, my mother received a late-night phone message. It simply said to be in kibbutz Ein Hamifratz the next morning at nine, with clothes for Moshe. The prisoners were told to pack their belongings that night and be ready to leave the next morning. Both my parents spent a sleepless night, Mother cleaning and baking and pacing and crying, and Father counting the slow hours in his Mazra hut, not quite believing it was to be his last night there. On February 17, the prisoners assembled near the gate, had their palms stamped with a release symbol, and walked toward their waiting families. My father put on the black-and-white pullover Mother had knitted him, and they went home. His greatest wonderment, he said, was at how well I could talk. I would never again say "Aba" to strange men in prison garb. Of the three of us, I was the happiest, as I was ignorant of the fact that what brought my father home was a war that would soon take him away.

My father drank of his freedom in large gulps. He laughed and played with me on the floor, read me stories and recited nursery rhymes, pushed my pram on Saturday to gather cyclamens, which covered the deserted Shimron Hill, and worked as a hired hand building troughs when not busy helping on his father's farm. He ate well, and made love, and soon bracketed as a remote memory his two-year prison term. Rommel's advance toward the Egyptian frontier and the presence of Vichy forces in Lebanon were more than reminders of Hitler's success, and my parents both knew a new separation was inevitable.

The Haganah established a country-wide force, trained to defend the Jewish population from possible Arab attack, and at the same time able to participate in British operations to repulse a likely German invasion. Yitzhak Sadeh was the force commander, and since he himself was an initiator and follower of the Wingate style in tactics, it was natural that his choice of field commanders included my father. When, on a May evening, the door opened and Sadeh and Zvi Spector appeared in the living room, my mother knew that the holiday was over. The three men sat and talked, and my mother put me to bed, fed the dog, and prepared tea. When Sadeh and Spector left, my father had a general idea of what his assignment was. D-Day for the planned Allied invasion of Syria was set, and my father had to form his own unit, train, equip, and brief them so they could spearhead the securing of a passage along the seacoast. Together with an Australian unit, they would cross into Lebanon, seize the highway bridges, and guard them until the Allied forces got there.

A base was established in kibbutz Hanita, men were recruited, hand-picked mostly from moshavim and kibbutzim in the valley, and arms were procured from Haganah arsenals to add to the unsuitable ones supplied by the British command. A reliable Arab guide was recruited, and with him my father spent the last couple of nights before D-Day on patrols. This was his pleasure, walking wordlessly along mountain tracks, through rough terrain and thick vegetation, taking in the smells and sounds of the cool nights, which sharpened his senses and prepared him for the task ahead.

The day before the invasion, I was left with Dvorah, and my parents drove together to Hanita. This was the last time I saw my father with both his eyes. A good friend, Zalman Mart, was visiting in Nahalal, and it was only natural for him to accept my father's invitation to join them, in Naharia, Hanita, and—why not—in Lebanon, too. Naharia is a quiet resort town on the coast, north of

Haifa, and the three stopped there for a relaxed hour. My mother had a sudden desire for strawberries with whipped cream—a rare luxury then—and playing big shots, they walked into the lobby of the best hotel in Naharia for a little celebration. The craving for strawberries was explained later by the fact that she was pregnant with my brother Udi, but she wasn't aware of it then, and they proceeded to stroll along the beach hand in hand, until it was time to take the uphill, curving road to Hanita.

Hanita was a second home, populated by many ex-Shimron friends. The dining room was crowded with Australians, Haganah officials, kibbutz members, and units about to leave for the front. Three units were packing ammunition and explosives, ready to move along three different tracks into Lebanon and Syria. My father's unit was composed of several Australians, including three officers; five Israelis, including Mart; and the Arab guide, Rashid. Spirits were high, and shortly after nine that evening, they were ready to depart. Mother walked with them for a distance, until they reached the Lebanese border. My father talked about me and suggested, as he'd be back in a few hours, that she wait for him in Hanita. They would drive to Nahalal together in the morning, he said.

She walked back to the dining room, for olives and tea. A short while later, the first bursts of fire could be heard, through the night. The first unit returned with dawn, and as the day broke, the rest of the groups joined, for a rich breakfast and the telling of success stories.

My father's unit was missing. He had crossed the mountain ridge with his men, to reach the bridges with first light. The unit split in two, each headed toward one of the bridges. Rashid, my father, and the Australian, Kyffin, found the northern bridge unguarded. They were both relieved and disappointed at seeing no action. The invasion force was due at 4 a.m., and they were supposed to wait for it. But it was nowhere in sight. They decided to look for a less exposed site for their wait, and Rashid suggested a police station a mile away, which could easily be taken from the few men guarding it. A few people were left under the bridge, and the rest followed Rashid.

The station was manned by uniformed French soldiers, who were quick to spot the approaching platoon and opened fire. A stone fence offered some protection, but ammunition was running low and my father decided to storm the building. Together with Mart, he ran to a nearer stone cover and threw a hand grenade through the open window of the ground floor. With the second grenade and an explosion, the machine-gun fire stopped, and the rest of the unit joined them and seized the station. The soldiers inside surrendered, and while reinforcements were surrounding the building, my father took ammunition and the machine gun to the roof, which made the best observation point. The station proved to be a Vichy HQ for the area, and the prisoners talked of roadblocks and ambushes along the planned invasion route. This information was vital, and Mart was sent on a motorcycle to try to make contact with Allied forces. His tires were shot up, however, and he returned, luckily unhurt.

The building was surrounded now, and there was little they could do but prepare to defend it and await the arrival of advance Allied units. My father returned to the roof to man the machine gun and drew heavy fire from the orchard. He took the binoculars to try to trace the source of fire, and hardly managed to focus when a rifle bullet smashed the field glasses, and his eye and hands. His loss of consciousness lasted only a brief moment. Mart came up to the roof and found my father on his back, covered with blood. He bandaged his face and hands with whatever he had. A stretcher made of blankets was used to lower him to the ground floor, where he lay in pain, bleeding, but by then fully conscious.

The post held out, with mortar fire and with Mart at the machine gun, and they managed to seize and hold a French convoy heading south from Beirut, but there was no way they could evacuate the building. Hours later, the first Australian units which were part of the invasion force arrived, and along with two other wounded soldiers, my father was evacuated in a captured French truck. Rashid and Mart joined him, and struggling against the Allied convoys moving in the opposite direction, they managed to reach a British field hospital. The doctor said not to touch the original bandage, and procured an ambulance. Twelve hours after the bullet hit his face, my father reached the Hadassah hospital in Haifa. The surgeon, before putting my father to sleep, said: "Two things are certain. You've lost an eye, and you'll live. What is not clear is the condition of your head, with the glass and metal embedded in it."

A couple of hours earlier, my mother had received a message in Hanita. Moshe is wounded in the hand, it said, and he is on his way to Haifa. It's not too serious, but you should try to get there. During the long trip along the jammed road to Haifa, my mother had the sensation of not being told the truth. On arrival, she saw Shmuel and Dvorah and her own parents, who had to reassure her that my father was alive, and being operated on. Very late that night, a hot, stifling summer night, he was wheeled into a room, and my mother was allowed to go in and see him. There was not much of him to see. His head was one big bandage, except for the hole above the nose where a tube was inserted. Both his hands were covered with bandages soaked in fish oil. The smell was unbearable. He couldn't see, he could hardly breathe, and safety pins held his nostrils open to prevent choking. He was still under the effect of anesthetics, and not being able to communicate with him deepened her sense of help-lessness and anxiety.

My mother spent the night on a bench outside the hospital. Sporadic shots could be heard, and only with sunrise was she allowed into his room. What mattered was that he was alive. But what if his brain was damaged? Would he be able to see, was his first question when she entered his room. He was awake, and there was no doubt as to the clarity and full functioning of his brain; he didn't know if both his eyes were damaged or how badly. Mother told him the surgeon had assured her that he would have full use of one eye, the right one. The left was lost, so was the socket and part of his nose bridge.

I was brought in to see him, and his familiar voice, faint but humorous, reassured me. It was my father, under the bandages and the tubes. He couldn't touch me with his hands, so I was placed near his chest and apparently was most intrigued by the safety pins in his nostrils.

How relative priorities were in those days! Within months, prison, which had been a trauma and a long agony, seemed like a secure, well-protected shelter; the bombing of Tel Aviv, which left me shoe-less, a fairy tale; and a near-fatal wound, sheer luck. He had the use of one eye. The hands were a pulpous mass but would heal. Haifa was bombed incessantly throughout a second night, but very little serious damage was inflicted and the hospital remained untouched. My father was alive. Freedom had acquired a special taste and meaning after Acre, and now life itself, breathing and sensing and being, was no longer taken for granted. This was mostly the reasoning of those around him. I doubt that he indulged in meditations over divine intervention, chances, or odds, or in an "I could have died" state of mind. He felt great gratitude to Mart, derived some satisfaction from the success of the invasion, and soon began to sink into pessimism, if not despair, assessing his chances as a one-eyed cripple.

A rough classification of people as "dreamers" and "doers" would certainly include my mother in the first category. Yet, several times in their life together, she was the decision-maker, on intuition, with a sudden burst of self-confidence. After the air raid on Haifa, Mother decided they should move immediately to Jerusalem. The surgery over, the Hadassah hospital on Mount Scopus was more pleasant; she could stay with her parents; and, most important, there was a general trust that Jerusalem, being the holy city for all religions, would never be a target for bombers.

My father, well bandaged and very weak, was installed in the back seat of my grandmother's little Morris; my mother sat in front; my other grandmother took me on a bus—and we all went up the winding, beautiful road to Jerusalem. It wasn't the horrible scent of fish oil that made my mother faint when the bandages were being changed. She was a few months pregnant, too late for an abortion, and my father's reaction when he found out was violent. Never in his life before, or later—until shortly before his death, when he was losing the ability to see with his one good eye—did he indulge in self-pity. He did now. Recuperation was slow, the maiming of his face depressing, the prospect of metal and glass fragments forever embedded in his head and body terrifying. His hand was still deformed and partly paralyzed, and the empty eye socket discharged pus and was painful. The end of the war was nowhere in sight, and it was obvious that another war would have to be waged to acquire a national home for the Jews in Palestine. Moshe Dayan found himself a farmer without a farm, a soldier without an eye to focus with, or hands to pull a trigger. He saw no way of providing for his family, and the thought of a second child was a frightening prospect. He was a war hero, but he had no country which could reward, compensate, or even acknowledge its heroic son, and recovery was painfully slow.

Pouring tea from the kettle to the cup without missing it was a major task for him; reading was blurred; the judgment of distance was totally inaccurate, which made driving impossible, and attempting to focus was almost always a miss. Treating life itself as a God-sent gift, and measuring the daily shortcomings against its grandeur, could not last. Normal proportions resumed, and my parents, not being religious or even remotely believers, could not resign themselves to an abstract, humble "This is God's will" and accept. The world was fighting for its sanity and life, and although the magnitude of the Jewish tragedy under Hitler was not yet grasped, Jews in Palestine were determined to secure a state for themselves. Meanwhile, my father was taking night walks to force himself to adjust to his handicap. It was the quiet, realistic insistence of my mother and her parents, their trust in him and in his ability, and to a small degree my existence that gave him support. His recuperation meant spending a lot of time with me. I didn't seem to mind too much the absence of one eye, and was not in any way repelled or frightened by the sight. I was a fast learner, and with the excuse "Why should I read these stories to her, let her read herself," Father taught me to read and write. The fact that children under three years of age do not read didn't impress him. I talked well, I remembered well, and I soon learned the alphabet and the numbers and mastered the writing of a small vocabulary.

I learned to read, and he taught himself to live with one eye. Soon he could drive, learned to adjust to the change from light to dark, and he knew it wasn't an act of charity when Reuven Shiloah, then in charge of Special Services at the Jewish Agency, offered him a job. A real job, for a salary, and additional pay for the rent of a small apartment, and not least in importance, the chance to be absorbed again into the war effort, in its political and military aspects.

The threat of a German invasion was all too real, and it was essential to prepare an intelligence network for transmitting information to the Allies in case of a German occupation. My father submitted a detailed plan, which was approved by the British. "Moshe Dayan's network" was centered in Jerusalem but had cells and substations all over the country. My mother, by this time showing her pregnancy, participated in a training course for wireless operators in which she didn't excel, although the sight of her in khaki uniform and protruding big stomach had a cheering effect on the general morale.

We moved to a large flat in Jerusalem. Part of it was used as a wireless station. Two rooms were occupied by "Ginger" and Ron, British sergeants assigned to the intelligence plan; and when Udi was born in January, they volunteered to administer his late-night bottle. We were a family of four now. Udi (short for Ehud, the Bible hero) was a handsome, gentle, easy baby. His birth did not cause the excitement mine did, but there were no nervous tears of inexperience and uncalled-for anxiety either. I showed no symptoms of jealousy, then or at any other time, because I obviously felt secure and superior. The attention and love bestowed on me were fully and dominantly mine. I was not asked to share and never begrudged my brothers what they got. I always knew that in my father's heart, as much as he loved Udi, and later Assi, I occupied a special, unique place. I don't know whether it had to do with being his only daughter, or being his first child.

His wounds were healed. The shrapnel was mostly static, and though he suffered from pain, he learned to live with it, for the time being. We all thought in terms of the "time being." Obviously, this was a transitory period. We had no home of our own, we were mobile and adjustable, and the war engulfed our lives on a temporary basis, allowing no time or state of mind for any planning or even dreaming about the future.

Although Mother was a Jerusalemite and she loved her city, she longed to return to the farm. One day, she hoped, they would own their own farm. In contrast, Father, a Nahalal farm boy in his thoughts and behavior as well as background, fell in love with Jerusalem, especially with the Old City. On Saturdays, we walked the narrow alleys, shopped in the bazaar, and ate sumptuously at the National. Father was not interested in archaeology then, and his sense of "belonging to the Middle East" was a sensual thing. If anything spiritual supported his sense of continuity, it was the

Bible, which he knew and loved—not for its values or strict morals as much as for its prose, precision, and wonderful stories of Judges and Kings. When he walked the walls of the Old City, he could see King David and King Solomon, the way he thought of Gideon and heard Deborah and Barak in the Valley of Jezreel.

Jerusalem was smells and tastes and sounds which were home for him, not an exotic Orient but his own language, an extension of his spirit which was never in conflict with his beloved Nahalal, with the orchards of kibbutz Hanita or the flowers on the Hill of Moreh.

The Germans did not occupy Palestine, and some of the network trainees were recruited for missions into Nazi-occupied Europe. In the summer of 1942, we returned to Nahalal. Deganya, Nahalal, Shimron, Jerusalem, Hanita, Nahalal again . . . Farming on a moshav, on a commune, fighter, intelligence officer, sailor, truck driver—how and where did my father see his future? Clearly, he had no ambition whatsoever to achieve any of the things that made him famous a few years later. He was never surrounded by an entourage or aimed at leadership. He wasn't a loner, but didn't encourage jovial friendships. He did not think of himself as a brilliant future strategist or even an exceptional farmer; and his scholarly inclinations were satisfied with improving his English with the help of my mother. In one of the last letters from Acre, he tried to sum up his thoughts, dreams, and plans: "About our future, after all we are not children, and we have Yaël, and it's time we had planned our life. I know that plans and reality may be too different things, but I've given it a lot of thought. Basically, I think that my demands on life are minimal. If once I thought that social activities were central, that one should search for 'fun' and 'content,' that in order to find life satisfactory one should be active and perhaps even a leader, today I ask for much less. The subject is happiness, and to achieve it I imagine a way of life— We are sitting in our cozy room, listening to the radio, reading a good book or poetry, Yaël rolling on the rug and you knitting. We sip tea and talk . . . I know this is an exaggerated romantic idyllic picture, but these are my daydreams.

"What work to do? Whatever, as long as it does not disrupt the scene I've described. I could be the village driver, or a watchman, a builder or a farmer, in a kibbutz or a moshav, even a trade-union functionary, as long as I can have the peace of family life, the good books and the two of you. You probably think I am naïve, I must sound more like a Boy Scout than a father, but these are the desires I want to share with you. I feel I've lived for so long, and went through so much, that all I want is calm and rest. Good night, and a kiss in the middle of your forehead . . ."

Returning to Nahalal, to a small cabin famous for its leaking roof, offered the beginning of the peaceful life he coveted. Farm chores and duties were resumed, as if nothing had happened in the interim —except my father's black eye patch.

My father hated the black patch. He hated it physically—it irritated and upset him—and he hated the symbolic value it had acquired. For many years he didn't abandon the hope of replacing it with an artificial eye, and he underwent several operations—each less successful than the other. The villagers soon were used to it, and children, once their curiosity was satisfied, didn't give it a second thought. My own schoolmates wanted to know whether there was a deformed sick eye under it or a deep hole, and at home, the instant he walked in, he removed it, and we were accustomed to the scar and the deformed skin under it. Only later did I realize that his real fear had to do with the one healthy eye, that it might be injured and leave him totally blind.

I was sent to the village kindergarten; my mother tried to earn some money making children's dresses; Father worked on his father's farm, waiting for a chance to buy his own farmstead and basically seeing his future as a member of the Nahalal cooperative.

I remember nothing of the kindergarten. I was reading and writing already, and my world was rich with stories and tales rather than toys. My mother's efforts to earn extra income were not successful, as she worked without patterns and put too much effort and material that was too good into products which the spartan, stingy, poor Nahalal families considered luxuries. I was to remain, for many years, the best-dressed little girl in the circle, and the sewing machine was put to other uses—patching and mending and making sheets and curtains. My Grandfather Shmuel regarded the experience as degrading. We were farmers, people of the land gathered from the Diaspora to reclaim and cultivate the soil, not to indulge in frills.

He would not have a dressmaker for a daughter-in-law. My father tried in vain to fix the leaking roof, and perhaps one of my early real memories has to do with the obstacle course from door to bed, as one hopped around or over pots and buckets placed on the floor under the holes in the roof, to contain the rainwater.

But before we got our own farmstead, we moved again, this time to Tel Aviv. As before, this was not my father's doing, but a move prompted by higher Haganah circles which thought there was a job that "Moshe Dayan from Nahalal was the right guy for . . ."

Two years earlier, Sadeh had come to recruit Father for the Syrian operation, and now into the cabin one afternoon walked Eliahu Golomb with a new assignment for my father. Golomb was Supreme Commander of the Haganah, and the mission he wanted my father to perform had to do with Jews rather than Arabs or Vichyites. Father would be a full-time officer in the Haganah headquarters in Tel Aviv, and participate in the attempt to stop and curtail the independent dissident undergrounds. The Haganah advocated "restraint" and cooperation with the British against the Nazis. The war was still on, and Ben-Gurion believed there was no call for acts of violence, such as the Irgun and the Lehi were engaged in, against the British or, for that matter, against innocent Arabs.

Of all the battles, intelligence work, or political endeavors my father engaged in, this was certainly the least pleasant, emotionally the most taxing, and spiritually exhausting and trying. He rather liked some of the Irgun and Lehi leaders, respected greatly their self-sacrificing devotion, and understood, even shared, their motivation. But he knew their methods were wrong. Rather than "hunt" them—the Haganah tactic during the so-called Saison of 1943—he tried to negotiate with and persuade the dissidents, but he was unsuccessful and was unhappily forced to follow the official approach.

Father insisted we all move to Tel Aviv, and to his father's expression of discontent, he replied that loyalty and proximity in marriage were difficult enough to sustain and he was not going to risk it by physical separation, or take chances. Shmuel, of course, thought the big city was bound to corrupt us small children, and he was sure we would pale and weaken without the fresh farm eggs, the smell of fresh hay, and the famous Nahalal fresh double cream.

We lived in one shabby hotel room, then in another, and Tel Aviv was harmless and cozy compared to my grandfather's predictions. I was nearly five, and it was time to think of proper schooling for me. My parents paid a visit to the best school in Tel Aviv, talked to the teachers and the headmaster, and found out there was no room in the first grade. My father suggested I was overqualified for the first grade, and when it was ascertained that this was indeed the case, I was enrolled at the age of five in the second grade. I was two years younger than my classmates, which didn't bother me then, or later, and even offered certain advantages, not the least of which was my parents' pride at this enormous leap. Udi was accepted in a nursery school across the street from my school; Mother enrolled in a French course; and I proved to be a responsible "big sister," taking Udi to and from his school, before and after mine, and babysitting with him in the afternoon. I was not only the youngest in the class but by far the smallest. Of small frame anyway, thin-limbed, and rather short, I nevertheless was strong and pretty in a regular way, and had no trouble keeping up with the others.

By the end of my first school year, the Saison, to everybody's great relief, was over, and a farm was available in Nahalal. Resources— mostly those of my mother's parents—were put together, and farmstead number 53 on the Nahalal circle was ours. After ten years of marriage and two children, my parents had their own home, and if they worked hard, a stable source of income—another dream— would come true.

F O U R ✖ T H E

P R O T E C T I V E

C I R C L E

Every time my family returned to Nahalal, they had the illusion that it was forever. The year in the Haganah HQ did not lead my father to think in professional terms, to wish to climb higher in the hierarchy or contribute more than he did. Lack of personal ambition, which distinguished his behavior all his life, did not necessarily stem from a sense of inferiority or inability. Even at those times when he knew himself to be superior, he never indulged in self-promotion. "They" knew where he was, "they" knew his worth and how to get in touch. More than availability he didn't wish to offer, and when it was taken, he would devote himself totally to whatever the mission was, reaching deep and high without regarding any of the positions as a step in a ladder which would advance his career.

Number 53 farmstead had a small house on it, consisting of two rooms, a living-dining room and a kitchen. Toilet facilities were, for the time being, in the back yard, and the walk there at night with a lantern was scary. Altogether, this shaky aluminum structure, hiding a dug hole covered with a provisory wooden "seat," the square cuts of newspaper for tissue, the unpleasant odors that stemmed from the wooden floor—all these were signs of poverty, a reminder of primitive beginnings and an inspiration to try harder, as we all did, so as to be able to install proper facilities in the house, running water and the like. (This was to be installed several years later, for at the time all efforts were concentrated on the actual farm.) In addition to the citrus grove that came with the farm, my father bought some cows, built a chicken run, and planted vegetables. There were dogs, German shepherds, and a mule called Lord which was our means of transportation when tied to a two-wheel cart. For fun we had a donkey named Menelaus, chicks under the brooder, small rabbits to play with. I had a baby brother on the way, for my mother was happily (and my father was contented this time) carrying Assi.

Both my parents, on various occasions, referred to the years following our return to Nahalal as their happiest. These were the years between the two wars. The one had destroyed our people, and the other secured our national home. If this was happiness on borrowed time, my parents didn't realize it, and as far as they knew or planned, life was going to consist of making the cows produce more milk, fighting insects and worms that bugged the cauliflower, and harvesting a better yield of wheat. Hopes had to do with rainfall, farm machinery, and a new coop for the chickens, and disasters meant drought, a cow giving birth to a dead calf, or a foot-and-mouth cattle epidemic, which hurt our farm badly.

My father's involvement with public, military, or political affairs was minimal. His father was active in Zionist councils and in the Labor movement, and, at the time, young people were not encouraged to replace their experienced elders. Heated arguments at home were for argument's sake, a verbal involvement after milking or before plowing.

They were happy years for me too, and when I think of "childhood" in the abstract, before the impossible painful teens and after the little-remembered dramatic first years of my life, I recollect a rainbow dotted with pleasurable moments, delightful events, and enriching experiences.

An active partner and contributor to this happiness was my Grandmother Dvorah. I was the oldest of her eight grandchildren, and her favorite, and I daily walked the quarter of the circle separating my parents' farm from my grandparents'. There, her time was mine, and her world shared with me as if I were a savings account into which to pour and invest all precious knowledge and accumulated wealth of experience.

My grandmother was not an easy woman. I had the time, the desire to learn and listen, and if not the mature understanding, the love for her, the way she was. Her dreams and aspirations were never to be fulfilled. Small and frail and very beautiful, she was ill for as long as I can remember. She fought cancer all her life and tried not to be dramatic about it. Dvorah was an artist, a serious, talented writer who had to be satisfied with expressing herself in short stories and vignette essays for the Labor-movement women's weekly, in a language which wasn't the language of her heart. We would sit under the grapefruit tree making butter from creamy milk till my arms ached, and talk about Pushkin. We skimmed the froth from the big bubbling pot of rose-petal jam, and talked of Anna's suicide. Anna Karenina, Raskolnikov's guilt, Tolstoy's ideas, Turgenev's men, and Chekhov's women populated our world, and my enthusiasm waned only when she attempted to teach me Russian, of which I retain a couple of nursery rhymes. Grandmother's Russian romanticism was well encased in a stubborn, almost tough external behavior. Her approach was cerebral, her posture in the village aloof, and her manners quite pedantic and calculated. She called me Yulinka, my parents called me Yula—a nickname I carried till I was married, and both she and Shmuel spoiled me rotten.

Shmuel, my grandfather, had nothing sophisticated about him. He operated and functioned on a basic level. A handsome, strong man, he idealized farming and the "return to the land," even when he was away on peculiar missions to the Labor Zionist supporters in Toronto or the Zionist Congress in Basel. On his return, he would proudly switch to old patched work clothes and boots and enjoy the smell of the cowshed and the touch of the wooden plow handle, as if his trips abroad were a burdensome sacrifice. He had a hearty laugh, and in an endearingly naïve way, his love for Dvorah was mingled with humble adoration. He knew he had deprived her of a fulfilling intellectual life, and his dogged insistence on working hard on the farm, washing dishes, and writing long, apologetic letters was his way of offering a small compensation.

The gap between the ideology my grandfather preached and the way he lived his life would, he hoped, be bridged by the fact that his firstborn son, Moshe, and his family would epitomize the success of the new Zionism. Although my father, for reasons beyond his control, was to be unable to fulfill these hopes, in 1946 we could pass for a model of Jewish renewal.

Our little house was very modest, but matched my parents' dreams of a warm nest. The curtains were handmade, with appliqués; the tablecloth hand-embroidered; and the atmosphere was cozy and welcoming. Though we were as poor as the other farmers, there were little luxuries to indulge in. We children had a radio, had toys; we were meticulously dressed, and we each had shoes, boots, and sandals. Work was shared by all. I had my list of chores in the house and on the farm. I helped by picking fruit and vegetables, cleaning and sorting the eggs, and feeding the chickens. I walked to the bakery every day, munching on the fresh loaf as I returned home, and tended my brothers Udi and the newborn Assi, who was a delightful, happy baby. The entire family spent afternoons in the farmyard, busy with the livestock and the plants, Assi in a packing crate with his bottle, and even Udi running around trying to help.

Education was something that more or less just happened. School was a few short hours a day, the class an odd mixture of age groups, and if the teacher was good we considered ourselves lucky. We were taught the basics, and I doubt whether any of us or our teachers and parents thought at the time of higher education or the need to prepare for it. At the same time, Father put a great deal into our education, not systematically but in his way of sharing his loves and interests. I never missed the birthing of a cow, no matter how late at night, or a new book of poems by Alterman or Shlonsky, the two great poets of that period. To this day, I carry exciting memories both of a newborn calf being pulled out and emerging, trying to stand on its frail legs while being licked by his mother, and of the rhymes of Alterman and Shlonsky (still my favorite Hebrew poets), I can hear their rhymes the way I did then, sitting high on a haystack, listening to my father recite them to me.

There were no whispers at home. There was nothing that could not be said in front of us children, and if we "understood" the times we lived in, or loved our farm and homeland, this was the result of my parents' honesty. We were not "indoctrinated." Rather, formative experiences like climbing Mount Tabor on a Saturday, Assi in my father's arms and Udi in a pram, picking flowers, the sunsets over the Carmel ridge, the smell of the thirsty soil responding to the first rain, the taste of the first tangerines in late fall were all particles in the larger composition which produced love of land and country. Arabs from neighboring tribes visited us often. I was never told an Arab was the enemy. British soldiers were still safeguarding the Mandate. Security was not questioned, and as far as we were concerned, there was no other homeland and the gathering clouds of the looming war did not darken those joyful days.

I had schoolmates. They came home, and I visited them, though my father was not particularly friendly to the other children. We mostly met in back yards; we had a tree house, where we played for hours, each of us bringing her own toys to share. We also made new friends when a group of Holocaust survivors was brought to Nahalal. They were known as the "Teheran children," although most of them were of Polish origin and many were orphans. Each family "adopted" a child, and so our family of five was enlarged and Tzippi joined us, bringing with her the smells and fears of a tragedy still unknown to us.

Tzippi was older and much larger than I. An intruder at first, she soon found her place among us, and if she was jealous of me, I was not aware of it. Several of the "Teheran children" were in my class, and they represented the outside world in a way that was both curious and frightening. Names like Lila, Vera, Sammy were names from novels; their accents were strange; and they spoke mostly Yiddish. They had no families but spoke of their parents and longed for them. They told us of wealth and large houses, of the big cities and large farmhouses where they had hidden, but they talked little of the deportation. They were possessive and often unkind, and we were told to be generous and patient, to share and to understand something which, of course, was beyond understanding or grasping.

The war also meant postcards from Zorik and Aviva, my father's brother and sister, who were both abroad with the Jewish units of the British Army. I adored them both and missed them, and when

Zorik stayed on at the end of the war to help with Jewish refugees,
I could connect Tzippi's presence with his absence.

All recollections of my childhood are a little suspect, but I think
mine are probably genuine in part because of two sensations that
dim them which have remained with me. One had to do with the
Dayan family status in Nahalal, and the other with the stifling
feeling the circle had on us. We were not too popular in the moshav
community. My grandfather was often criticized for high preaching
and poor performance; my grandmother was pitied by many for
having to endure by herself but envied by others for her rich and
deep intellectual life. The Dayans as a clan were too independent,
too nonconformist, too stubborn, and not generous enough to fit the
pattern. Though less rigid than the commune, the cooperative demanded a certain conformity from each individual. The villagers
resented Dvorah for trying to sell her homemade jam privately, my
father for trying to cultivate new strains of vegetables, my mother
for dressing me in "city" dresses, and all of us for being slightly
different. Jealousy did not breed sanctions, and we derived strength
and self-confidence from one another, ignoring the gossip. If we were
indeed different, we were not ashamed of it.

Of the Dayans, only my mother was truly comfortable in the
closed circle. She who was not born into it found security in offered
friendships, had no desire or need to excel above others, was
tolerant, and accepted human shortcomings and even failures. I was
competitive and eager, but not for one minute did I see my world
as limited to this circular, muddy dirt track, though I was happy to
be protected by it. I read like a maniac, daydreaming about dramas
and romances that could only occur away from the village circle. I
didn't feel trapped in the circle, but I never ignored the way out of
it. Somehow, my family made it clear that the optimum in quality—
of people or opportunities or possible achievements—existed mostly
outside.

The Dayans were founders, and hardworking farmers. We had our
own farms, and Nahalal was undeniably and inextricably our one
and only home. Yet, more than anybody else, we had secret or open
"escape routes" to the outside world, bloodlines and sources to widen

our scopes: Shmuel's travels around the world, and his frequent trips to Tel Aviv; my mother's parents coming, and us visiting with them; Father's Haganah activities, which continued intermittently and kept us from taking his daily presence for granted; Dvorah's illness, which resulted in long periods of disappearance in hospitals or the Motza sanatorium. Zorik was in Europe, Aviva back from Egypt, my mother's sister Reumah was in London, Tzippi's father was in Europe and expected to come and perhaps take her away. The world did not end at the wide perimeter of the cultivated fields of Nahalal. The Carmel ridge to the west, the Hill of Moreh in the east were as far as the eye could see, but the Dayans had wings and the sky was the limit. Or so I believed whenever I thought of my future life.

The Valley of Jezreel was celebrating its twenty-fifth anniversary, and I was selected to read a poem "On behalf of the grandchildren" in a large ceremony in Ein Harod. Dressed in a white dress, with dangling embroidered cherries sewn on it, I made my first public appearance. To reach the microphone, I was placed on a chair, and to the proud delight of my grandparents, I read the poem and the greeting loud and clear. The success led to another appearance at the Nahalal anniversary celebration. This time I composed my own speech, encouraging the Diaspora children to join us in the sacred project of returning to our land, offering to share with them our homes, joys, and sense of freedom. I was eight, a fast learner and an impressionable child, and no doubt I easily digested some of my grandfather's high-key, enthusiastic, and oversimplified truisms.

It was at this time that my father, with little enthusiasm and many doubts, took his first step into the local political arena. Very few young people then found party politics attractive or enticing, and the first line of leadership in Mapai (Ben-Gurion's Zionist Labor Party) was composed of men and women in their late fifties. There was a call for more involvement on the part of the younger generation, and candidates were recruited to participate in committees and councils. Ben-Gurion encouraged the Young Mapai members, as they were sure to back the activist line he urged when the world war was over. A sense of duty rather than a desire to embark on a political career, then, motivated my father to present himself as candidate, and together with Shimon Peres he was elected in 1946 to represent the Young Guard at the Zionist Congress in Basel. Shmuel was an official delegate to the congress, and enough funds were raised and scraped to enable my mother and Dvorah to go along. Zorik was to meet the family in Switzerland; my Aunt Reumah planned to join them from London; and we were left with Aviva and a young woman from the village who moved in.

The preparations, the packing, and the arrangements were a source of great excitement and pride. I was unaware of the political implication of the congress, which was, in fact, going to vote to choose between Weizmann's moderation and Ben-Gurion's activist policies. My parents were going to Paris after the congress for corrective surgery on my father's eye socket, hoping to be able to get rid of the black patch and use an artificial eye. I was promised a watch and chocolates—the two predictable Swiss gifts—and I promised to write daily.

The trip was only a partial success. My father's speech, his first to a large assembly of "strangers," won him minor fame and the complimentary acknowledgment of Ben-Gurion, which he treasured. But, while Zorik returned to Germany and Reumah volunteered to work with UNRRA at the DP camps, my father's operation was a disaster. His body rejected the bone transplant. For days, he hallucinated in a high fever, nursed by French-speaking nuns in a miserable hospital, and my mother shared his pain and disappointment. Shmuel was injured in Italy in a car accident on the way home and was brought back on a stretcher. My parents returned exhausted, bringing me, as promised, my first watch.

In Palestine, the British Mandate was about to terminate, and for all Jews the formation of a trained and equipped force was the central objective into which all efforts went. My father was summoned by Dori, Commander in Chief of the Haganah, and agreed to return to the military to work on intelligence projects.

Though we didn't move again, and the only major change in our daily lives was the hired laborer who helped with the heavy farm work, our family's feeling of permanence and stability was disturbed. Father came home most nights, still worked on the farm many days, told us bedtime stories, and was as interested in details of schoolwork as before, but something had changed. The major competitor for his love, attention, and time—the "state"—had appeared, never to be fully removed. Time was the main thing. He had enough love for his family and his country, and his attention was totally undivided for each in its turn. He was never absent-minded or remote, or taken up with other thoughts while being with or listening or talking to us. But he was there less. Zorik was back, and married his fiancée, Mimi, in a lovely triple wedding where the whole village danced and rejoiced. Again, there was a feeling of borrowed time and stolen joys, and it touched us all. Many of the men were away training most of the time, and the women worked harder but distractedly and with terrible anxiety. Tzippi's father arrived with other survivors of Bergen-Belsen, and the reunion was disastrous. The man frightened us all, with his stale chocolates, unshaved cheeks, and leather breeches. He was unstable and talked of a plan he had to save the Jewish state. He must meet with Ben-Gurion, he kept repeating, and Tzippi was hysterical, clinging to my parents and refusing to go near him. My father reassured her, but her world of expectations and dreams collapsed pathetically within minutes, and the man left, talking to himself. He was later hospitalized in a mental institution, and Tzippi continued to live with us as long as we were in Nahalal. His visit was a sign of the times and for me in part the slow filtering in of the knowledge that the dark side of life was not limited to Russian literature.

Yet, before we wept, we danced again.

On the night of November 29, 1947, the United Nations' General Assembly voted to partition Palestine between Arabs and Jews. The partition resolution anticipated the establishment of an independent Jewish state, the culmination of age-old yearnings, of two thousand years of hopes and prayers—the fulfillment of a messianic dream.

My father's strong hands lifted me from my bed and sleep. Mother woke up Udi, and we dressed in a hurry. I half knew what was happening, and the excitement was contagious. We hurried—leaving Assi, who was still a baby, to sleep—to the community hall in the center of the village. Everybody was there, old and young, dancing to the music, kissing and embracing and crying with joy, until the rising sun painted the sky pink and it was time to milk the cows.

If there was a vein of sadness in the faces of the dancers, it was a small indication of the price that would be paid. How many of these young people would be dancing here next year? How many of the children would be orphaned? How many mothers would be without sons? These thoughts could not be repressed, as, by the end of that week, thirty-six Jews were killed by Arab terrorists. The term "Arab" itself was gaining a new meaning. War was imminent, though not yet declared, and growing up had to be speeded up for us.

My father never dramatized these things. Before, during, and after wars, he talked and wrote about them matter-of-factly. Even his deeply felt compassion for the casualties and their families was low-keyed, reverent. He was enthusiastic about the personal courage of others, ignoring his own, or taking it for granted, and did not indulge in the romantic or morose aspects of fighting.

By the end of 1947, a full-scale war was on, though the official invasion of Israel by all the Arab countries was launched a few months later, when the British left and independence was declared. We dug trenches by the tangerine tree, for protection from shelling and air raids, and we knew that if the village siren sounded, we had to get into them. Jerusalem was cut off from the rest of the country, and for many weeks we lost touch with my grandparents, as the phone lines were down. Zorik and Mimi had had a baby boy, Uzi, and they were living in a suburb of Haifa. Zorik was serving as an officer in the Northern Carmeli Brigade, and it was clear he was never going to settle for farming in Nahalal. Aviva, Israel her husband, and their two children lived with my grandparents and were working on the farm. Israel was an officer, too, coming and going in much the same way my father did.

We children played war games, talked in military jargon, and bragged about our fathers and uncles. The realization of what it was really like came with the shock of the first death in the village, in the family, someone we knew—and the first grave. The agony of this war shattered me with the cry of my Grandmother Dvorah when she was told that her youngest son, Zorik, had been killed. I had never seen her cry before, or I didn't remember. I had never thought of her as old before, or even vulnerable. But after Zorik's death my wise and all-knowing grandmother, disciplined and brave, was a broken person. Indeed, we were all helpless in our anguish. Zorik was special to each of us. He was not a typical Dayan, with his optimism, his jolly, unmalicious humor, his vitality and sensitivity. Zorik kidded me and made me laugh; he teased me and told me funny stories. With Zorik I rode a horse for the first time. Zorik was Dvorah's baby, my mother's young brother, a friend to Reumah her sister, the village's naughty darling. Zorik's body was left for three days in the fields of Ramat Yohanan, unapproachable because of snipers. It was a warm May, and the last of the spring flowers, poppies and wild chrysanthemum, covered the fields when my father went to identify Zorik's body. Mimi and Uzi, only a few months old, stayed with us, and Mimi insisted in her sobbing that Zorik was still alive. I knew the baby would never know his father, and I panicked. It could happen to me, and to my brothers. I had no control over the things that mattered, and there, in the coffin draped in black, could be my own father. The proximity of death was frightening. The candles burning in my grandparents' house, the sobbing turning into screams by the grave, the disbelief on Shmuel's pained face, my father's inability to ease his mother's anguish—memories were told and retold, as if talking about him, or reading his poems, or remembering things he said would resurrect him. I was never lied to, and reality was never bent in order to accommodate my age. Storks did not bring children into the world, and the dead did not disappear into the clouds in the sky to dwell with angels. Zorik would never return. He was buried in Shimron, and we laid fresh flowers on his grave. Mimi was a widow, my beloved grandparents were bereaved parents, and I found little if any comfort in my father reassuring me, time and time again, that he was not going to be hurt. He had got his bullet already, he said, and he survived it. Now he knew how to avoid them and he had no intention of being hit again. There was no god in our lives to pray to, so I had to take his word and try hard to believe what he said.

Maturity has to do with not taking anything for granted. Zorik's death gave me a shocking blow in this direction. All these good things bestowed on us, the obvious, the God-sent, the natural, had a price tag on them. And on a shelf in a corner, not too exposed but ever present, Mother's peach-pits necklace made in the Acre prison, Tzippi's screams at night, Zorik's photo draped in black, all were warning signals that I was too young to understand but old enough to be alarmed by. The phrase repeated at cemeteries every day was suddenly real: "In their death they bequeathed us life . . ." Family, my little brothers, the pretty room the three of us shared, the cowshed and the smell of clover I chopped, my schoolmates and my watch and my own life, nothing, not even the change of seasons in the valley or rainfall in the winter, could be taken for granted again.

On May 14, 1948, we listened to the historical radio broadcast of Ben-Gurion reading the Declaration of Independence. The blue-and-white flag of Israel flew everywhere, and even we children held our breath in awe when Ben-Gurion spoke the words "Medinat-Israel" —the State of Israel. Born in Mandate Palestine, we would grow up and have children in the independent, free, and, we hoped, secure State of Israel.

By May 14, the line of graves in Shimron was long. Zorik did not rest alone there. The all-out attack on Israel by six Arab countries on May 15 hadn't taken anybody by surprise. The British had left, the Haganah had officially become Zahal—the Israel Defense Forces—and my father was assigned to organize and train an elite commando battalion. He had a khaki uniform; a revolver dangled from his belt, legally and openly; and he had the rank of major. The state was three days old when General Yadin summoned him to command the Jordan Valley front. Deganya, Father's birthplace, was under heavy attack. It had been seven years since my father actively participated in a battle. Physically he was fit, and the absence of his left eye was a fact he had adjusted to. "To aim and hit, you need one eye only, and one good finger," he said.

He arrived in Deganya on the eighteenth. The Syrians were preparing for a major onslaught with an infantry brigade reinforced by tanks and artillery and some air support. The defenders had home-made explosives—Molotov cocktails—a few anti-tank bazookas with limited ammunition, small arms, and dedication. Two of the settlements nearby were deserted, which added to the gloom, and when representatives of the settlers appealed with tears to Ben-Gurion, he said: I'm sending you Moshe Dayan as reinforcement . . .

According to my father, he wasn't instrumental in saving Deganya, but what was obvious was his contribution to morale, his inspiring courage, and a few well-timed and inventive tactical decisions. My father ignored the chain of command and was not bothered by who was subordinate to whom. His orders were carried out because they were given with confidence and self-assurance. There was no time to check whether a written authorization was on hand. He moved about quickly in his jeep, inspecting each trench, changing positions, placing the few bazookas at the flanks. Luckily, a 65mm gun, initially on its way to Jerusalem, was diverted to Deganya and helped save the settlement.

The battle took place at the kibbutz gates. A Syrian tank made its way into the main square but was stopped in time in front of the trenches. When shells began to hit the approaching Syrian infantry, they started to withdraw in panic. Father was surrounded by close friends, some of whom had no business being there but followed him faithfully. Nahalal fighters, his brother-in-law Israel, friends from the settlement of Yavniel—all hand-picked and capable. The assault on Deganya lasted nine hours, with brief intervals. The danger to the Jordan Valley was removed, and that evening Father, with a few friends, drove into Zemach, the small Arab town across the river which served as HQ to the Syrian forces. Later he talked often about this night visit. There was no way of knowing if there were troops still in the town, but his curiosity was stronger than his sense of caution. He didn't have to leave the bridge during the Allied invasion and go look for the police station where he lost his eye. This time the risk proved worth taking, for Zemach was totally deserted.

He returned to Deganya with a Syrian radio car and some guns and was deeply affected by the ease with which the enemy had abandoned everything, including their wounded and dead. "They knew they outnumbered us by far. They knew we couldn't attack the town, and yet, at the sound of the first shell, they broke down and fled. Like the birds in the corn field, when we chase them, banging on empty cans."

If he needed a boost to his self-confidence as a fighter, the battle of Deganya did it, and he reported back to Sadeh reassured in his acceptance of the command of the special commando battalion.

Although Nahalal was only a short distance away, we didn't sense the danger. Mother was sent for one night to visit Father in Deganya, something that recurred in every battle thereafter. When he was away more than one night, he would send a jeep for her to join him; he would take her around the trenches, talk with her and inquire about us and the farm. There were no camp followers, but no full-time soldiering either, and it seemed only natural for him to have her around.

The only one among us who was nervous was my grandmother. Since Zorik's death, she feared for my father, and her fear was not irrational. She knew his daredevil courage, and she counted the minutes to his return. My visits to her were less frequent, as I felt I had to tiptoe in the presence of a great grief. She said to me one day: "You don't have to whisper. Zorik is not asleep, he is dead," and cried. Later, better adjusted, she read me Zorik's poems, showed me pictures of him, and talked to me of my father's boyhood as if passing on to me secret information which would be precious if her prayers weren't answered and the same fate befell my father. For his part, Grandfather said to me: "Your father is a hero"—a sentence that bothered me no end then, as in those days it was almost like saying "Your father was a hero" to an orphan.

Battalion 89, plainly known as the Commando, was organized, equipped, and trained in unconventional methods. It had in its ranks a mixture of fighters. The nucleus, composed of volunteers from Nahalal and from other farms, was joined by ex-Lehi dissident underground fighters, by a group of eager Tel Aviv youngsters, and by a few volunteers from overseas. It was a heterogeneous battalion: nobody was forced to join, but the prestige of the group and its commander soon spread, and other units started to complain of the miraculous disappearance of men and equipment who deserted to join "89." The unit embodied informality at its best: no rank badges, no salutes, individually designed uniforms, and a sky-high spirit that was toughened and solidified by hard training. The weaponry consisted of jeeps with machine guns attached, for the key word was mobility; and the tactical instructions were to race forward, surprise, destroy, and move on. Each individual soldier counted, and each had to be relied on to act with courage, initiative, and precision. My father was in his element as a field commander—surrounded by friends, free of textbooks and conventions, and ready to go. And when they did go, they reached far.

The battalion's first objectives were to capture enemy posts around two Arab villages not far from the airport and the city of Lydda. Another brigade was to enter Ramle and Lydda later and disrupt the enemy line in the central sector, between Tel Aviv and Jerusalem.

At dawn, Battalion 89 moved out. The two objectives were soon achieved. During the short battle, my father left his scout car, ran under fire to the company commanders, took command of one of the companies, and demonstrated what he meant by storming with full fighting power. The battalion had five wounded and was resting when my father was summoned by Ben-Gurion. He drove his jeep to the Tel Aviv HQ and found B-G worried. He was upset mostly about Jerusalem, unhappy with its command and the morale of its defenders. He wanted to appoint my father commander of Jerusalem.

Father, in fatigues which bore traces of the fighting he had just been in, was amused and irritated. This was Ben-Gurion's way, and later his own, too. He wanted to see Dayan there and then, and he had to be found and summoned—from wherever . . . My father rejected the proposal outright. He was fighting with his own men; he was not about to relinquish this command and go somewhere where he was bound to send others to fight. Not right then, not in the middle of combat. Ben-Gurion asked for details of the morning's battle, and dismissed my father. It was understood that the Jerusalem appointment would be brought up again.

"89" proceeded to Deir Tarif, which was held by the Jordanian Legion, and my father found his men engaged in a static battle not to his liking. He ordered his driver to zigzag to the top of the hill, avoiding sniper fire, "to get a better look at what was happening and what's next." He quickly assessed the situation, and a devilish brain wave went through his mind. They were dillydallying. There was no element of surprise in besieging Deir Tarif. The real target was down there in the flatland, surrounded by olive groves—the city of Lydda. Tens of thousands of people, large stone buildings, a well-armed military force defending it—the idea seemed completely crazy. His eye caught a nearer target, crazy enough, too, in the shape of a beautiful armored car equipped with a two-pounder gun! It took a few hours under Jordanian artillery, the ingenuity of a mechanic who volunteered to help, a tow cable, and some luck, and the vehicle was towed down, to the applause and cheers of the fighters. A few men were put through the fastest artillery training course ever, and were able to operate the gun. The radio was re-paired and a suitable name was painted on the armor: The Terrible Tiger. Many of the vehicles bore written phrases—the best-remembered of which was Nahalal–Amman Express.

Encouraged by the condition of the Tiger, my father casually said in a loud enough voice for the company commanders to hear: "Let's finish up here and make for Lydda!" Those who thought he was joking didn't know their commander. In a short while, with the Tiger in the lead, the half-tracks following, and the jeeps in the rear, they stormed the main street of Lydda.

The successful attack on Lydda and Ramle has been told and retold many times. The use of shock tactics, crushing by surprise, the speed and fire element, all have been analyzed in textbooks and debated. Many tend to belittle the victory by emphasizing the luck element while criticizing the risk-taking chutzpah. It could have been a disaster . . . But my father was no trigger-happy, daredevil hero taking chances. The risks taken were calculated ones within a battle plan that, though perceived and worked out on the spot, was clear and quite detailed. The breakthrough lasted less than an hour. The column proceeded from Lydda to Ramle as the radio system failed and the leading half-track lost its brakes. When they stopped, both cities were behind them. Then they retraced their route, return-ing to the point of departure. A sweeping, storming, surprising move which enabled Yigal Allon's brigade to engage later in a final battle at the end of which both cities yielded. My father himself was everywhere. Jumping from vehicle to vehicle, shouting orders when there was no functioning radio, encouraging, helping to load casualties for evacuation, and operating small arms when advancing.

In this short, exemplary battle, my father thought he demonstrated many qualities and methods which should typify—and did later—the "something unique" of the Israeli special units. The reactions to the battle were various. Yadin was angry but added: "Nothing succeeds like success." The brigade commander who completed the takeover of the cities said: "Moshe acted according to his character; he did his demonstrative bit, and walked away." Sadeh criticized and praised. Ben-Gurion listened to a full report and commented at the end: "This is not the way to fight a war." Father thought then that this was the only way to fight this particular battle with this particular unit. Still, Ben-Gurion insisted that his choice of my father as commander of Jerusalem be accepted, against the better judgment of Yigal Yadin, Ya'akov Dori, and the other active generals. A delegation of officers from Battalion 89, threatening a "strike" if my father was posted elsewhere, didn't change Ben-Gurion's mind, and the appointment was finalized. August 1 we were to move to Jerusalem.

After the battle of Lydda and Ramle, having visited the wounded in the hospital and reporting to HQ, Father came home to Nahalal. He always did this in the days and weeks that followed, when, before taking command of Jerusalem, the battalion participated in the breakthrough that prevented the Negev from being cut off from the rest of the country. He would be in Nahalal for a few brief hours, take a bath, change clothes, and refresh himself. These short visits were a boost of life to his mother and father and a source of security for us. My mother managed to see him more often, as he arranged reunions in the battalion's headquarters.

His presence at home was very physical. He always kissed us on the mouth, hugged and embraced and patted. The three of us would climb into his bed when he was resting, and he would find a moment to play a favorite game, listen to what we had to say, and tell us what he'd been through. We never suspected that a goodbye kiss could be the last one, because he seemed so infallible and so fully protected. Not because I was an innocent. I went up the cemetery hill, not to gather flowers as before, but to lay fresh ones on grave-stones of young people I knew. Nahalal was bombed from the air, by Iraqi light planes, and the silly-looking ditches we helped dig came in very handy. We were covered with dirt and gravel while sitting crouched in them as a shell hit not far off. Our next-door neighbors on both sides lost a son and a prospective son-in-law on the eve of his wedding. My mother's spells of crying had to do with the agony and pain of other people's losses, not with her own anxiety for our father, and when a truce was announced and there was a ceasefire in Jerusalem, we sensed the relief of the adults around us, and shared it.

We were told we were to move to Jerusalem, and though I didn't find the prospect appealing, there was the knowledge that Father would be with us, every day and night. I didn't want to leave Nahalal, the school, or the farm, or my grandparents or my school-mates. It wasn't a move to an unknown place, either. My other grandparents lived in Jerusalem. I visited the city often; I didn't fear a change of school and wasn't particularly excited or frightened by what a big city had to offer. But Nahalal was always home.

I was not aware that, breaking away from the protective circle, I was to enter a new world where, from the start, I would be referred to as "Moshe Dayan's daughter." I was a precocious child of ten, and whether this new epithet would be an unbearable handicap or a springboard was not yet up to me.

F I V E ❧ G R O W I N G U P

A N D A W A Y

The main road to Jerusalem was blocked and we took an alternate route—an unpaved, dangerous, bumpy track known as the "Burma Road." In the heat of August, it meant hours of riding in a thick cloud of dust. We first lived in my grandparents' house, while my parents were apartment hunting. The Abkarius Bey house was not exactly my father's idea of "a small warm nest." It had belonged originally to a rich Greek lawyer, whose widow left Jerusalem when the war began. The house, like other deserted houses, was taken over by the Custodian of Absentees' Properties. When we moved in, I couldn't believe my eyes. It was a palace from the pages of a novel, a mansion of princes in St. Petersburg, or a castle from a wicked fairy tale. Each room was painted in a different color, and we couldn't stop counting them. There was a pink room and a green room, and a green-tiled bathroom, a blue bathroom to match a blue room, and two enormous living rooms. There were bay windows, and a downstairs with a huge kitchen, and more rooms. There were long corridors and terraces and a walled-in garden with a water cistern and a couple of fruit trees. My parents chose furniture from the Custodian's warehouse and paid for it with a loan from my grandparents. It was made clear to me that this pink-stone, spacious dwelling was not permanently ours. Somewhere there was a woman who owned this house and who might return one day to claim what was hers. For many weeks I imagined a beautifully dressed woman coming to the house and ordering us out with a royal gesture. The wineglasses were pink crystal, the furniture mahogany, and the beds huge and comfortable. The change was unreal and sudden, and so many adjustments had to be made in a short time.

My father was by now brigade commander, with the rank of lieutenant colonel. Beyond his military duties, he assumed diplomatic missions as well. Nothing had changed in his attitude to us, but there was a new commotion about his comings and goings. There were drivers, other officers, telephone lines, and vehicles, which more or less turned the house into a second HQ for the brigade. There were revolvers and maps and binoculars and sandbags piled on top of the outside wall. If, before, the war had been brought home by the radio or through men on leave, or by the dead, now we were in its midst. Our home, and it soon felt like home, with my mother's graceful touch applied to it, was also an outpost. The carpets, crystal, and velvet were not out of bounds for tired, dusty, dirty men from the field, and the kitchen operated around the clock to provide meals and sandwiches to what seemed like a micro-kibbutz assembled in the Abkarius residence. The empty rooms were filled with people who joined my father to form a semi-official entourage. These included, among others, my Uncle Israel, Mart, an old Shimron friend—Nachman—Alex, his loyal adjutant, and Uri and Akiva from "89," who managed to join.

Commanding, cleaning, and feeding us all was Simcha. She was there when we moved in, scrubbing and preparing the enormous house for its new residents. My mother realized that there was no way she could cope with the housework by herself. Simcha's excellent cooking soon spoiled us all, and reluctantly my parents agreed that she should stay as a hired maid. Her son was killed in the war, a small daughter was living with her downstairs, and she soon became part of the family, pampering my brothers, treating Assi like a royal prince, and enchanting us all with her natural wisdom and bedtime folktales. I don't remember my father treating anybody with the respect and humble obedience that he accorded Simcha. She couldn't read or write, and she worshipped him in a way that he must have found embarrassing at times.

If HQ was partly based at home, the actual front line was around the corner. So much so that we had to sleep in the basement many nights when the siren sounded, and use the back driveway entrance to avoid sniper fire. The trenches facing the Old City walls were a short distance away. My father thought no more of taking us with him on inspection tours than he had of putting me on top of a haystack. Or teaching me the names of wild shrubs or flowers, or climbing the Hill of Moreh or Mount Tabor. The same reasons that had led him to share a night with my mother during the Deganya battle or to make us move to Tel Aviv with him during the Saison still motivated him. Not because he needed me there, on ladders and steep tunnels leading into trenches, or because he thought it was good for the morale of the soldiers or educational to us. He didn't give it a thought. We were his family, this was his life, and he didn't wish or know how to separate the two. I certainly felt important. There I was, facing the walls of the Old City, a pair of binoculars held to my eyes by my father, and he explaining to me where we were and what I was seeing. Through the binoculars I could see the Jordanian soldiers in red-and-white kaffiyehs, posing with their guns at the ready. My father told stories of King Solomon and Absalom, described Jerusalem's ancient water system, and made a few remarks concerning the tactical position we were in. Was he talking to me, or to all those around us? It didn't matter. He made a place for me so I could look at the map. He lifted me up when I was unable to reach an observation hole, and held me tight when we were speeding in a jeep on a bumpy road. I drank water from canteens and ate army rations, and nobody seemed too concerned with the presence of the thin little girl in these unlikely places.

Courage must be contagious as well as built in. I don't know whether I was naturally courageous, but I don't remember being afraid, either. There were nights of explosions, there were bullets that missed me by a few meters, there were night walks in the old Moslem cemetery not far from our house, there were visits to Ramat Rahel in a half-track shot at along the exposed road, but there was no fear. The kind of confidence my father inspired in me was lacking in bravura or exhibitionism. It was more the certainty of being in control. He assessed a situation, took everything into account, and the logical conclusion ruled out emotional or even instinctive reactions. The other person I knew who was capable of rationalization that resulted in fearlessness was my Grandmother Rachel. On these two models my own behavior was formed, and when they were no longer physically around me, I suppose my "courage" was already a conditioned reflex.

I was vaguely familiar with Jerusalem when we moved there, and all explorations ended in cul-de-sacs that announced the proximity of the border or a mine field. I did not feel for the split city in a religious or historical way, but sensed a deep frustration whenever I had to turn back because the road I took led to no-man's-land or ended in a "last trench" on the roof of a "last house." As small as Nahalal was, we could walk in any direction as far as our legs could carry us, and the circle we left behind felt less claustrophobic than this wounded city. The transfer from the provincial village to the cosmopolitan city didn't affect us much. My mother felt at home, my father retained his farm-boy charm and informal manner without being ill at ease when the occasion called for a change in tone, and my brothers simply ignored whatever restrictions the new life presented. If there were complaints, my parents dealt with them with patience and humor. I suspect my father was rather satisfied to hear that Udi set free the doves from a locked dovecote that belonged to a friend, and was not too worried when Assi wandered off into no-man's-land, to be returned by UN observers. My Aunt Aviva moved with her children to the top floor in the Abkarius house. Shmuel and Dvorah came whenever they could, with fresh farm eggs and cream. And Simcha soon served daily meals to a dozen people or more. By the time school resumed, we knew the city well. Udi and I explored it on bicycles, and Assi joined us for the shorter walks. I had my own hideout, on the roof of one of the buildings overlooking the Old City walls. I managed to sneak an old blanket there, along with a pair of binoculars and a few books, and I spent hours watching the Jordanian soldiers, at times waving to them, pretending this was "my place," as the rest of the house was badly damaged and deserted.

The fighting in the Jerusalem area was not renewed, beyond two minor and not too successful operations, and my father, who had been posted there for his combat qualifications, found himself involved in an entirely different type of battle. The ceasefire was mostly observed by both sides, and supervised by Ben-Gurion directly. Father was in charge of negotiating local arrangements with the Jordanian commander of Jerusalem and participated in the ongoing discreet talks with King Abdullah.

Life acquired a new pattern for us too, as the outside world, or its dignified representatives, gathered in our house every Friday afternoon. Franciscan monks, UN observers, foreign consuls, and a variety of journalists were permanent and welcome guests at what was referred to as the Dayans' open house on Fridays, which soon became the focal point of Jerusalem's social life. Simcha baked pitta bread and made hundreds of little sandwiches every Friday. Tea and coffee were poured into beautiful porcelain cups, and I helped to serve, shaking hands, being kissed, mumbling in English, and enjoying it all. We didn't have to climb anywhere socially; we didn't have to copy anybody or be jealous or want to reach higher. We were parachuted there, at the top, and the world was ours. We definitely were not village people who had to acquire some sophistication and reach from the perimeter to achieve centrality. My mother was in her element, and my father was the center for the best of reasons. His position was well earned, and he proved as successful in Abdullah's palace as he was in the breakthrough to Lydda and Ramle. Fortunately, both my parents managed to retain a Nahalal-style informality at home, even when the guest list was imposing. Lower ranks, family, visitors from the valley, our own new friends were all welcome, and if my father praised somebody, or categorized him as "an idiot," it had nothing to do with a person's position or title.

Food and water were rationed, but with occasional fresh supplies from Nahalal and Simcha's miraculous touch, we were never short. For fresh fruit, my father introduced a new pastime on Saturdays—family visits to deserted fruit orchards in the Jerusalem vicinity. The ventures were not illegal, but there were very few families, if any, who went where we did. On dirt roads, near deserted Arab villages, the five of us in a jeep would climb the side of a mountain to discover ripe figs and the sweetest of grapes. Father was a fruit maniac, and each of these wild, overgrown, unattended "bustans" was like a new Eden.

He taught Udi and me to shoot, and if at the beginning we could hit a tree trunk, we were soon good enough with a revolver or a light rifle to blow a ripe red pomegranate to pieces. We talked about Nahalal and the farm, as if we were to return happily there the next day, and Father told us about King Abdullah's palace as if late-night dinners there were a natural part of his life. We recited Alterman together, and he shared his daily experiences with Mother. We watched pheasants and drank spring water, and if the wireless on the car summoned him back, we were involved.

The school year began, and Udi and I went to the Rehavia Gymnasium, which was within walking distance of our house. Assi was taken daily by Simcha to a nearby kindergarten, and my mother started to work with the Jewish Agency. Both, school and Mother's work, did mean changes for me. School discipline was difficult to take at first. Nahalal classes had offered little challenge, and farm work always had priority over scholarly occupations. Here, school meant studies and education as well. The pupils were from affluent Jerusalem families, sons and daughters of lawyers and doctors, and a snobbish touch was not lacking. I was supposed to consider it an honor to be in the Rehavia school, and adjust to its rules unquestion- ingly. We had to stand when a teacher entered the classroom, address the teachers as Mr. Yonah and Mrs. Fuchs rather than by first name, and being late or talking during a lesson or not doing homework was, naturally, not tolerated. I soon found out it was easier to obey the rules than to fight them, and rather liked the competitive spirit. I was still younger by two years than my class- mates, always the smallest and least developed, so that being able to excel in studies and sports was doubly rewarding. I made a few friends—two girls, but mostly boys—with whom I shared my secret rooftop and a variety of afternoon activities. My father took great pride in my high grades, and it proved profitable to invest a little effort and be a very good if not a top student. I soon found out our name had acquired fame, and attached to this came an obligation. Udi, being younger and less interested in formal schooling, didn't notice it at all, but I was made to understand that "being Dayan's daughter, you are expected . . ." or not expected, according to the specific propositions. My parents laughed it off; my father said I shouldn't do anything I didn't feel like doing, but he said it with the knowledge that I would always be good in school. I was curious and intelligent and aware of the importance of good schooling. I did not have to become ambitious to fulfill expectations; I was ambitious almost in a cunning way. Being better, I knew, would secure me liberties if not privileges, and certain popularity.

Fame was not a burden. It was not a false fame, and not mine in a way I had to forever justify or keep up with. It was all my father's, and there wasn't yet any jealousy or malice attached to the appraisals. Although his name and picture were often in the newspapers, his own attitude was neither aloof nor boastful, and the full credits for the political achievements were undisputedly Ben-Gurion's. The Army hierarchy itself limited Father's scope of action, and he never pushed his way higher in the echelon or grumbled about not getting there sooner. For me, being referred to as Dayan's daughter was not a stigma or a handicap, and if expectations were attached, I didn't feel obliged to justify them. I showed my schoolmates the special telephone connected to the Jordanian colonel Abdullah el-Tel, with a childish wonderment rather than as a boastful gesture, and they lined up for rides in the military jeep because it was fun. Still, though fame, and Father's position, didn't hinder or advance me, I realized it could. It could give one wings or be a weight around one's neck; it could open doors or expose weaknesses, make you fly or drown. One thing was clear: I couldn't fight it or reject it, and there was no way to be anonymous; but then, the Nahalal circle didn't offer anonymity or privacy either.

Mother's absence from home was not at the expense of anything important. Simcha ran the house, and we were busy with school, homework, and the youth movement, and she carefully explained to me what her work meant. Women from old established moshavim volunteered to work with new immigrants, initiating them into a style of work and life they had never known. My Grandmother Dvorah had been doing it for a while already, and my mother joined in, going every day to the moshav not far from Jerusalem to which she was assigned. My father encouraged her, and she was always home in the evening, to settle our quarrels, look at our school reports, or engage in the social activities my father's position required. I never resented her taking a job, and soon she shared her experiences with us, her failures and satisfactions, and we were more than enthusiastic. What was supposed to be simply guiding agricultural work turned into a series of discoveries and added a new dimension to Mother's life and ours.

These immigrants, from Yemen and Hungary, from Bulgaria and North Africa, had a talent that was taken for granted, that of superb mastery of handicrafts. My mother had no sense for business, but she could tell one embroidery from another and the value of a handmade silver chain. She noticed in their homes the hand-drawn lacework and the extraordinary needlework and soon found out they could make these beautiful things at home, in their spare time, and thus add to their meager income. It took a while to convince Jewish Agency officials to allocate a small budget for her endeavors, but she was soon working with two dozen settlements, all over the country, reviving ancient crafts, preserving traditional arts, and creating a national framework for artistic home industries.

My father was more than cooperative, and she managed to work long hours without failing to be home when he needed her. The tremendous challenge to absorb, settle, and train more than a quarter of a million new immigrants in 1948–49 was of national dimensions, and it was soon given top priority as the War of Independence came to an end and permanent armistice negotiations commenced.

By nature and upbringing, my father was a patriarch. He didn't mind who was in the kitchen, as long as somebody was there, and he didn't resent the idea of women working at anything. He wasn't concerned with questions of equality and took it for granted that the last word was his. Not because he knew better, or felt superior, but being in charge was natural to him and unquestionable. My mother's lack of confidence and natural humility served both of them well. He was the master, the supportive shoulder, the shelter, while she was able to assert herself, work, and be independent. They both knew that his needs, his desires and comforts and plans would come first with her.

On July 20, 1949, the last of the armistice agreements was signed, and for all intents and purposes the war ended. My father headed the Israeli delegation to all four Mixed Armistice Commissions which negotiated the demarcation lines—in fact, the borders of the State of Israel. For a short while, I thought we would return to Nahalal—by now a thought which, although not unpleasant, was not exciting, for it was clear that my father would not stay in command of Jerusalem. It was Ben-Gurion, this time too, who decided for us. The Southern Command had the longest borders with two Arab countries, and the influx of immigrants was mostly destined to settle there. The return of the Jewish exiles and the renewal of the desert were the immediate goals, Ben-Gurion declared, and my father was promoted to major general in command of the south.

The southern part of Israel was like a foreign country for me, like a trip back in time. The valley in the north was all soft contours, many of the trees evergreen, and each season delicately adorned the black soil with flowers. Nahalal offered shelter in the muddy earth and in flows of water; insect life was abundant; and I didn't have to look for living creatures or signs of the perpetual cycle of life. Jerusalem was man-built out of stone, perched on rocks, with a sense of eternity. The city had an ambiance all its own, as if it hardly mattered what people inhabited it, or how many armies stormed it. It was indestructible on its firm foundation, and offered hospitality and protection behind walls, in cellars and courtyards and alleys.

The Negev meant total exposure, from the flat, bare desert patches to the deep craters or lofty peaks of the central range of mountains. It had a life, but one had to search and discover it; it had plants, but they were thorny and dry, and the landscape was harsh and imposing. A country without shade, forever trying and surprising. The eroding, sweeping winds, the sudden, yearly, violent floods in the wadis, the moving, treacherous dunes, the scorching heat during the day and the freezing cold at night offered no comfort or shelter or a firm foothold. There were no footsteps or tracks to follow; civilizations were buried or exposed at random by the forces of nature; and any thought of taming this wilderness seemed a hallucination.

My father fell in love with these very qualities that others found sinister and forbidding. His resentment of frills and excuses, his search for the basic and the essential was satisfied in the desert. He was eager to adjust rather than dominate, and set to learn the language of the place rather than impose on it his own. For a variety of reasons, which didn't apply to Southern Command generals who succeeded him, we did not move away from Jerusalem. The road to Eilat was not built yet. Beersheba was a small, Wild West-style town, a desert trading station. Desert agriculture was still a dream, and all in all, the south was no place for women and schoolchildren. Father's HQ was south of Rehovot, in a large camp, and an old one-room trailer served him as living quarters. To be sure, our life pattern did change. Mother was working. Simcha took care of us and the house. A few of the rooms were rented out to students, and Father stayed a few nights a week in camp. Since his imprisonment in Acre, he had always been home at night, but now his side in the large double bed was often vacant. We didn't question it, or even miss him all that terribly, but there was an adjustment to make. We were five people, I realized, not one conglomerate, and each of us had a life, whether already shaped or being formed. Each of us had independent choices to make and decisions to take, and eventually we would be five different streams flowing in the same or in separate directions, crossing or parallel, self-supporting, even if we all stemmed from the same source.

The cocktail parties and receptions stopped, or rather became smaller in size, moved to my grandparents' house on Friday afternoons, and though Father now was a major general, he was not a newsmaker, and some privacy was restored to our daily life. Just in time—for the "international" touch to my life was premature, and if I benefited, by learning English and feeling at home in a variety of surroundings, I doubt that I was equipped with the right sense of proportion to cope with the many temptations it offered.

My father, too, needed the trimming effect the south offered. He was no longer a farm boy, and not yet a full-fledged statesman. The active war was over, and he was aware of the gaps in his formal education—military, diplomatic and general. Ben-Gurion promised him a period of study, but it had to wait. Securing and settling the Negev had first priority, and my father was to deal with civilian as well as military development plans. Ben-Gurion spoke of a road to connect the Mediterranean and the Dead Sea, a road to Eilat, railways, a large military training base in the Negev, fishing in the Gulf of Eilat, agricultural settlements, and small towns based on local industry. These were national goals, and my father, still a farmer, was happy to take time from military duties and work with the civilian authorities in charge of Negev development. The operational activities of the Southern Command in 1950, a quiet year, consisted of preventing border crossings, of reconnaissance patrols into the Sinai, and of dealing with some hostile Bedouin tribes.

My father's sense of freedom was intensified in the wild region he commanded. If in Jerusalem he had been called a Bedouin, as a derogatory remark, it now was an advantage. As much as he loved his home and a certain routine, he was a spartan nomad, and at thirty-four was still uncorrupted by material comforts and worldly possessions. He took every opportunity to join patrols and excursions across the dunes, down the ravines, and up the steep mountains. Very often, he had me along. Away from my mother, Simcha, my young brothers, and school, I discovered this new territory and learned to love it the way he did.

We would leave the camp when it was still dark, with me wrapped in a blanket over a windbreaker, my head covered with a kaffiyeh, and my small frame huddled between my father and other soldiers. The best vehicle for these desert trips was a four-wheel-drive command car which had enough room for supplies, sleeping bags, and ammunition, and I didn't take any more room than a jerry can. At sunrise we would stop for breakfast, and my father explained to me, over 1:100,000 maps I was familiar with, the route we were about to explore. It was usually a wadi, the dry bed of a watercourse. We would follow one as far west as the Egyptian border and return along another—all the way east, crossing the Negev along ancient caravan trails and creating new ones. What seemed to be static, glorious, but dead scenery came to life as soon as we moved into it.

What I didn't notice, my father pointed out to me, and he often stopped the car, took me by the hand, and led me to a hidden cave, a top of a hill, or for a closer look at a desert tree. Deer rushed past; wild rats were caught in the headlights of the car; and majestic camels appeared from nowhere, going nowhere, it seemed. I never exclaimed aloud or cried with joy, but we exchanged looks and we knew we were excited and moved by the same things. The trackers with us told of their adventures; the officers talked defense plans; and there was always someone who knew the names of birds and plants to initiate us into this magic world. An eagle flying to its nest was justification for a whole day on a dusty track; a cave dug into the white rock, used as a cistern in ancient times, was a cause for joy; and the best part of these trips was the nights.

Father arranged our sleeping bags or blankets near one of the cars, making sure no sharp stones or scorpions or thistles were under mine. "The princess and the pea," he would laugh, and get me a fresh canteen to wash with. The men cooked dinner, opened cans of army rations, and boiled water for coffee, and we would all gather around a small fire, barely talking, listening to the occasional sounds and relaxing. I took it all in with a sense of gratitude. I was the only female, the only child around, and I felt honored, as if allowed a glimpse of the world of giants.

These men, my father's friends and subordinates, were new to me, too. He took command of the south, arriving alone. His old followers dispersed or stayed in Jerusalem or returned to their farms, and he didn't need the security of a familiar entourage. He didn't need them, and some were probably not qualified for higher rank. Soon Father assumed authority over and even developed friendships with the group of officers he found in HQ, though most of them were loyal, close associates of the previous commander, Allon, and perhaps resented Dayan replacing him. But all these men had a special love for the desert, and my father's lack of discipline in minor matters, his resentment of routine, and his sense of adventure appealed to them. If Gandhi (a nickname given one of the able officers for his looks) was surprised when his commander, on their first meeting, took him along to steal fruit from a nearby orchard, he still joined with pleasure, and it never occurred to my father to comment on the way he looked, barefoot or in sandals. Discipline for Father had to do with battle routine, behavior under fire, devotion to a friend and a cause, and not with salutes, rank, or paperwork. If he learned to appreciate the importance of these external disciplines later, it was because the Army itself had changed, was less homogeneous and couldn't count on a friendly "gang spirit" as a common denominator.

One evening, in Wadi Hiani, Gandhi showed up with a goat tied to a rope and presented it as our dinner. A lively discussion followed as to the proper means of slaughtering the poor thing, and the choice fell on a spade, which chopped off its head. It wasn't a sight for a little girl to behold, and my father felt uncomfortable. "You don't have to eat it," he told me. We looked at the animal as Gandhi skinned it with one expert yank. "I doubt that I could eat it either," Father added, and we went to our blankets.

The cloudless sky offered an ethereal sense of proximity to the stars. His bedtime stories had to do with our ancestors who walked this desert, or very close by, and filled my imagination. Abraham and Isaac, Jacob and his brothers, Moses and the Children of Israel . . . I knew my Bible, and my father added his own compassionate version. This was the land that offered men nothing but trouble, and the only motivation to move on had to do with faith. No water, no livelihood, no shade, moved by a promise of a God they could not see, hear, or touch. Yet he could understand, if not explain very well, why the desert was conducive to the creation of monotheism: it was bare, imposing, and its strength rejected plurality. If in Nahalal he taught me the wisdom of the Judges, who in war and in peace united the tribes into one people, and in Jerusalem he made me feel the grandeur of Kings, here we were back where it all started. Abraham was a Bedouin, Jacob had flocks of sheep, Joseph went to Egypt and his brothers followed, and Moses liberated us. Between slavery in the green pastures of the Nile and the promised land of Canaan lay this desert. Only those who traversed it deserved freedom.

Before dawn, he woke me with a cup of tea, drove me to a less exposed spot to relieve myself, and on we would drive to what always seemed new horizons. I could have gone on like this forever (so could he, perhaps), but these trips never lasted more than a couple of days, and I always knew there would be a next time. After each trip, I returned to school with a note from my father, excusing me and explaining my absence as "inevitable, for special reasons." He rightly felt I was learning more on these days of absence than in school, and if my teachers didn't agree with him, they didn't show it. There were no other privileges or demands stemming from my father's rank or position.

I was growing enchanted with school. My father and mother came to hear teachers' reports and always left with a smile, sharing equally their pride in my advance and the few complaints, which had to do with behavior. "Unsuitable behavior" reached a peak when at the end of the school year I managed to bring nearly a hundred small frogs from the Moslem cemetery pond, with the help of Udi, and install them in the classroom, all over. "There is no room for her in our school," the headmaster told my parents, but at the end agreed to accept a written apology.

My occasional bad behavior was an expression of childish naughtiness rather than of a need to attract attention or establish leadership. I was surrounded by friends in school and was immersed in the youth movement, was loved though not spoiled at home, and was left alone when I wanted to be. There were no rules as to home-work, regular hours, or my whereabouts. I had my parents' trust, and as long as school reports were good, it didn't occur to them to forbid, or prevent me from doing whatever I wanted. I read a great deal, and when I ran out of books in the school library, I borrowed from friends. A collection of horror stories was lent me by a boy-friend, who told me to hide it from the grownups. It had no sex but plenty of bloodsucking by vampires, dissecting of limbs, and burials in double walls. I could tell it was cheap, vulgar, and rather violent, and in no way took it seriously. My father did. He found it next to my bed, gave it a long look—the picture on the cover sufficed—and slapped my face strong and hard.

Shock rather than pain brought tears to my eyes. He had never done that before, and although my brothers, for good reasons, were often spanked hard, I never expected such a strong reaction, not for anything, least of all for reading a book. "Why?" I screamed. "This is trash, and I forbid you to read it." I stopped crying and assumed a new tone. "I will read whatever I want. It's a nonsense book, but it's thrilling and fun. All my friends read it." I was slapped again.

He threw the book on the floor and left me hurt and puzzled. He never referred to it again, and after I returned the book to its owner, I remained puzzled for a long time by this outburst.

He tried to make up, but behind the kissing and hugging, the funny stories and small gifts, he sensed my hurt. He wouldn't admit he was wrong, and neither could I. During the years that followed, we both developed ways of indirectly admitting wrongs, almost by a code. Right then, it was clear to me that I had to watch out, that his tolerance was not total and his reactions not always predictable. Did he feel his absence meant a loss of control? Did he notice something I hadn't yet which had to do with growing up? Was he beginning to feel guilty, or was it just "a bad day at work," which was my mother's explanation for just about everything.

The freedom he discovered in the Southern Command definitely contributed to a loosening up of the tight family unit. He enjoyed the space, he loved the mobility and the speed, he took minor liberties, such as stealing chickens from a moshav nearby, and, I was told much later, he discovered he could survive the guilt he felt when indulging in extramarital affairs.

He was Ben-Gurion's favorite general, and the old man's door was always open to him. On many occasions he ignored the chain of command and approached the Prime Minister directly. It was clear to those around him that he never did it to show off or assume authority he didn't have, but only to save time and achieve results. At times, even the straight line between two points was too long for him. Ben-Gurion saw in him a natural candidate for the supreme military post—Chief of Staff—and it was clear to all of us that any plans for a return to the farm in Nahalal would have to be set aside. His life, our lives, would exist within the framework of the Army.

PART

Three

S I X ❊ A D O L E S C E N C E

In 1952, my parents went abroad, not on a vacation, but for a six-month stay. For me this was a significant separation.

My father was to attend a senior officers' school at Devizes in England, and my mother would accompany him. "Arrangements" were made for us children. Udi and Assi were sent to close friends at kibbutz Maoz Haim; Simcha stayed in the Abkarius house to run it and take care of a variety of tenants who occupied some of the rooms; and I moved to my grandparents' house so I would not have to change schools.

My mother often compared me with my father, and, at times, with my grandmother. The second comparison had to do with what she thought was our cerebral approach to behavior. She said I never played with dolls and never cried. She said she didn't remember seeing her mother cry either. And there was some truth in the comparison insofar as it summed up Mother's inability to communicate with either of us. She feared confrontations with us, where we supposedly remained cold while she expressed herself emotionally and often by crying. Of course, I did play with dolls, a big variety of them, and I certainly cried, as often as was natural for a girl my age.

My first night at my grandparents' was a night full of tears. I slept on a couch in the dining room. Everything had to be carefully folded and neatly arranged, and all the traits I was supposed to have in common with my grandmother did not come in handy. I was alone and lonely, and this was anything but home. My Grandmother Dvorah had a physical warmth about her that radiated and engulfed me whenever we were together. My father was always fondling and kissing; my brothers were all over each other and everybody else. My Grandmother Rachel was different. I didn't doubt her love, her caring, her ability to supply me with all I needed or even wanted, but if she didn't cry, she didn't kiss either. Most of all, I missed my mother. I knew my father had to go away; it was his duty, part of his training, and this I could grasp. But though I wasn't jealous of Mother for being with him, I felt a self-pity which took some effort to overcome. My imagination didn't help much. What if something happened to them? My brothers were so young and dependent, and I was not capable of taking care of them yet. I soon relaxed. Letters arrived regularly, and I realized my parents were not exposed to any dangers and that six months was not an eternity.

My grandfather took enormous interest and pride in my studies, and my grandmother encouraged my independence, and relied on me and respected my privacy. She treated me as a capable adult, and I soon learned not to interpret her balanced, coolheaded, controlled behavior as a lack of love. I was very much on my own, for both Rachel and Zvi worked during the day and were usually busy in the evening. I doubt that the ability, and later the need, to be alone is inherent. "She is like her father, she likes to be alone," my grandparents said, and it was true enough, even if I had acquired the need there and then because of circumstances.

School grew more and more interesting, mostly because I was lucky to be taught by two great teachers. One, who is now the head of the classical history faculty at Tel Aviv University, not only opened for me the fascinating terrain of Greek and Roman history but basically taught me how to study. I learned from him how to ask questions and where to look for answers, how to choose among the given and at times contradictory answers, and how to analyze and draw conclusions from a series of interrelated facts. Pericles and Aristotle, Socrates and Alexander, as well as Marius and Cicero, Julius and Trajan, filled my life, and if he drew

analogies to modern times, he gave us the scholarly tools to dis-
agree with him, too. The teacher who taught us literature and
poetry, now one of Israel's leading poets, was unknown and un-
published at the time. He encouraged me to write, taught me that
imagination had no rules or limits, and led me not only to love the
beauty of words but to appreciate their power as well. School was
not a duty when these two teachers were around, or a pastime, but
a challenge and a pleasure, and my grandfather's beautiful library
provided me with additional hours of inexhaustible search for
knowledge.

Youth movement activities supplied the necessary physical outlets. We hiked and walked and camped, and though I missed the
Negev excursions, I delighted in smaller discoveries of caves hidden
by olive trees, secret streams with transparent waters in the winter,
and treasures of edible mushrooms under the Judean pines. We sat
around a bonfire every Saturday evening, planning and dreaming,
and even when we laughed or played games, we took ourselves
desperately seriously. I was thirteen, my classmates were fifteen,
and what I lacked in size or years I had to make up in brains and
behavior.

My mother shared an apartment with her sister Reumah in
London. Reumah had married Ezer Weizman, then a young Air
Force officer and pilot (the wedding had taken place a year earlier,
in the Abkarius house garden) who was now attending an officers'
course in Andover. My father and Ezer came home for weekends,
and during the week my mother took courses in weaving, basketry,
and other handicrafts. She was going to continue her work when
she returned to Israel, and it was clear to her that what had begun
as a job would be a lifelong occupation, a mission. Both my parents,
each in his own field, were filling in gaps in their education. With
all my father's dashing natural talent, he was not a dilettante, and
his admiration of excellence and proficiency, in whatever field,
equaled his contempt for pretentious amateurs.

Three major events took place in my life while my parents were
away: my first menstrual period, the acquisition of my first brassiere,
and my first kiss. The first two were treated by my grandmother in
a very matter-of-fact way. She rightly presumed I knew all about

it, and bought for me what I needed. I washed my own underwear anyway, and she added a few remarks on feminine hygiene. I suspect it was a nuisance for her, just as much as when a lice epidemic hit my school and she had to wash my hair with kerosene. My first kiss was a treasured secret, and I was quite glad my parents were away at the time.

Most of my friends had boyfriends already. They danced together, held hands, and kissed. Saturday night, when we returned from our gatherings, most kids went home in couples; and these couples were more or less steady. When a boy from a higher grade offered to walk home with me, I was naïve enough to say I lived in the opposite direction, a long way away. He insisted, I accepted, and a few days later we walked beyond my grandparents' house down a hill to a hidden site surrounded by bushes which we called ours. He had dark curly hair, delicate hands, and the beginning of a mustache. He was sixteen, and what seemed most important, he was the favorite student of both my history and my literature teacher. His kisses were wet and long and clumsy, and I participated and contributed, as this was my entry ticket to maturity. He was aroused sexually, but I was more interested in talking than in necking, and I was sure that this was an everlasting, deep love. Or I thought I should be sure. For at that time I discovered how often I tended to separate myself from any experience I was going through. First, this frightened me. Later it offered the escape of an observation post, and eventually I accepted it as part of my character and took advantage of it. There I was, in shorts and sandals, with the boy in question, Avi, holding me or fondling me in our secret corner, and we were whispering sweet nothings in each other's ears. There I was, the same me, looking at myself mercilessly through a magnifying glass. There and on many other occasions. Inevitably as an on-looker, I saw the pathetic, ridiculous, or, at best, humorous aspect. I was in the frame, and at the same time behind the lens, taking snapshots and cataloguing them in my mind. I wasn't playacting, and most of the time I was carried away and involved in the experience itself, but I had this defense mechanism, a control knob at my disposal.

My boyfriend visited me at home. My grandfather cross-examined him briefly and was satisfied to learn that he was the son of a respectable Sephardic family, that he was a good student and generally a pleasant young man. It was my good luck that my grandparents were liberal and not too inquisitive, and I had no desire to share my early romantic indulgences. Not with a girlfriend, not with a diary, and least of all with my parents. Permissiveness was an unknown word then, and my father was prudish and old-fashioned even by the innocent standards of the early fifties. Words like "sex," "homosexual," "prostitute" were never heard at home, not to mention four-letter words. There were no references to intercourse or even lovemaking. Not in front of the children. When my father was angry, his vocabulary did not exceed words like "idiot," "a bastard," or "hell," and language at home had to be kept clean.

The course in Devizes ended, and my father underwent another unsuccessful operation in Paris on his eye, and was soon on his way home. Mother went to the States, the first of many trips on behalf of the United Jewish Appeal. The fact that Father returned alone was well compensated by suitcases full of gifts he brought us. I would have liked, then, to be dramatic and say: My father had left a little girl and returned to find a woman; but this wasn't the case. His return threw me back in time into more relevant proportions. I was what he expected me to be, and as intimate as we were, there was no way I could talk to him about a boyfriend, let alone kissing or necking. He attended a parents' meeting at school, was happy with the reports, and didn't notice any changes in me.

He wrote to Mother daily, sometimes twice a day. One four-page letter was mostly devoted to the small radio he brought me. He bought it after she'd left, and he described in detail his inability to choose between battery-operated and other models, the color, the size, and the price—£14, which was a great deal of money. He bought Assi bicycles and Udi an air gun. He wrote: "Yaël has everything, a watch, a fountain pen, binoculars of her own and now a radio. If she wants a revolver I'll give her one from my collection." He was mirroring his own childhood, for he had no reason to think I wanted a revolver . . .

Another letter, five pages long, recommended another shopping list, a tea set for the kibbutz friends, some games for the kibbutz school, a hot-water boiler for Nahalal, and winter shoes for all of us. He wrote suggesting she should buy herself some clothes for the next season and announced that the sandals she sent me were too small. "Yaël's feet are enormous, and I'll draw the boys' feet on paper and send it to you for size."

What seems trivial now must have preoccupied him, and between the shopping lists and news of Assi losing his first tooth, and taking me to the beach on Saturday, with the boys, and Assi not being able to swim because he had a cough, he mentioned that he would probably be getting the Northern Command, which would be ideal since we could all return to Nahalal.

It was at that time that my father was touched by a passion that would consume him more and more as the years went by: the passion for archaeology. Not in museums or shops or private collections, but the personal, possessive, physical sense of himself doing the excavating. He went pigeon shooting with Udi one Saturday morning, and while walking among the ruins in Tel el-Safi, he noticed a row of jars sticking out of the mud wall of the wadi. The jars were exposed by heavy rains a few days earlier and they looked new and whole. He took one home, had it examined by a friend, and discovered that it dated back to the ninth century B.C., the period of the Hebrew kings. The following Saturday he returned to Tel el-Safi, better equipped for digging, and exposed a few more jars, some oil lamps, and handles of larger jars. There is a whole world down there, he exclaimed to us. As tangible and real as ours. Beneath the fields and the roads and the houses, in the walls and caves of wadis. A world of our own ancestors, their tools and vessels and weapons, their houses and their graves, a silent world which comes alive with these potsherds and sooty handles. Within a few years, this hobby became a consuming preoccupation, at times an obsession. I think the philosophy behind it, the spiritual justification—like the learning in depth about the subject—was secondary. At first, it was the physical pleasure of digging, the almost childish joy of discovery, and the wonderfully primitive creation of a bond between himself and his own history. Skipping the Ukraine, jumping over the shtetl mentality of his Zhashkov grandparents, not touching the

Yiddish-speaking Diaspora, flying over generations of devastated communities, bypassing Inquisitions and exiles.

There was Abraham, a wandering Bedouin, and his wives and his cattle, and his overwhelming discovery of monotheism. There was Moses and Joshua, and the Judges and Kings who drank from the dishes my father unearthed and touched the clay cups we were touching. Then there was Deganya and Nahalal and Lydda and Jerusalem and Alterman and Ben-Gurion. The spiritual dimension followed but it was not the central motivation. In the early fifties—I was not fourteen yet—digging was not an escape but the occasion for a happy expedition where family was welcome, and we enjoyed it as we did picking flowers in the spring or stealing fruit in the summer.

The Northern Command brought us back to home ground. We lived for a while in Tivon, near Haifa, and when the house in Nahalal was ready, we moved back. Only I didn't. My father's HQ was in Nazareth; Udi and Assi went to the Nahalal elementary school; and I was enrolled in the Reali high school in Haifa, as other high schools in the area were not considered good enough. My parents never completed their formal high-school education and naturally wanted to make sure we all graduated properly. I was in the ninth grade, and in subjects like mathematics, chemistry, physics, or even geography, I had more knowledge than they had. Not that it mattered to me. I treated and thought of both of them as superior even if they couldn't help me with my homework in algebra.

I lived during the week with an uncle and aunt of my mother's. They were a gentle, simple couple, and again, I found myself using a bed in someone's living room. Meals were bland and conversation banal, and I looked forward to Fridays when I went home to Nahalal for a short weekend. I was not enthusiastic about our return to Nahalal, as it was obvious to all of us that we would not stay long. The Northern Command was to be another step in Father's career, and if he became Chief of Staff, we would move again.

I did miss Jerusalem, that city which I had grown to love and enjoy. My boyfriend wrote me long letters for a while and then stopped. I didn't like the regimented attitude of the new school, hated the khaki school uniform, and fancied a boy who never so much as looked at me. I was still an excellent student, but my happiest hours were spent with books. Ezer Weizman's parents lived two blocks from the Reali school, and their library was at my disposal. Flaubert, Proust, Romain Rolland, and all the Russian classics were all waiting for me, uniformly bound, badly translated, but magical.

There were still a few trips with my father, visits to Arab villages rather than to Bedouin tents, and to the Syrian and Lebanese borders. Lush-green Galilee, with its abundance of water and thick vegetation, did not appeal to my sense of adventure, or his (as the Negev did), and we both missed the freedom and mystery of the desert, where survival was a challenge rather than nature's offering.

The following winter, in December 1952, we were packing again to move to Ramat Gan, near Tel Aviv. My father had been appointed head of the Operation Branch of the General Staff, and we lived temporarily in a small apartment not far from HQ. A place without character or grace or even space. Udi and Assi found it difficult to adjust; they didn't like their new school, and two growing moshav boys on the third floor of a suburban apartment building meant trouble. I was given a room on the ground floor. My own place, my own key, total privacy for the first time. It was a good beginning to a disastrous year.

From the open fields, from provincial Haifa, from friendly area-command atmosphere, I was tossed into a whole new scene. My father was now engaged in raising the standards of the Army combat units, setting new criteria for officers in which top priority was given to those elements meant to engage in actual battle. Since the War of Independence, organization and routine threatened to dull the sharp edges of the commando spirit, and he felt obliged to reinstill it. It wasn't that he was away more often, but as his sphere of action and interest changed, I felt he was drifting away from me— from us. Being part of the General Staff meant more salutes, more discipline, more channels to go through to reach him, and he seemed to be climbing toward a place where I would not be included. The freedom I should have appreciated was interpreted by me as neglect;

the trust that was put in me I read as a brush-off. I was fourteen, well developed, and smart. I wasn't beautiful, but I was attractive, and what earlier had been considered precocity was now taken for flirtatiousness.

I was equipped for many things. I could walk up to Massada and reach the peak first, I could read a 1:100,000 map and navigate, I could identify wild herbs and build a good fire. I knew how to be polite with UN generals and ambassadors and how to respond to the greetings of an Arab sheikh. I knew my Bible and history and could recite most of Alterman and Shlonsky, but I was totally immature and spoiled when it came to real life. To coping with my equals, asserting myself within the framework of normal daily activities, finding my place in a high-school society, and enjoying the simple offerings of an ordinary existence. I was excellent as General Dayan's offspring; I was praised for courage and sturdiness; I was complimented on my quick absorption, good memory, and brightness; but something was missing. My father chose to ignore the fact that I was growing up. My mother developed a strange inability to communicate with me. And the façade of resembling my father attracted grownups to me and definitely deterred my peers. I was alone again, and still needed and liked to be alone, but I was suddenly lonely, the loneliness that exists between two worlds, the childhood we are afraid to relinquish and the adult world, attractive but frightening.

My new school was extremely liberal—no uniform, open student-teacher relationships, very little discipline, and many lectures on free society, socialism, and individualism. I joined the Tel Aviv Scouts and was welcome, but remained slightly on the outside. The two-year difference between me and my classmates suddenly mattered enormously. All the girls had steady boyfriends; they had grown up together and shared common backgrounds and interests. My father's status in the Army didn't seem to interest any of them, and I had to work to fit in. In Tel Aviv, I encountered for the first time the differences between the haves and the have-nots. Not a class society in the usual sense, but a way of appreciating people by the size of their apartments and the make of their cars. The Scout group I belonged to in the north of Tel Aviv was typically bourgeois in values and possessions, and the competitiveness among the youngsters was based on family income and the ability to afford luxuries rather than on personal merit. There I didn't want to compete; I didn't care for brand names and clung to my own criteria. I had no jealousies, but I did cry into my pillow on many nights.

But something about middle-class Tel Aviv family life also attracted me, as unexciting and almost revolting as it seemed a few short years later. Life was set for them. They didn't build an army, they didn't steal fruit, they didn't hoist a flag every morning in the name of Zionism, they didn't absorb immigrants, and their treasured memories didn't have to do with shaky jeep rides in the Grand Crater. They had radios and record players; they had shiny bicycles and tried on their mothers' lipsticks and makeup. The girls had delicate hands and many played the piano or studied ballet, and I seemed clumsy and pathetic, trying to share their interests. This was perhaps the one year in my life when I wanted to be like the others, to fit into a line, and the line declared me different. So I took a sharp turn. If different, then different to an extreme. If among other teenagers, egotistical and self-centered as they were, I was not too welcome, I would try my luck with the adult world, which was tolerant and curious and not afraid of competition. I began to keep a diary, write short stories and bad poems, and I even found a certain relief in writing a few essays. I wrote long letters to nonexisting friends, and the drawers of my desk were full of pages in which the imaginary was mixed with reality. I frequented an artists' café in Dizengoff Street and was made welcome there. Among the writers and poets and journalists I sat with my school bag or in my Scout uniform, drinking tea and taking in their anecdotes and stories, feeling very comfortable. I was well read, offered an opinion when asked, and was not treated as an oddity. I was young, true, but it made them feel closer to youth, and their interest and care were genuine. My father's name was obviously my entry ticket, but once in, I was accepted and liked in a pleasant, patronizing, nonchalant way. I was offered a part-time job on a children's magazine, and this gave me an alibi

for my strange choice of "friends" as far as my family was concerned.

Among the many journalists I met in the café was the editor of
a weekly magazine which was widely read and as widely resented.
It was considered a scandalous yellow sheet and probably was,
which didn't curtail its large circulation among those who supposedly "wouldn't touch it." The man was fun, interesting, and
gentle, and if he paid attention to me in order to obtain information
about my father, he disguised it well, as he seldom mentioned him
and we talked mostly about Camus or Sartre, about general political
trends and some gossip. I volunteered some information occasionally, but in an innocent and rather ignorant fashion. I was too busy
with myself in those days to bother with the goings-on in the General
Staff. I had no access to papers, and my father didn't bring home
classified material. At the most, I was in possession of minor facts
concerning his own whereabouts or lively quotations of social-gossip
value only. I learned later that this man was considered a "dangerous
type" and that I was soon put under surveillance—unaware as I was
of several highly sensitive topics my father was concerned with at the
time.

I was paid for my work on the children's magazine, and I didn't
think much of accepting a small payment for a couple of items which
appeared in the social-gossip column of the magazine. In an effort
to widen my circle of acquaintances, I put a letter in the pen-pal
section of the paper, and two dozen or so replies followed, which
pleased me no end, though I pursued none.

I was restless. Layers of new worlds were unfolding before me,
and I wanted to have access to them all simultaneously. There was
school (I never lost interest in the act of learning); there was the
youth movement, which by now I regarded with slight superiority,
and there was my new circle of acquaintances, which supplied
polar stimulants, from Alterman to crazy, homeless painters. Surely
I belonged to none of these worlds. They mattered to me, but I
held no position in them, and the entanglement was time-consuming
and exhausting, a wild chase for something I couldn't define and a
running away from something I didn't care to evaluate.

In the summer, I went to a kibbutz camp with the Scouts and the physical work did me good. I was healthy, I looked well, I enjoyed rising at dawn and picking apples, and I didn't think twice when one of the popular boys in the group suggested we date. "Dating" meant walking along the Jordan River holding hands during the day and mostly necking after sunset. On the second evening, he took me to a eucalyptus forest not far from our huts and we sat talking for a while. When he asked me to take off my blouse, I hesitated, and did so reluctantly, as he said the magic words "But we are a couple, a steady one." Just as I finished unbuttoning the blouse, three flashlights flooded over me, throwing yellow beams at me, through me, scorching me shamelessly as the boy produced an ugly smile of victory. This should teach you a lesson, he said, standing up. You shouldn't give in so easily, and we have heard you do, to men who are your father's age! Behind the flashlights, three boys appeared, giggling, and the four walked away, proud and aloof. I was more angry than ashamed, and my tears were tears of protest. What a fool I was! Humiliated and degraded as I felt, I didn't feel guilty or even ashamed. I had been taken advantage of, and what I lost that evening was not my innocence but my trust, not my self-confidence but my confidence in others. I was stupid enough to convey the incident, adding some fictional melodrama, to my diary. The next day, I looked them all straight in the face. I worked harder, associated with some kibbutz young people, and proceeded to act, for the rest of the summer, as if nothing had happened.

Back home, I was again the little girl, studious and curious and presentable, and a new school year began. In November, my father participated in the Israeli mission to the UN as an advisor to Abba Eban. The UN Security Council was discussing a very serious complaint by Jordan concerning a reprisal operation against the village of Kibya. Ariel Sharon, an outstanding paratroop commander at the time, was in command of the attack, leading his legendary Commando Unit 101 and other paratroopers. The planned assault was in answer to an attack on an Israeli settlement in which a mother and her two small children were killed. Sharon and his people, believing that the civilians in the village had been evacuated, blew up fifty of Kibya's houses, and the tragic result was the death of many innocent villagers, including about thirty women and children. Father was extremely upset but not apologetic. Strict orders were issued for future cases, whereby Israeli soldiers, even at a risk to their own lives, had to verify that there were no women and children before launching an attack on a house which harbored terrorists. Meanwhile, Father backed the special unit involved and faced an unpleasant Security Council session on the subject.

In the meantime, a series of articles appeared, published by the editor who had befriended me. The authorities were very upset, and when Father was in New York, all hell broke loose. Some clues concerning a security leak had led the Intelligence Service to me. They searched my room, read my diary, and went through my school copybooks. They cross-examined my mother, and she was dumbfounded. There was no way she could face me, and hectic cables were sent to my father to return home. He was reluctant to do so, and as the whole affair was highly classified, he wasn't even sure what it was all about. He wrote letters twice a day, to my mother and to me, and I claimed partial innocence. Yes, we were friends. Yes, I occasionally told him about a party or a social gathering, and no, nothing more. What's more, I didn't care or know details about any of the subjects I was asked about. "Asked about" in a roundabout manner. A friend of my parents was given the unhappy mission of questioning me, an assignment later undertaken by my Uncle Ezer. The questioning was pathetically naïve and obvious, an attempt to drive me to tell things that didn't happen. I was rebellious, I was different, I was treading on dangerous ground without knowing it, perhaps I was taken advantage of by smarter people, but I did not say or write or give away anything that was damaging or secret.

My father was wild with frustration and anger. He wrote Mother: "I couldn't understand anything from our phone conversation, though it was long and cost fifty dollars. I can't understand why I should cut my trip short because of our 14½-year-old daughter, and how to explain it to others. Can't you, your parents, Ezer or my parents put some sense into her? If you think I should return immediately, I will, but this will create an even greater scandal, for me and for her, which may mark her for life. It makes me blush to think I will have to go to Eban and tell him I have to cut my trip short because something happened with my daughter. I cabled Yaël asking her to listen to you and enable me to finish what I have to do here. I asked her to terminate her friendship with you know who, and put it to her as if she was doing me a great favor . . ." etc., etc.

A letter a day, telephone calls and cables, and yet he didn't cut his trip short by one day. I was terrified of his arrival and was forever grateful that he didn't cancel any of his "national obligations." Though I wasn't worried about the actual "scandal" or any of the public aspects, I was not looking forward to a confrontation with him. My mother was sick. Unable to cope with, or face, or even understand the circumstances, she became physically ill, which was probably a combination of shattered nerves and too much crying, and moved for a few days to her sister's house. Now another guilt was loaded on me, by my uncle, who pointed her out to me through a curtain, lying in bed, swollen-eyed and red-faced. "Look what you did to your mother." He explained that her entire world was shattered, that my behavior was a blow to the strong foundations she had so carefully built for our family, that she was in a state of shock and felt hopeless about the future, too. At that point, rather than melting with shame and misery, I felt that I was forming a shield. I hated sacrificial attitudes, I couldn't stand the missionary approach, I didn't feel guilty and wasn't even falling into the trap of self-pity. I promised not to see the man in question. I said I was beginning to feel like a scapegoat, maybe someone was guilty of leaking something to somebody, but, as it wasn't me, they were wasting their time, and interfering with my studies and playing spy in the wrong arena. I derived from my absent father the strength to answer back, and from the fact that he was far away and less alarmed now, and from a night-long decision-taking analysis of the situation.

When Father returned, the scene was brief, painful, and enlightening in many ways. I found him in my room. My diary, which he had obviously just read, was open on the desk. He kissed me warmly, as we hadn't seen each other for a long while, and then he slapped my face, so hard I was almost thrown across the room. He threw the diary on the floor. I cried from the pain, and all I could mutter was

"Why?" "What did I do?" He wasn't very clear when he tried to answer, and I managed to compose myself and even assume a certain detachment. "I am not talking about Kibya, or Lavon or the Intelligence Service report. You are fourteen and a schoolgirl, and you are not yet smart, or wise, or experienced enough to know when you are taken advantage of. So don't take risks until you are fit for them." He was furious about the incident in the Scout summer camp as read in my diary—shocked and somehow hurt.

"It is partly fiction," I said, "and I learned my lesson."

"Oh, did you? And went on to sleep with a man who could be your father?"

The use of the term "who could be your father" from my own father made me smile. At my smile, he slapped me again, and this time I could detect regret in his eye as he did it.

"I didn't sleep with him. I am a virgin, for what it matters, and I'm not even interested. I can't say the same about many of my girlfriends, and that isn't important either." I was afraid to smile, but I felt a devilish grin inside when I added: "One of the intelligence officers who talked to me, in a very fatherly way, and made me cry, also tried to kiss me in a way which was not fatherly at all. So I'm on guard now, Father, and I am in control, but so many people around me are not, and maybe you should handle them first."

"And so I will. But you'd better watch yourself." It was obvious that the conversation was over. He was uncomfortable. We both let out steam and were aware of the dangers of melodramatizing, and he was looking for a way out. "Come up and see the dresses I bought you. I hope the sizes are right."

"Don't you want to talk some more?" I tested him.

"The subject is closed as far as I am concerned."

It sounded like "Roger and over and out," and I was grateful. We walked up the stairs, and before we entered the apartment, he kissed me again, and said, "I love you very much, but don't take advantage of it."

The dresses were beautiful, and so were the other gifts. My mother managed to relax and pretend it was all over for her too, and no apologies were exchanged at any time. Though we had all handled the given situation badly, the nearness between my father and myself was not impaired, and the distance between Mother and me didn't diminish. I had a notion of the price I had to pay for fame, notoriety, and independence, and the "straight talk" with my father was satisfactory only to him. There were things he couldn't ignore but wanted shelved, and he absolved himself rather than support me. He, too, wanted to be free of guilt and anxieties as a father, and I offered him an easy way. No blames, no psychology, no question marks as to how we ever reached this gap or rift, and, above all, no moralizing. Two slaps, five sentences, a diary which was to be burned and forever discontinued and a renewed façade of happiness and unity which supplied a good alibi for both of us. We both wanted, with different degrees of legitimacy, not to be slaves to the confining dictates of family routine.

A month later, my father reached the top of the military pyramid and was appointed Chief of Staff of the Israeli Armed Forces, and we moved to our own new house in the suburb of Zahala.

S E V E N 🙰

P E R S P E C T I V E

The house in Zahala was home. It was to remain so until my parents were divorced almost twenty years later, and it was a home we all loved. Nahalal was more than a memory—the farm was ours and someone else lived and worked there; we visited the village often enough—but I knew I should never live there again. It would remain a loved birthplace, having given me a basic sense of security, simplicity, proximity to the land—whatever the term "roots" is comprised of—but it would not present me with obligations, only the privilege of belonging. The Jerusalem house was an episode. We couldn't afford and, in any case, we didn't really care to live in the Abkarius Bey style. Both in Nahalal and in Jerusalem, I had grandparents in whose house I was always welcome, and Zahala was just in between, both geographically, being a suburb of Tel Aviv, and in life style.

The house was bought with a loan granted by my mother's parents. The entire suburb was state-subsidized to enable Army officers to buy and own their own houses. It had three bedrooms, a large garden, a small kitchen, and a living room, and Simcha joined us from Jerusalem, as Mother resumed her work with the Ministry of Labor, developing handicrafts.

I had my own room, and this time there was no change of schools. Most of my friends lived in Tel Aviv; the youth-movement club was there too; and even the daily ride to school and back was time-consuming, so in fact I was a commuter, but it had its advantages. I frequented Tel Aviv less, devoted more time to studies, and started writing feuilletons for an evening paper, using a pseudonym. I was more than careful now, having learned my lesson, and kept a low profile. I was going to work doubly hard and reassure myself time and time again that my achievements were my own, that no advantage was taken of me, and that I was treading the thin line into self-assertion safely, and on my own merits.

My father was Israel's number-one soldier. His face, so easily distinguishable because of the black eye patch, was synonymous with tough bravery and pride, and I wasn't going to ever try to wage that losing battle for anonymity or even privacy. I didn't need to test my father's love; it was fully there and mine. What had to be proved was my own capacity, my own talent and persistence. The doors were open, the obstacles obvious, and I knew there was no way to avoid exposure.

In Nahalal, my father had sworn not to be the "average Nahalal farmer," and now he was set on not being the "typical Chief of Staff" either. When it was suggested to him that he should change his style, "become more respectable and circumspect and fashion a new Moshe Dayan," he answered: "It is not I who would change; the image of the Chief of Staff, and if necessary, the Army itself would change." And it did. He moved into a smaller, less formal room in HQ, replaced the furniture with a plain wooden field table covered by a khaki blanket, and a few simple chairs. He cut down on ceremonial and established direct contact with lower echelons in the fighting units.

He felt restless confined to the office. He was often bored with long meetings concerning issues he felt others on his staff could handle. He needed to remain on edge and preserve his restlessness and mobility. He was often absent at night, waiting in a remote post or distant camp for soldiers to return from night exercises or an operation. He didn't need intermediaries; he wanted to hear direct reports and make his comments directly to the young officers, in his own style. His principal objective was to overcome mediocrity and not allow lethargic routine to take over. His unexpected presence, dressed in fatigues, munching on fruit, brought more than a smile to the faces of tired soldiers returning with dawn to some out-of-the-way border post or settlement.

His informal style and unpresumptuous behavior affected the family, too. We were part of the scene. I could call or enter his office whenever I wanted; I was always welcome to join him on inspection trips or visits. The house in Zahala was open to private visits from military and civilians, and there were no office hours or any attempt at privacy at home. His effort to remove all barriers between himself and the troops antagonized many officers along the chain of command, and his informal, direct, and at time impatient style was often interpreted and criticized as irresponsible.

The driver, the secretaries, the members of the General Staff, officers of commando units, and favorite "fighters" were all welcome. At the same time, my father resumed his ardent interest in archaeology, and whenever he could, he went digging or sat in the garden putting shards together. His collection grew, and the garden acquired a special near-magic when among the shrubs and flowers he placed Corinthian pillars and ancient millstones. The delight he took in his discoveries was still childlike and appealing, totally free of materialistic considerations. He would wake me up in the middle of the night to show me a new piece, or at the crack of dawn to look at the garden in first light. We all helped push and pull and place the sometimes ton-heavy sarcophagi and pillars, but what for us seemed an interesting hobby was becoming for him an addiction.

Ben-Gurion resigned as Prime Minister in 1953 and retired to Sde Boker, and there was constant friction between Moshe Sharett, the Prime Minister, and Defense Minister Pinhas Lavon. My father was not close in spirit or even ideology to either of them, and his relations with his ministerial chief he defined as cool and proper. Sharett believed in diplomatic solutions to problems like Egypt's ban on all cargo to and from Israel, while Lavon was an activist anxious to use his authority over the head, almost behind the back, of his Chief of Staff. This was intolerable to my father, who presented his resignation, withdrew it when Lavon asked him to, and eagerly awaited the return of Ben-Gurion after the failure of an attempted act of sabotage in Cairo referred to in public as "the security mishap."

Ben-Gurion returned to office in the winter of 1955, and the intangible web of suspicions and trustlessness that had begun to form was removed. I had a feeling, which became stronger with time, that as powerful, self-confident, and independent as my father was, he did need to share responsibility with a number-one, above him. As long as it was Ben-Gurion, it was understandable and reflected the admiration, respect, and love he felt for the old man. Later, his need and acceptance of the authority of lesser leaders reflected a strange, paradoxical reluctance to stand alone at the pinnacle of power.

The main security concern of that period, other than the Egyptian blockade, was the recurring attacks on civilians by guerrilla infiltrators. The Jordanian, Syrian, and Egyptian borders could not be hermetically sealed, and defense alone was no solution. Reprisal operations were accelerated, and as my father put it, "We cannot totally prevent the murder of an innocent family, asleep in its moshav home, or the blowing up of a pipeline. We can, however, quote a very high price on our blood, a price too dear to be worth paying by Arab villages, Arab armies, or Arab governments. We can fight the infiltrators if they understand that the killing of a Jew in kibbutz Ruchama endangers the life of the inhabitants of Gaza." However, he chose military rather than civilian objectives and made it clear that his was not an "eye for an eye" policy. His intent was not to punish but to deter. It was up to the Arab governments, and much in their own interests, to control the terrorist activities launched from their territory. The small, extraordinary, special Unit 101 was integrated into a larger force, that of the paratroopers, enhancing the morale and setting standards for other regiments as well.

"Dayan is stripping the Army of its fat, it's all muscle now," a government minister suggested. Although it was not meant as a compliment at the time, the remark aptly defined my father's intention. The set standards and criteria were highly demanding. "Officers of the Israeli Army do not send their men into battle. They lead them into battle," Father said to cadets graduating from an officers' course, and 50 percent casualties was a very high maximal price before withdrawal or retreat. The tough demands produced results. The paratroopers drew volunteers, and this large force, all muscle, was, as Ben-Gurion put it, a "nursery for heroes."

These developments, debates, conflicts, and achievements were never limited to camp or office hours or staff meetings. They constituted our life. I was in my last year of high school, alert and political-minded, and though Father didn't seek my opinion, or consult with me, or treat me as an equal, I was no longer a child and I was a good audience. He liked to air his views, he gave me his speeches to read before he delivered them, and talked about operations and reprisal acts, returning red-eyed and smiling or anguished, according to the number of casualties. He decided all officers should be trained to parachute, and he was going to do it, too. Jump he did, and fractured his knee in the night jump, but if some were surprised or saw in it some typical Dayan stunt, we did not. He would never send a soldier where he wouldn't go himself, and if the ability, the courage, or whatever it took, was to be the standard of an Israeli officer, it was natural for him to undergo it himself. The day he got his paratrooper's wings, pinned to his shirt by Sharon, then the paratroopers' commander, he felt proud and joyous like a little boy, and we felt as proud. For myself, I felt invigorated and truly privileged at this sensation of belonging, allowed to share, not only witness, this world of purposefulness.

I have always been a light sleeper, and the phone ringing in my parents' room would wake me up many times most nights. After a few calls, when it was obviously going to continue, I would wander into the kitchen, to find Father peeling an orange or slicing a watermelon—depending on the season—and he almost always felt like talking. Not long discussions, no philosophies or preaching or bombastic historic declarations, just small talk, a few rhetorical questions, an indication of an idea—counting on me to complete the obvious or assume the relevant end. His pride and admiration of the acts of bravery of some of the soldiers he recounted as if these were tales of ancient biblical heroes; his sadness when speaking of someone who died in action was unfathomable even if his voice hadn't changed or broken, and I learned to detect the fine emotion that underlined each expression, though for an outsider his face would have seemed a static mask. He was forty, and not as slim, but he was very strong and sturdy, and being sixteen myself, I tried to look at him the way other women probably did. I didn't regard him as physically attractive, but I could well see that he appealed to women. The scar of the missing eye pained and troubled me, and his physical behavior in the privacy of home was clumsy, gauche, and a subject for teasing. He would clean his ears with a well-selected key, clean the dirt from between his toes sitting barefoot near the garden table, walk around the garden in shabby, baggy underpants, urinating in a corner if he felt like it. "So don't look," he would say, or: "What's wrong with a key? Is a ball-pen better?" He had no inhibitions, and while he didn't act to spite one, he was definitely not out to please either. There was something endearing in his genuine lack of consideration as to "what will the neighbors say."

I think of those years as years of harmony. A teacher-pupil harmony, at that. It was easy to admire him, and I did so without reservations. He looked his best in uniform; he inspired confidence and, in me, trust as well. Qualities that drew criticism and were regarded by others as appalling or distasteful, I found endearing, exciting, and worthy of imitation. He was snappy and impatient with people as well as with certain red tape and even legal procedures. He held in contempt the stupid, the mediocre, the coward, and the meek. They were referred to as "idiots," "worms," and what they had to say was "bullshit" and "utter nonsense." Sensitivities, human shortcomings, and the mere fact that most people are not endowed with above-average talents or qualities were not taken into account. He placed the traffic lights, the white lines, and the stop signs along his way, and often removed them according to changes of mood or circumstance. He didn't feel superior, he *was* superior, but he totally lacked the tolerance and respect for fellow humans who were less lucky. I, at sixteen, was a perfect audience for his "humorous," often degrading remarks about people.

Of course, a certain minister was an idiot. Obviously a particular ambassador was a moron. Very funny to have told a policeman when caught speeding: "I have only one eye. Do you want me to look at the road or at the speedometer."

His judgment of character was superficial, and this went for the people he liked or respected, not to mention his taste in women, which was downright vulgar. But he taught me to be selective and discerning, and at the time, I applied it to everything and everybody, except him. He was above reproach, he could do whatever he wanted, he was the epitome of a "free man."

I soon learned his way could not be imitated. Not because I didn't have his record, which led people to tolerate him, but because I didn't have it in me. I liked his manner and style, and he didn't mind paying a price and taking the consequences. I felt sorry for the idiots, rather than contempt, and where he was irritated, I was often amused. His lack of sophistication produced narrow-mindedness, though never on military or political issues.

Assi and Udi reacted differently. Udi left Zahala and studied in a farm boarding school a short drive away. He refused to be driven there by Father, didn't want the other kids to know he was Dayan's son, and though it didn't last long, he tried to grab small chunks of anonymity whenever he could. Like Zorik, Udi was an adventurous nature lover. Being an excellent sportsman and an able mechanic gained him the reputation of being a poor scholar. Laziness made him accept the definition, and it took him and us many years to realize that he was as capable of scholarly, even literary and artistic, achievements as the rest of us. Assi was more of an extrovert as a child, temperamental and sensitive very much like Mother, but he, too, tried to fight for an identity apart from the famous name he carried. He was easily elated and as easily depressed, and in elementary school, when filling in a questionnaire about home and family, he wrote: "My father is a plumber, my mother is a dressmaker from Rumania," and added at the end: "I don't want to be a guinea pig." All our teachers told our parents that the three of us were suffering from a "Dayan complex." The school psychologists offered us remedies or guidance, but my father, in his usual style, laughed it off as "two-cent psychology" and suggested they themselves had a "Dayan complex" and they should worry about their own children.

Mother loved us and thought the earth of each of us and felt there was no cause for serious alarm. We were great, we were good-looking and healthy, we had talents and abilities, and she was there to protect us, which basically meant to give and spoil and permit and supply our needs. The emotional, intricate level, or whatever complexes we did develop, was ignored and suppressed in self-defense.

All along our separate routes, Mother managed to distinguish our achievements, regard them as dream fulfillment, and exaggerate their worth, and simply treat failures and disasters as "bad luck," to be blamed on others and later on my father, or simply ignored. I seemed to take the Dayan complex for granted, as a biological fact. I couldn't and didn't choose to fight it, and I didn't waste energy trying to shake off something that couldn't be shed and didn't disturb me. Very often I heard, behind my back or in conversation: "She is very much like her father." The fact that, more and more often, it was not meant as a compliment didn't upset me. It inevitably meant being different from the others, and it pleased me to think that I ran no risk of fitting into some sordid mediocre routine of average dull people. I was "somebody," and I didn't have to deliver anything or work for the title.

The last year in school was pleasant enough. We mostly worked to prepare for the matriculation exams, and discipline was lax. School authorities treated us as adults and spoiled us, especially the boys, as a way of saying: "Let them enjoy the freedom and not burden them, it's their last year before the Army." Often, that was meant with a touch of sadness, as if they might add: "And maybe their last year altogether . . ."

This sadness was made more melodramatic in our talks among ourselves. The borders were restless, reprisal acts were becoming major operations, and there was talk of escalation, perhaps of an all-out war. My classmates were all set to volunteer for the paratroopers and other special combat units, and the list of dead from among the past graduates grew longer, adding white hair and deepening wrinkles on the teachers' faces. They looked at us with compassion and pity, remembering a dead pupil's liveliness or mischief or promise, and muttering: "Only yesterday . . ."

The boys in my class hid their fears under a thick but transparent layer of humor. "I'd rather die on the Egyptian front; in the sand you rot slowly." Or: "You'd better find a spare boyfriend, someone with a green thumb who can cultivate the flowers on my grave." Or someone would suggest that next year's class reunion should be held in the military cemetery.

We had fun, we went to the movies and admired Lana Turner and Grace Kelly or whoever was blond and buxom and elegant; we ate corn on the cob on the beach and licked ice cream while talking about what we would do after Army service, unless there was no "after."

I was younger than the others. I had almost two years before I was due for military service, and I planned to study a year at the Hebrew University in Jerusalem. I was more involved than the others, and what was to them an unknown, demanding yet exciting world was almost home for me. Uniforms, weapons, drill, camp, the after-battle smell and the nervousness preceding it, the red berets and the heavy boots, the light aircraft and the topographical maps were all part of my daily life, and familiarity breeds security.

We had heated political arguments, and most of my friends leaned to the left. They thought of life on a kibbutz, of total equality, and oversimplified pure socialism. I was for the moshav system. Ben-Gurion's policies were socialistic enough for me, and I was satisfied with the equality of opportunities. We were free of materialistic desires, and none of us thought then in terms of future income, the size of apartments, the make of cars, or even of our own clothes. Simplicity, a modest appearance, basics were "in." Girls didn't use makeup; the boys wore shorts and sandals and a clean, rolled-up-sleeve white shirt on festive occasions.

My father was satisfied that I'd pass the final exams without difficulty and was trying to convince me to study agronomy at the university, "or something else that is useful." He knew I wanted to write; he liked my short articles that appeared occasionally in the evening paper. He didn't think I lacked talent, but he thought I could do all this on the side, and study something "real," have a profession and support myself. Agronomy, archaeology, zoology were worthwhile studying. The subjects I chose like international relations and political science were a "waste of time and money."

In the very long run, he proved right, and I shall always harbor a frustration at not having studied medicine or biology. Many years later, I worked doubly hard to complete some courses in science and genetics as some small compensation. At fifteen, I didn't believe I had the stamina or even the gift for math or science and chose the easier way. It was not his money, or his time, so, without a major confrontation, Father let me have my way and I enrolled for the following university year when all my girlfriends were preparing themselves for military service.

My girlfriends had boyfriends their own age or older. Some talked about marriage; a few had made love; and I watched with envy as, at the end of a Scout meeting, couples drifted off holding hands, sharing sweet secrets, leaning on one another, drawing strength from intimate friendships. I consoled myself with the fact that I was popular, even courted and "loved" by a couple of boys, but I waited for the "real thing." I was mature, I looked older than my years, I was attractive, but I was not interested in flirting. I longed to fall in love; I waited for an explosion, for a rainbow to break through, and wasn't settling for less. What I witnessed around me was pure and beautiful, and somewhere along my teens I missed the age of innocence. My two closest friends were boys, and we mostly studied together, often in my house. My father asked whether they were clever, which they were, and studious, which they were, and occasionally exchanged a few words with them, showing us a piece of ancient pottery or inquiring about their future plans. He didn't ask me whether I dated; he didn't suspect that girls my age made love, and definitely didn't want to know more than he did. I wouldn't lie to him and he knew it. He wasn't after excessive information, and for the time being there was nothing to hide. My mother was fully involved with a major project, the fruit of a few years of work: Maskit. Maskit's purpose was to trace and develop handicrafts and other local artisanal activity, improve design or preserve the traditional and original, and create a proper outlet for it commercially, thus supplying a source of income for the artisans and craftsmen. At the same time, Mother's priority was still my father, and she made sure nothing was changed in his routine. He showed sufficient interest in her work and encouraged her, and she was soon flourishing under heaps of rugs and carpets, samples of handwoven materials and embroidered dresses, boxes of Yemenite jewelry and lace collars. Between my father's accumulated pot-sherds and handles and stones and Mother's beads and sweaters and ceramic creations, I entertained dreams of an empty house, bare walls, and uncrowded space and developed a certain antipathy to any sort of "collection." She was busy and I found comfort in it. If I had a young woman's dream of love, or coveted an engulfing huge emotion, it was not something I cared to share. Both my parents, even if they felt guilty momentarily for not being more inquisitive about my emotional life, didn't really want to tackle anything that might prove complex. It suited me fine. We called it independence, trust, respect of privacy, whatever. My father said often: "You do what you want; it's your life, and I trust your judgment. Most important, don't do anything you don't want. But if you need me, you should know I'm always there, with all my love, and not such a bad brain . . ."

There was something deterring in his offer of a "shoulder to lean on." He meant it fully, but in my mind I could complete the sentence, adding: "As I love you and trust you so much, I'm sure you'll never get into trouble serious enough to use this shoulder. The knowledge of its being there should suffice." Only after his death did I count the many times I was on the verge of appealing to him and didn't, the times I wanted to lean and didn't dare test the validity of his offer. Many years later, and he kept repeating this key sentence, my image as independent and self-sufficient was so strong that preserving it was my minor contribution to his well-being.

Mother watched me grow up and away, make progress and fall and stand on my feet again, as if through a barrier that I myself created. A barrier she was afraid to cross and I didn't care to abolish; we were both remiss. "She is like her father, she doesn't need people," she would say, and left it at that.

Travel is second best to being in love, or so I discovered when my maternal grandmother offered me a graduation present—a trip to Europe. My first trip abroad, something that during those years of austerity we could never afford on our own family income. School

was over, the youth-movement experience was over, the university
and Army service had not yet begun, and it was time to collect a
dividend on the fact that I could read and write at the age of four. I
gained a year and I was set to discover the world beyond Carmel
and the Old City walls, beyond the Mediterranean. With my parents'
blessing, a few new outfits, loads of practical advice, and my grandmother's car, we left the port of Haifa for Marseilles. As the lights
of Haifa disappeared in the dark, I sat on the deck hypnotized by
the trail of white foam in the water. The stars were the same, most
of the passengers were Israeli, and the language was the same, but
the strange sensation of being carried away from home, by a large
hand, to be deposited on a distant shore, excited me. The nightly
emergency phone calls for my father, the morning news, the headlines, the permanent, almost obsessive preoccupation with what was
happening all around, the microcosms of retaliations, declarations,
borders, curfews, my mother's Yemenites and Moroccans, my
father's brave young commanders, all faded into the steady sound
of the waves, and I felt guilty. This feeling that was strongest then,
as I went abroad for the first time, has never left me during years
of extensive travel. As if I ran away from a besieged and surrounded island, as if I was a deserter. A few days passed before I
could pull out of this mood and begin to look around and take new
things in.

The trip was all I dreamed of and expected, and more. A constant
revelation of layers unfolding and presenting themselves to me, to
touch, to look at, to taste, and to experience. Pages of everything
I'd learned and read and imagined came to life intensively and nothing was familiar or remotely resembling what I knew at home. We
drove to Paris, to Amsterdam, to Stockholm and Oslo, and crossed
the North Sea to Newcastle, arriving in London a few weeks later.
We stayed in youth hostels, as my grandmother was in charge of
youth hostels in Israel and was attending an international congress
in Oslo; we bought local foods and ate in forests and near rivers and
lakes. It wasn't a luxury trip, but the abundance of luxurious
offerings made me feel like a princess. I wasn't feeling guilty any
longer, but I was jealous. Envious to the point of crying. The green
huge forests, the streams and lakes and springs I compared with the

pathetic flow of the Jordan, and our dry wadis and yellow desert. The small villages with their pebble-paved alleys and their church towers, the monuments of Paris, the art of Amsterdam, the cherries and the raspberries, the politeness and the cleanliness, the calm of people, and their complacency, the aesthetic quality of everything from shop windows to public parks. It was all too much for me to absorb. Villages in Israel were hurriedly thrown together in the fifties, and scarcity of water and lack of expertise gave it all an appearance of something provisionary. From the perspective of a Danish village, my own country seemed a huge transit camp of refugees slightly hysterical in behavior and hopelessly pathetic in their efforts. One room of the Louvre, one corridor in the Rijksmuseum, one lake outside Stockholm, seemed to equal what we have nationally in art and resources. And people were not nervous, or so it seemed. I suddenly discovered there were people, intelligent and cultured, who didn't switch on the radio every hour on the hour, who didn't read three newspapers a day, who didn't hurry or raise their voice or perspire or push their way to the top of a line, or even bargain. I was so bewildered by comparisons that much of the actual experience would have been wasted, had it not been for my grandmother. I could have choked on pure oxygen and mineral water, if she hadn't forced me to look a little deeper and stop comparing. She showed me slums; she pointed out miserable beggars and primitive dwellings. She distinguished for me between calm and boredom, complacency and purposefulness, striving and taking for granted, age-old achievements for which a very high price was paid and results reached in a short time against all odds. I learned to enjoy things without the need to possess them. None of it was mine, or would be mine, and it was all very beautiful, and I was able to take in and enjoy and appreciate. What was mine was not degraded by being different.

For the first time, I felt Jewish. What was inherent in being an Israeli suddenly acquired its own reality. I was an Israeli; I had a blue passport, and I was born in Nahalal. In the forms I filled whenever we crossed a border I wrote: Nationality, Israeli. When I visited a synagogue in Amsterdam or Paris, when I heard Yiddish spoken, when I said I was from Israel and a stranger added, "You mean you are Jewish," when I saw the sign KOSHER over butcher shops in London's East End, it was as if something from inside me was extracted and exposed as a second skin. I didn't believe in God, never had a Jewish education in the orthodox religious sense, never was observant. Being Israeli, speaking Hebrew, studying the Bible as my national history book, as geography and poetry and philosophy, touching my father's oil lamps and having Tzippi for a sister, were all components in my being, and there was no need to dissect or analyze them. When we were in Stockholm, someone said: "Oh, but you don't take bacon with your eggs." I'm sorry, I had to give it a thought and an answer. I do eat non-kosher food, I do drive on Saturdays, no, I don't speak Yiddish, yes, Jerusalem is my capital, yes, the Jews dressed in black praying in the small synagogue are my brothers, yes, the Nazis did kill my people, yes, there are Israelis who are not Jews . . . leave me alone. I don't know. No, it's not a religion—I'm not religious. It's not a race; we are not biologically homogeneous; we are a people. We are custodians of a great culture. We are a civilization. Some of our people have a state; the others are minorities in other countries. I found out, never having all the answers, that I was not defensive about it. The "others" thought of me as Jewish and applied their terminology regardless of my identification with it. Only in London did I begin to sense what it meant to belong to a minority, what kind of insecurity it produced, and in turn what Israel meant to the Jewish people. That's when I seriously missed home and felt saturated with the formal, confining, slightly hypocritical "European civilization." I absorbed to capacity and was on the verge of giving up, but just as I was ready to go home, I found a part-time job and decided to stay for another couple of months. So when Grandmother crossed the Channel to drive south alone, I had to force myself not to run after her like a baby. Staying was a self-imposed test which I didn't enjoy and yet didn't regret.

I rented a room in the apartment of a lovely old lady my grandparents knew, in Swiss Cottage, and took the bus every morning to Fleet Street, to the offices of the *Jewish Observer*, a weekly magazine which was quite an authority on Middle Eastern affairs thanks to its brilliant and knowledgeable editor, Jon Kimche. I did some translations, but mostly research on Hungarian Jewry under the Nazi occupation and on the attempts to bargain with the authorities to "buy" a certain number of lives. Kimche directed my research as if I were a qualified university graduate, the Wiener Library had files and papers on everything relevant to the period, and I trained my eye and brain to select, to read between the lines, put together facts from different sources, and create a pattern, as if I were completing a fascinating jigsaw puzzle. I lied about my age and easily passed for an eighteen-year-old, and my salary was raised to five pounds a week. With this fortune, I could indulge myself.

For a very brief while, I playacted the woman I wasn't. I painted my fingernails red, wore eye makeup, dared high heels, and even attempted a change in dress and hairstyle. My friends were people I met through the magazine, mostly Jews, and a few journalists I met in the pub near the office.

Letters from home were sweet and loving. My father suggested the "British experience" should soon be over, and I couldn't have agreed with him more. I disliked most of it, other than the actual work. The smell of fried bacon and kippers in the block of flats, the indifference of people I saw daily on the bus, the condescending attitude to foreigners, the anonymity which I appreciated at the start became an imposition rather than a choice. The aloof remarks of friends who were not Jewish about "your poor little country," plus an undercurrent of traditional admiration of the exotic Arabs, annoyed me just as much as the apologetic discomfort of my Jewish friends. I missed my brothers, I missed my parents and grandparents and the beach and the sun, and I was nervously unhappy about myself. Men courted me, I was fun to be with to a point, but I was on edge. The slightest question about my "famous father" threw me off, and any humorous reference to my "brave little Jewish country" produced an outburst. I hated red fingernails, I craved sandals and tanned skin; the duffel coat was heavy and itchy, and Fleet Street suffocating and dark. I wanted to go home, away from the dry sherry before lunch, the posh shop windows on Bond Street, the cat-loving landlady, and the heap of pretense I felt buried under. Back among the aggressive natives, surrounded by other aggressive maniacs, where I belonged, where I could get up in the morning and cry out: I am a majority! I spent my savings on gifts to bring home, and some books, and landed in Israel as if I had escaped from a wrecked ship, almost kissing the soil.

But the bug of travel had installed itself in my system. My curiosity was not satisfied, and I knew I should forever try to break away to explore, to feel lost in a crowd, to be an uninvolved stranger. The marvelous sensation of homecoming reassured me of the roots that enabled me to spread my wings.

I returned just in time, for my Grandmother Dvorah was dying. She wasn't dying; she was gradually fading away. My father, who held a dialogue with death all his life, could not contain his agony. In desolation, he almost ignored her sickness, which steadily progressed, devouring her. Since her youth, she had fought cancer, had undergone operations, but clung to life and stubbornly refused to give in. Her small frame was the size of a child's now; the beautiful face wrinkled; the long braid of raven-black hair of which my father was so proud was lusterless and meager. She bent under the blow of Zorik's death but forced herself into a renewed vitality with a bravery and resolution which had astounded us all. Of her grandchildren, only I was really aware of her condition, and I soon realized I couldn't talk to my father about it. While she was still alive, he turned her into a holy, perfect memory, and with all his cool reasoning, the man who could distinguish so well between imagination, wishful thinking, and facts could not accept the obvious proximity of her death.

I found a room to share in Jerusalem and, not yet seventeen, became the youngest student at Hebrew University, supporting myself on a meager salary from the Department of Tourism, where I had found a job. A room and a job in Jerusalem, home and family in Zahala, forty weekly hours at the university, and a good number of friends in Jerusalem and Tel Aviv. Enough to keep anyone busy and content, and mostly I was.

If clouds were gathering and there was tension in the air, it was over the national sky. The word "war" was mentioned often at home, and when my father talked of "war" he did not mean an isolated act of retaliation. The Czech arms deal supplied Egypt with massive quantities of heavy tanks, guns, jet fighters, and bombers,

Dayan with his mother and sister, 1926

As a schoolboy, 1929

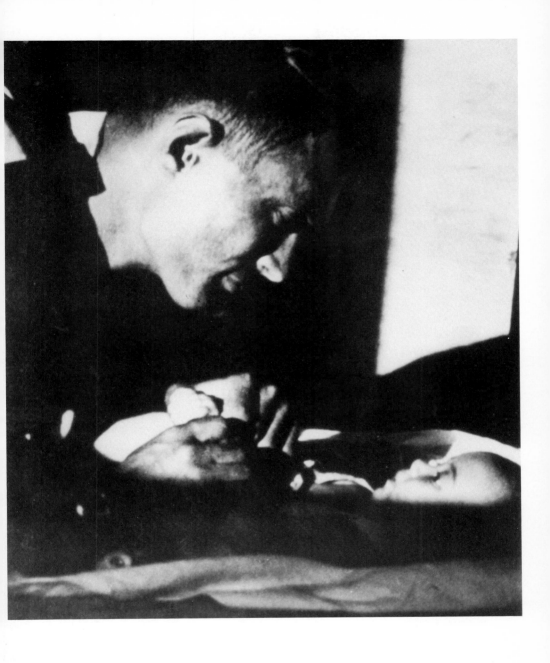

(opposite, top) Moshe and Ruth as newlyweds
(bottom) As a prisoner in Acre prison, 1940
(above) With Yaël, 1940

(top) Yaël and her paternal grandparents, 1946
(bottom) With brothers, Assi and Udi

(top) With her mother in 1956, during basic training
(bottom) Cadet school graduation ceremony, 1957

(opposite) In Paris, 1961
(above, top) At Udi's wedding, 1963
(bottom) A dinner in Athens, 1965

(clockwise, from above)
With Ariel Sharon in the Sinai, 1967
At Yaël's wedding to Dov Sion, 1967
Dov and Yaël on their honeymoon in Rome, 1967
The brith of Yaël's son Dan, 1968
Dayan with his grandson Dan in Zahala, 1972

*Dayan and Ariel Sharon
during the Yom Kippur War,
1973*

*The archaeological collection
at Zahala*

*Dayan with Henry Kissinger,
Zahala*

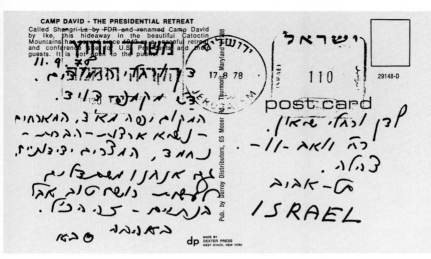

*A postcard from Camp David
in 1978 during the peace talks*

*Yaël and Dayan at the White
House for the signing of the
Egyptian Peace Treaty in 1979*

*Moshe Dayan, Anwar el-Sadat,
and Menachem Begin in Israel*

(top) Yaël with Rahel at Dayan's memorial service
(bottom) Mourners at Dayan's funeral, October 1981

and by the summer of 1956 these arms were absorbed and operational. The Soviet weaponry came with full political backing, and Nasser could feel confident and ready, controlling this formidable might. France was our only supplier of arms, and in April the first Mystère warplanes arrived, followed by AMX tanks and an agreement with Britain for the purchase of Meteor night-fighter planes. There was no way we could match Egypt in quantity, but in quality we were superior, both in equipment and in fighting ability.

My father set new priorities concerning the Egyptian war challenge. The acquisition of arms was tops, from every possible source —excluding the U.S.A., which adamantly refused to change its embargo policy. Next was the reorganization of civil defense and emergency services, and the fortification of settlements. The Army itself, an alert, capable fighting machine, was ready. At the end of June, Father left for Paris, with Shimon Peres, who was director general of the Ministry of Defense, and returned satisfied, with a firm agreement for an additional supply of arms. This trip, and others that followed preceding the Sinai Campaign, were shrouded in secrecy. At no point did my father conceal these "secret" missions from the family, or at least from my mother and me. He mentioned, almost casually, that it was classified, that he was going under cover, in a military plane, but didn't fuss with "Don't dare tell" or "Let there be no leak," and didn't dramatize. He confided in us, shared his anxieties when he left and his accomplishments when he returned.

He showed only a vague interest in my studies, and almost no interest in my social life. Some of my friends visited me at home. They were students, a young journalist, a painter, and a couple of classmates who were in the Army. The fact that all were men and a few years older than I didn't seem to bother him, and I didn't regard it as unusual, either. There was no serious romance, and if there was, it was one-sided. I had a strange feeling of a growing capacity, though not a desire, to hurt men who were involved with me. I was not ready for any form of attachment on an exclusive or long-lasting basis and was not sexually attracted to any of them. The greatest friendship I developed was with a homosexual, as this satisfied both of us and was free of expectations, jealousies, and plans. It intrigued my father, who refused to acknowledge the fact that homosexuality existed. It can't be, because it's unnatural, he said naïvely. Yet he wondered: What did they do when they did? And pulled a face expressing disgust when I tried, avoiding all words which were unmentionable at home, to graphically suggest it was possible. I often went out with a young student of economics. My feelings toward him swung between near-love and a fear of hurting him. Because he was in love with me, because he was a devoted friend, because he was intelligent and honest and fun to be with, he was bound to be hurt, since I wasn't ready for him. I was a mixed-up, restless, self-centered young woman, and he couldn't wait the length of time it would take me to come to terms with myself, my surroundings, my family, and my plans. I was honest enough not to mislead and secure enough not to tease. I knew no jealousies, as I didn't allow myself a deep love, and I didn't want to own or dominate; touching was sufficient.

My father wanted to know more, but was afraid to find out, and I volunteered nothing. He ignored and simply regarded as non-existent many phenomena and people he didn't like, and it was obvious that the thought of someone touching me, or, God forbid, making love to me, was shelved as something unpleasant, preferably impossible. I was touched, and I did make love, and not necessarily with the one man I cared for most at the time.

I had begun to work as an assistant to a film director who came to make some documentaries for the Tourist Department. He was married, separated from his wife, fifteen years my senior, and extremely wise and gentle. We worked around the clock, and it seemed only natural when lovemaking followed. I didn't look forward to it, I didn't expect much, and there was no room for disappointment. Not such a big deal, I thought, and though I learned to enjoy more as I cared more for my partners, it basically remained so. It was fun to taste the first clementines of the season; it was great to swim at sunset on a hot, still day; it was superb to have a real, precise, totally honest conversation, and sex was okay too. So were some good passages in Malaparte or Camus; so were solitary walks. So there was no promiscuity and no obsession, and it rather surprised me when the man said to me: Did you know you are marvelous?—meaning in bed. They say it to all women, I gathered, and was satisfied to be a good, average, easy-to-fulfill partner.

To my enormous surprise, word of the "affair" got to my family, and for all the wrong reasons they were alarmed. Part of my salary was a ticket to the United States and back, and somehow this was transformed into a story of elopement, maybe even a kidnapping. As nobody dared face me with straight questions, least of all my mother and father, I had no chance to laugh it off or explain. And then, in the least suitable circumstances, I had an opportunity to do so.

My Grandmother Dvorah had improved after the removal of a tumor, but, toward the summer, her condition worsened. My father visited Nahalal as frequently as he could, to spend a few minutes at her bedside and distract her from the pain and agony, but mostly she was taken care of by Aviva, Shmuel, and my mother. Toward the end of June, she asked to be transferred to a hospital. It was too much work for everybody, she said; let professionals do it. She knew that, as much as she wanted to die at home, she was leaving Nahalal for good. On the way out of the village, she lifted herself up in the ambulance to look at the Hill of Shimron, a farewell to Zorik, who was buried there, which also meant: I'll soon join you. My grandfather, who sat by her bed in the hospital, wrote down every word she said, every conversation she held, in a shaking hand and in tear-smeared ink. She talked of Ben-Gurion, wishing he were gentler in personality; of Sharett, whom she liked but disagreed with; of her work and the future of the Labor movement; and she talked about me. Of Grandmother Rachel, who visited her, she begged: "Yaël has to be saved from the trap set for her. She is so clever and talented, how come she doesn't realize? She is Moshe's daughter, how can she do it to him?" I visited the next day, and she asked my grandfather to leave us alone. She was crying and in pain, and I held her shrunken, tiny hand in mine, trying in vain to calm her. "I hear dreadful things about you. How can you live with a married man? How can you go with him to

America? His wife will make a scandal; you'll be rejected by everybody; your reputation will be ruined, and it may even destroy your father's position. I talked to your father about it and saw a tear in his eye, just as when you crawled to him in the Acre prison . . ." I was crying, but I managed to compose myself. I had to bring this uncalled-for scene to an end, and I was furious and irritated. This exceptional woman, in her dying bed, was anguished by some idiotic distortion of reality. I must have sounded cold and harsh, but I had something to put across through the morphine and the physical pain. "This is nonsense, and I beg you to believe me. I'm not living with him; I'm going to America because it's a chance to go and I've earned it, working pretty hard. I'm not surrounded by evil people. I am seventeen, and a student, and I'm not doing anything you, or I, or my father should be ashamed of." She was crying and nodding, and I felt the distance between us grow as if a hand were pulling her away from me. "Please," I said, "don't let it worry you, please get better, I love you so much." She stopped crying and for a minute resumed a posture I could relate to. There was wisdom and acceptance of reality in her eyes. "Don't disappoint me, or your father," she said, with great fatigue. The nurse came in and gave her an injection when I left; she was tortured by unbearable pain.

My father visited when he could, but she was under the illusion that he was there every day, morning and night. "Brave Moshe," she said. "If he were in my place, he would have shot himself. When the pain is so strong, all I want is to make it to the window and throw myself out." She begged my father to help her terminate her sufferings. She was burning slowly. The cancer in her liver spread quickly to the lungs, and a lump in her throat made breathing difficult. She alternated between hallucinations and clarity, and kept insisting: I'm not afraid of death, so why the torture? Yet she fought and held on to whatever hope she could. She wanted to return to Nahalal, promised the visiting grandchildren—only Udi broke into tears—that she would soon be well and with them. Toward the end of July, she was unconscious with painkillers most of the time, and asked for my father whenever she came to. The doctors said it was a matter of hours, but it took a few long days, during which she had an angry, bitter expression on her face, much the same as my father's on the day he died.

On July 26, 1956, Nasser announced the nationalization of the Suez Canal. The possibility of a combined French–British–Israeli operation against Egypt was still remote, but Nasser's action triggered a series of reactions that resulted in the Sinai Campaign a few months later.

July 28 was a Saturday. My father had a great deal of concentrated solitary thinking to do, and as was his habit then, he did it while on a dig. He left early in the morning, heading south, to a site he had recently discovered near Ashkelon, and I went with Mother to the hospital. At noon that day, my grandmother passed away. I looked at what was left of her, with great pity. Death was a blessing for her.

My father had to be found, and a helicopter was sent to search for him. When he was spotted from the air, a note was dropped to tell him of his mother's death. He arrived an hour later, dry-eyed and impatient with us all. There was nothing to say and very little to do, and I suspect each of us wanted to be left alone. There was something legendary about Dvorah, and her impact was stronger than her personality. Almost someone to admire rather than love, to approach rather than touch. Her self-discipline and honesty were so superior that they acted as a barrier.

My father had gradually developed into a "legend" very difficult to live with, but my grandmother was always a symbol of achievements and of qualities so perfect that, for fear of being put to shame or totally consumed, one had to keep away. Her disappearance left an accusing vacuum that nobody would, or perhaps wished, to fill.

She was buried in Nahalal, not far from her son Zorik, and my father hurried after the funeral to a meeting with Ben-Gurion. There was no way he would sit Shiva or share and expose the sense of loss he felt.

He proposed to Ben-Gurion a preemptive attack on Egypt, and suggested the Army could capture the Sinai Peninsula or, in turn, lift the blockade by seizing Sharm el-Sheikh. Ben-Gurion decided to wait till the heavier arms from France arrived and were integrated. In London and Paris, a resolution was reached to launch a joint attack on Egypt and hold the Suez Canal zone. The coordination of these two proposals was a question of time. Time enough, my father assured me, to go to the States, see, learn, and enjoy, and come back. "Don't worry," he promised. "I'll make sure you are here, as I don't intend to fight a war without you . . ."

EIGHT ✖ A SOLDIER IN HIS ARMY

The departure was easy. I wasn't leaving home but going on a well-deserved vacation. The man who had so frightened my grandmother left long before, and nobody thought I was running away, leaving home and country to join a married lover. I was given some money in addition to what I had saved, planned to stop in Rome and Paris, and my mother had Maskit make a beautiful wardrobe for me. My parents gave me a list of addresses and names of people to call, and it seemed to my father, though not taken for granted, that with three hundred dollars, a passport, and a suitcase, I could stay for a long while and profit from every minute. After all, I was seventeen and a half! Needless to say, youngsters didn't roam the world the way they do now or even twenty years ago. Travel was a privilege a few could afford, economically and emotionally. The world was less homogeneous and there were few common denominators, all of which contributed to a sense of fear, discomfort, and insecurity when faced with exposure to "foreign" things. But my previous trip, my "worldly" upbringing, and my knowledge of English eliminated any anxieties I might have had, and I was on my way.

I looked a lot different than a year earlier, when I left with my grandmother. My dresses were simple but of good quality and fashionable. I was slimmer and suntanned and didn't need any makeup or a special hairdo. I let my hair grow to shoulder length and have never had it shorter since. The only concession I made to feminine indulgence was hair removal from my armpits and legs; the rest was natural, clean, and tidy.

My first stops in Rome and Paris were, in a curious way, a revival of my artist's café days in Tel Aviv. A short, brisk, and this time amusing lesson in what was given me because of my father's eminence and what was mine regardless of him. By his grace, or rightfully mine. If I was invited to Cinecitta to watch the filming of *Ben-Hur*, guided there by a top PR lady, and given a ride in a Roman chariot driven by a famous star—that was listed under Dayan. When the star called on me in my small hotel room late that night, and swore all he wanted was a deeper and more meaningful relationship and tried to woo me into lovemaking, this was listed as a Yaël episode. A friend of the family, a journalist living in Rome, suggested I move in with his family and use the spare room. This was a Dayan offer. When his two sons competed for my attentions (they were both gorgeous) and I didn't really want either but found out they felt they were being played against each other, this was Yaël's dubious achievement.

During these months, Israel's security was a daily news item, and the Dayan name was again a door opener. What happened with me once inside had to do with something I had or hadn't, could or couldn't deliver. When in Paris, I met—connections again—a top Ministry of Defense official. The delicious lunch at Lapérouse I owed to my father's name. The flowers, phone calls, two more meetings, and what came very close to a marriage proposal were my own. I went out a few times with an Israeli journalist living in Paris then, who emphasized time and time again that he liked me despite my father. This, too, went into the Dayan list. My ego was well pampered, but I wasn't sure what to pin my "success" on. It wasn't sex, since few if any of these enthusiastic beginnings ended in bed. I should add, not because of morals, but due to a fear of pregnancy, and to inconvenience and my basic feeling that sex without deep emotion was overrated and a "complication." The only creed I seemed to have was the preservation of my total freedom and independence, and sex seemed a threat or hindrance to it. I wasn't irresistible in any way that could justify the courtings, the flowers, gifts, and confessions of love. I wasn't a femme fatale giving a little and taking it all back, or mysterious or even great fun. True, I wasn't an ordinary seventeen-year-old, but not a provocative Lolita either, and the only qualities that were fully there were a quickness of mind, a certain eloquence, being a good listener and an undemanding friend, and a freshness which must have been a bit different from the blasé, provocative, demanding ways of a typical European young lady. I lived and experienced and expressed myself, but I played no games, and this may have been appealing to some.

In all my travels, I cannot list anything as more exciting than my arrival in Manhattan. All the way from Nahalal, I thought in awe. Europe was a search, superficial as it was, into a past civilization. Not as far back as my father's archaeology, but a distance back in time that I could still relate to in a cerebral rather than mystical way. New York was a trip into the future. If this city existed, everything was possible and reachable. Free of gods and confining traditions, almost abstract in its lack of roots, it could reach to the skies, lifted to unimaginable heights by human talent and aspirations only.

I felt at home immediately. No one, or everyone, was a stranger in New York. Anonymity was offered not by the condescension of others but as a result of total acceptance of a lack of uniformity. The multitude of colors, styles, languages, customs offered a hilarious sense of liberty. The freedom to be different. Whether to belong or remain alone was my choice. Neither the solitude nor the involvement was imposed by those hurrying but friendly millions, their attitudes or norms.

I moved into a one-room apartment kindly offered me by someone I had met in Rome. His sister gave me the key and showed me how to operate the electric appliances, after reading a short letter of introduction. "You need some rest from the war over there where you live," she said, and asked no more questions. The apartment was on the East Side, the upper Forties, and I walked to the consulate for mail. It takes about five minutes to adjust to directions in Manhattan, and after Rome and Paris, where finding an address was an ordeal, I felt grateful for the American ingenuity of oversimplification. The assumption that, to be simplified, the system had to cater to the lowest common denominator of perception rather pleased me. Everything felt like a child's game. Instructions were spelled out to the full, and if that made me feel like an idiot, I soon realized that there were different layers, great depth of mind and heights of sophistication. Brain energy did not have to be wasted on filling out a form or finding an address. I found some mail at the consulate, and left my address, looked at week-old newspapers from home, and walked back to the apartment with a heavy shopping bag full of American foods, none of which I found to my liking.

A long letter from home was a family affair. My mother missed me, was longing for mail, and added the addresses of two more people to call. My brothers wrote a few funny sentences, and my father wrote as if he were talking. "It's been ages since you left, and so much happens every day. I miss you, but an American visit is quite something, so make the best of it. Try and read the N.Y. Times, as they report about the Middle East fully and quite objectively. The retaliation raid, as a policy, has outlived its usefulness. The surprise element is gone, and we are thinking of other ways to maintain security. I won't bore you with details, but I'll let you know not when I want you home, which is yesterday, but when I think you should come . . ."

I could sense the enormity of the distance, geographical mostly, between the continents, and felt discomfort at being so far away at times like this. The apartment was shabby, the city steaming hot and humid, and I was tired. Tired of being a collector of experiences, of cataloguing them and listing them without having time to digest or even take them in. I wrote a few articles for a paper at home, called a few people and saw some, and realized that my limited budget wouldn't carry me much longer. The superficiality and repetition began to bore me, and I started to explore the Village and Harlem for variations. The rest was a series of codes, based on very few letters, presented in a small variety of combinations. A code for food, for dress, for behavior, for musicals, for intercourse, and for routine conversation. I mastered the code and felt I had deciphered the simple pattern; the rest, the beyond and above, would take time and money I didn't have. Of the many people I met, I liked one. A woman and, not surprisingly, of European background.

Pauline Trigère was, is, a fashion designer of the highest stature, an artist and a fascinating person. She was, for me, the epitome of the American dream. A Jewish immigrant who started from scratch and made it because of pure talent, resolution, and a fighting spirit. Her home combined the best of European taste with the utmost in American comfort. She held both my parents in admiration, had two sons, which immediately made it complicated for me, and lived with a man I found unpleasant at the beginning, until I grew accustomed to his Latin American–Jewish characteristics. This was the "other New York." Chic restaurants and fancy gatherings, best-dressed women and elegant men, and the incredible power of money. This world, too, had its code, easy to learn but impossible to follow without the dollars, which resulted in frustration. Ordinary New York life bored me; the higher-circle style I couldn't afford, and the artistic world of the Village was a second-class version of the Saint-Germain and Montparnasse with which I was familiar. The role of Jews in all these circles was almost dominant, and again the name Dayan was a convenient door opener, though, unlike in Europe, doors were swung widely open, and so were arms. One of the doors that opened was the Israel bonds offices, and I was asked to address a meeting in Miami on their behalf. This was a first in a series of hundreds of fund-raising meetings which I have addressed in the United States during the twenty-seven years following.

When I think of this first speech, which was an immense success, I cringe with shame. There I stood, facing a group of Bermuda-shorts-clad, cigar-smoking, elderly men, and I "gave it to them." It wasn't only chutzpah, it was disgraceful. All the obvious banalities, I delivered in a fast, domineering tone. I did a Dayan on them, without having earned the right to do so, and they loved it. The flag I was waving was soaked in the sweat of pioneers and drenched in the blood of heroes. The sights I evoked, of poverty and austerity, of new immigrants in huts, surrounded by lice-ridden, trachoma-suffering multitudes of children, were true to an extent, but I was appealing for charity instead of for serious support. I offered the negative present instead of an optimistic, positive future, and my satiated, comfortable audience loved it all. "Isn't she something!" they exclaimed. "Only seventeen," they sighed, and the obvious "apple and the tree" remarks. To disguise my discomfort, I behaved arrogantly, almost unkindly, to my hosts, but my reputation as a speech-maker was established, and I was asked by the U.J.A. to address more meetings, which I handled in a similar way, refining my approach but not my off-stage behavior. What underlay this behavior was obvious. I hated being on the receiving end. I didn't feel like a charity case, and begging was not my style. I felt somehow degraded, and kicked. (When I returned, after two years' Army service, I corrected all my previous mistakes, and turned into a good, honest speaker, inspiring, informing, and moving.) While I was speaking for the U.J.A., my expenses were paid, and I even toyed with the idea of doing a university year in New York. A two-phrase cablegram put an end to any plans I might have had. It was signed by my father and simply suggested I take the first plane home.

Which I did, arriving in a blacked-out airport on October 29, the first day of the Sinai Campaign. Mother met me at the airport, briefed me on what was happening, and there was no question in my mind that I should join the Army as a volunteer, though my conscription was not due for another six months. When I saw my father, we were both in uniform.

The Sinai Campaign showed my father at his military and political best. In a series of secret meetings with the French and the British in France, his campaign plans were accepted. A French military delegation found the Israeli Army better trained, equipped, and organized than they expected, and Ben-Gurion's reluctance to join forces with France and Britain was slowly easing too. It was up to the old man to make the final decision, and take into account the possibility that the French—and more so, the British—might fail to deliver. For France and Britain, failure would mean a loss of prestige and perhaps a few casualties. What Israel was risking was her very existence, in case of defeat. According to the Dayan plan, our paratroopers were to be dropped close to the Suez Canal on D-Day, after dusk. On the first day, the battle, we hoped, would be localized, and the Egyptians would not deploy their Air Force to raid Israeli cities, which was Ben-Gurion's major fear and the cause of his hesitation. On the first two days, Israel would be fighting alone, and the French and British assault would follow, bombing

Egypt's airfields and taking control of the canal zone. Israeli forces were to reach and capture the Straits of Tiran and lift the sea blockade. The objectives were clear: to neutralize the armed Egyptian threat, end terrorist infiltration from the Gaza Strip, and break the Egyptian blockade, activating Eilat as a major port.

Father's idea to start the battle from its final objective by dropping a paratroop battalion in the midst of Egyptian formations, far from Israeli lines, was the kind of seemingly risky proposal typical of his thinking. He knew his units, he knew Sharon and the other commanders, and he wasn't wrong in his estimate of the enemy. What may have seemed momentary brilliance and a stroke of luck was an operational plan, worked out to the last detail, taking all odds into consideration and counting on the intangible quality of the Israeli soldier. For my father, the expanse of this intangible was as clear a fact to rely on as the number of tanks or the range of fighter-bombers.

My platoon commander woke me up almost hysterical on my second night in training camp. "The Chief of Staff—that is, your father—he is here! He wants to see you." I reacted in the silliest of fashions. I put on my uniform, my beret too, and as we were told not to part from our personal gun, took my rifle along from under my mattress. It was as if I were reporting to the Chief of Staff, which he of course was, not to my father, whom I hadn't seen in three months. He was too happy to see me to notice how funny I looked. We kissed and kissed again, and he was obviously delighted to find me just where I was, a soldier in his winning army. He stayed only a few moments. He talked about the campaign, promising me a trip to the Sinai on my first leave, and when he parted, saying, "Be a good soldier," he sounded very much like an ordinary father telling his daughter to "be a good girl."

It took the Egyptians a long while to realize that the paratroop drop and the crossing of the border by relatively small units meant war. The appearance of the first faultless fast moves as another act of reprisal was effective, and the slow enemy reaction afforded our forces freedom of movement for two days. My father himself drove around the battlefield in a two-jeep formation. He was present at all important events, on all fronts, and didn't think anything of changing directives on the spot and giving new orders to anybody, regardless of rank. What he had invested in training, concept, and planning was his to reap now. The Army was fit, eager, and ready. Morale was high, the officers in the lead, and the new equipment well integrated. When discipline was breached, it was as a result of enthusiasm. As Father defined it: "Better to be engaged in restraining the wild horse than in prodding the reluctant mule." Conventional General Staff officers thought he should make more frequent appearances in GHQ, but he simply ignored them. His jeep was shelled and almost hit; so was the Piper plane he used; but being shot at never deterred him from going where he thought he should be. "Dayan behaves like the battalion commander he was in the War of Independence," critics said, but this was not the case. The Army was employing tanks as a mobile assault force for the first time. The French and British involvement was a first, and the mileage covered, as well as the size of the Israeli force, left no room for comparisons with any previous wars. My father did not spontaneously roam the Sinai in a jeep, for the sense of freedom or in order to show off. He was studying these new elements, developing new tactical concepts, and making essential decisions. New textbooks had to be devised and conceived by an eyewitness, not based on dispatches while sitting in the HQ office.

The Gaza Strip presented another "first" challenge, which had to be handled with speed and wisdom. The occupation of a populated area meant some form of military rule. Father met with the notables of the Strip and granted them permission to resume all normal activities—fishing, agriculture, and business. The local municipal departments, and UN agency officials, were to resume their normal routine. Eventual good-neighborly relations dictated a policy of non-interference in Arabs' lives, as long as they did not endanger Israeli security.

On November 5, 1956, Sharm el-Shiekh was captured, and my father informed Ben-Gurion that the campaign was over. Ben-Gurion, perhaps jokingly, replied: "And I suppose you can't bear that, can you?" Father, naturally, didn't answer. When I saw him next, he was very happy indeed that the fighting was over. As proud as he was of the Army and its demonstration of top capacity, he was never trigger-happy, and never found exuberance in the exercise of waging war. Indeed, his efforts to perfect the war machine had the sole purpose of winning objectives with the minimal level of casualties and damage. Not for love of war, but as long as peace was not feasible.

When we next met, I was still in the recruit training base. The war was over, and he talked little about it. He described the Sinai as if he were a tourist guide. The inspiring beauty of the mountains, the changing colors at sunset, and the palm trees on the Mediterranean shore. He took out of his pocket a flintstone arrowhead and gave it to me for luck, and told me about the archaeological treasures in a site near Gaza where he had just been. He wasn't too interested in my own experiences as a recruit and a soldier, acting as if this for me was just another change of schools. I'd lived with the ingredients of Army life all along, and he expected me to feel comfortable and at home in the barracks.

It wasn't quite so simple. Becoming a soldier was not traumatic for me, but it took some adjustment. Military life was home ground, but so was individualism. I felt different—I probably was slightly different—and the regimentation was not to my liking. Nor the hierarchy of discipline and obedience. I didn't mind the uniform, the gun, the narrow bed in the barracks, the lousy, fattening food, or the drill. I liked getting up at dawn and rather enjoyed the physical exercise. I loved night watch and was not bothered by the cold and the rain and the mud that caused such discomfort. The platoon commander was a charming girl who was satisfied as long as I saluted properly, kept my hair tied in a bun and my gun clean. The company commander was strict with all of us but had a sense of humor and a boyfriend who kept her happy and satisfied most of the time. But the women who held the top ranks in the camp, a major and a lieutenant colonel, were frustrated bitches as far as I was concerned, and for a long while I felt, probably unfairly, that the only thing they had in mind was the taming of Yaël Dayan. The major summoned me often to her office, on small, insignificant pretexts, for inevitable dreary lectures. "You understand that all women soldiers are equal. We expect not to run into any trouble with you. We notice already uncalled-for familiarity in your behavior to your superiors. I say familiarity; I really mean an aloof manner, as if we owed you something because of your father." "So I want you to know, and don't say you haven't been warned, that there will be no privileges on this base. I am very unhappy about your father's private visits here, and I hope this will not recur. I accepted it because of the war and the fact that you arrived from abroad, but . . ."

I played the naïve innocent: "Did I do something wrong?"— which angered her more. "It's an attitude, I can see it in your eyes. Stuck-upness, whereas you ought to set an example to others . . ." She carried on like this several times, and the more I was lectured to, the more disassociated I felt and acted. Once again, I was an observer. I obeyed orders to perfection, my gun was the shiniest, my personal things tidy, and there was no reason to reproach me on any of the required routines. I made no friends, as it was the first time I was surrounded by girls my own age, all fresh from the hothouses of home and missing their mothers and boyfriends, and I felt I had very little in common with them. I drew a circle around myself and was simply deaf and blind to what went on outside it. Inside, I compensated myself for whatever I thought I was deprived of. I wrote and received many letters, I read books of poetry and philosophy to distinguish myself from the others, who read romantic paperback novels and journals. Under the heavy Army socks, I wore pretty white ones, and I used the best soap and eau de cologne, rather than Army issue. I did help the other girls in many practical ways, but I didn't share their world and I kept to myself. My mother came to visit, and we were both humiliated, as she was not allowed in, and we kissed and talked separated by a barbed-wire fence, which must have reminded her of the Acre prison.

The first four weeks of basic training, until the coveted first home-leave weekend, made the obstacles I had to face very clear. In order to retain some freedom and privacy, I had to be disciplined beyond reproach. I had to excel in order to be granted basic rights, and had to avoid the higher ranks, who were intrigued by my presence and frustrated by my "attitude." I applied, and was fully qualified and hence accepted, to officers' course. This, too, was taken for granted by my father, and for a brief moment, during a pre-cadet course, I developed an intense jealousy. I, for the first and last time, envied the "ordinary" girls. Not for what they were, but for being rewarded for their efforts, in a normal, touching, human way. Their fathers wrote to them to say they were proud; their mothers ironed and starched their uniforms; their little brothers looked up to them; and their boyfriends encouraged them. Where the others found support and enthusiasm, I was just doing what was expected of me, even when I was doubling my efforts. Moreover, they had post-Army dreams which I was jealous of. They knew what they wanted, and when they didn't, they didn't have to pretend, and were free to consult and share their doubts. Most of the other girls I was with were in love, and being loved, and many talked of the future in simple, delightful terms of home and family, number of children, a farm or a business or studying for a profession. They were not lacking in ambition, nor were they narrow or simple-minded. They were healthy, happy young women doing their duty for a couple of years and satisfying themselves with achievable aspirations. The number of children, the size of a home, or even marriage as such was absent from my pattern of future plans, and it made me feel inadequate. I felt jealous of all these girls who were treading solid ground, serving with patriotic zeal, seeing the cadet school as a highlight and a call, while I was restless, suspicious, and still a collector of experiences rather than a participant.

I also envied their simple sense of patriotic achievement. They sang "meaningful" rhymes when they marched. They shouldered the heavy packs and rifles as if the country depended on them; they saluted the colors with tears in their eyes. The girls in the cadet school, carefully chosen, were in fact a devoted, dedicated, un-selfish lot, and they were determined to "contribute to the country" whatever they could for the duration of their service. My own love of country was as great as others', but my ability to express it or join in group enthusiasm was limited. I was saturated. From baby-hood to maturity, I had been immersed and padded and injected with everything that meant love of country and roots and belonging. Now this added layer caused an overflow and a surplus—as if at birth I had been attached to an infusion bottle, and into my veins flowed all the good elements, in an overdose that almost caused an allergy.

I worked hard at becoming an officer, and the motivation was strictly personal. I did not think: Here, dear Israel Defense Forces, an added talent is on its way, an accomplished officer is about to join the ranks and contribute whatever she can. I simply had to be very good, for my own good feeling, and was quite ambitious about it. Every officers' course ends in an impressive ceremony, during which an "outstanding cadet" leads the parade and is the first to receive her or his rank's insignia. The name of this selected officer is announced on the last day of the course. Two days prior to the ceremony, the base commander summoned me. "I want to share with you my dilemma," she said uncomfortably. "You deserve to be number-one in this course, but we very much hesitate because of how it will look if we give the honor to you. You see, the obvious will be said, and you, too, will feel uncomfortable." I did not believe my ears. They are dumb enough, I thought, not to be able to handle the situation. "What do you want me to do? Run away, so you'll have an excuse to nominate someone else? Take sick leave? Or should we have a double ceremony, one for the outside world and one for those of us who know?" I wasn't going to facilitate matters, and I got up to salute and leave. I later learned that my fellow cadets heard of the hesitations, sent a delegation to the commander, and demanded that full credit be given me, as it was clear that I deserved it.

I led the parade with pride and perhaps even a tear in my eyes. I was proud of my mates, and loved them for their honesty and generosity. Obviously, in the final account, I could reach as far as I wanted. I had to come to terms with the fact that I had to put in double the work and the effort to achieve the same credit, and that the "height" was not always worth it.

My mother was delighted and touched. My father gave me a big kiss and a hug, and in his eye was the usual "as expected" look. He would never have reproached me if I hadn't been number-one. He simply took it for granted that I would be.

By then, we were withdrawing from the Sinai, and although the campaign's major objectives were accomplished, Father was bitter and frustrated. He thought little of the UN Emergency Force as a peacekeeping element and of the Secretary General of the UN as a mediator between Israel and Egypt. He did whatever he could to delay the withdrawal, if not avert it, but to no avail, for he was certain that in a short while the Egyptian Army would return to the Gaza Strip to encourage and support hostile infiltration.

When the Israeli flag was lowered from the military governor's house in El Arish, he told reporters: "Officers have to eat Army rations, the sweet as well as the bitter." Ben-Gurion thought Father's notion of keeping parts of the Sinai in order eventually to conduct direct peace negotiations was premature, and in fact only ten years later the Israeli flag was hoisted again in El Arish, and twenty years later it was lowered to trumpets announcing the peace agreement with Egypt. My father flew with Ezer Weizman in a Piper to El Arish on the day of the final withdrawal. He asked Ezer to fly over some of his favorite archaeological sites and land near the last column of half-tracks. He himself, in an uncharacteristically exhibitionistic act of protest, left the area with these last half-tracks. A rearguard, first to enter and last to leave, like the captain of a ship. The ship wasn't going down—it had given a superb battle performance—and my father forced himself to shrink back to size, away from the strategic depth the Sinai offered, away from the wilderness Moses crossed, back to the cage-size dimensions of the international border. When I saw him after the evacuation, he was adamant in his decision to leave the service. As a military commander, he had reached the top of his ability. The Army stood up to and above expectations, and it was time for him to go, he said.

Go where, I asked, knowing that there was no definite answer. He had to detach himself from the protection the uniform and rank offered. He was going through many changes of mood recently, and there was bound to be an in-between phase of reshaping and planning his life, which he conveniently chose to do as a student at Hebrew University in Jerusalem.

In a meeting with Ben-Gurion, he asked to be relieved of his duties, and declared his intention to enroll at the university. Ben-Gurion reluctantly accepted that he was determined to leave the Army, but if my father expected the old man to offer him a cabinet position or a head start in politics, he was wrong. Ben-Gurion did not as much as mention the upcoming elections of 1959, and displayed great interest in my father's chosen courses in the university.

To me, he simply said he wanted time off. He called it "freedom" and claimed he had no desire to pursue a political career. "You don't really think my heart's desire is to sit around the cabinet table with Sapir and Aranne?" he asked, and added a sentence I was to hear many times: "If they want me, they know how to reach me, and I'm not leaving the country." He said it before, he would say it again, but after the Sinai Campaign, shedding his uniform at the age of forty-three, he had good reason to believe it wouldn't be long before he was courted, if not actually coerced into office. He was no longer a potential, promising young leader, but a famous and recognized man. His quality as an important leader was independent, from now on, of the post he was to fill or the "power" he commanded. So far, he had been Dayan the battalion commander, Dayan the Jerusalem commander, Dayan the Chief of Staff. The rest of his life, his name alone carried the charisma, the controversy, and the power, regardless of title or post or position.

The period of adjustment was turbulent for all of us. My mother went to talk to Ben-Gurion, something she had done and regretted doing every time there was a change or a crisis in my father's career. "Moshe is facing a gap in his life, now that he is leaving the Army, and it can be terrible for him," she said. Ben-Gurion reassured her that "Moshe will not get lost," and talked about the value of a higher education. "It's a lot of nonsense. After everything he's done, I know he can't sit quietly in a classroom and read textbooks. It's just not possible and I know it," she insisted. Ben-Gurion said to one of his associates, after Mother left him: "I admire this woman, not for what she said, but for what she didn't say." She didn't say a multitude of things she tried to hide if not bury. She didn't say she was seeing a man change in front of her eyes, and naïvely hoped there was a formula that could be applied to stop the process and avoid a crisis. It was true Father had become increasingly introverted, and went about systematically severing intimate friendships. His moods changed swiftly, and he reserved his more gloomy, irritable hours for the family circle. He didn't reject the family, nor was he bored with us or loved us less, but he didn't want to keep up a façade at home, and his frustrations, pessimism, and restlessness were expressed where there was no risk of loss of popularity—at home. A knock on the door, the phone ringing, or the arrival of a visitor, anybody, would alter his behavior immediately and he would display a charming, enchanting disposition, becoming generous and humorous in a seemingly effortless way.

The basis of his attitude toward people was never love or hate, but respect. Respect of courage and respect of professional knowledge, whatever the field. We, members of his family, confused this set division. He loved us irrespective of our intellect, courage, or talent, yet he had to come to terms with disappointments. His mother fitted both categories; he could love and respect her, idealizing her both before and after her death. He loved his father more than he respected him, making no allowances for a generation gap which carried with it different sets of priorities. I came pretty close, at times, to this luxurious combination of someone who could be both loved and respected, whereas my brothers didn't show at the time (and Father didn't allow for a generation gap there, either) signs of greatness that could satisfy this emotional conflict.

Rather than calm his restlessness, or mellow his edginess, the period of study in Jerusalem, as my mother suspected, produced the opposite results. Lack of responsibility made him irresponsible, and his impatience turned to arrogance. Not being at peace with himself resulted in bad headaches, medically diagnosed as late aftereffects of his head wound, but clearly not eased by his state of mind.

I was transferred to the Jerusalem command, as an officer, and enrolled again at the university, hoping to finish my second year while in uniform. We were both in Jerusalem now, only in entirely different settings. Father was a civilian, living in a small apartment the Army let him use, driving a civilian jeep, and going home to Zahala for the weekend; and I was an officer, driving—since my eighteenth birthday—an Army jeep, making an occasional appearance at the campus, where we often shared classes, and being relatively busy and happy with my new Army duties.

I lived in Jerusalem and worked in Abu Ghosh, an Arab village

twenty minutes' drive away, in the regional HQ. We were responsible
for the current defense of settlements, mostly newly founded, along
the Jordanian border and the Jerusalem corridor. The settlers were
newcomers from a variety of Arab countries, and it was essential
to give them basic training, so that, in addition to feeling secure,
they could in fact protect their own homes and farms. The long
working hours in tough weather conditions, in villages remote from
the main road and in many cases not yet supplied with electricity,
demanded dedication and patience. I found both in myself and was
fully rewarded by results, as slow as they were in coming. There
was something miraculous in the adaptation of these people. Many
of the women were illiterate. There was disease and a rejection of
modern medicine. Farming was a mystery to them, and they had to
be coached into a new, taxing world with loving hearts and attentive
hands. What began as a dialogue between deaf and mute developed
into a common language, and I could actually see roots taking hold
in the rocky, bare soil, backs straighten, and faces change expression from bewildered despair to acceptance, to the pride of belonging. When I felt guilty about Nahalal or Deganya being what
they were, I had to remind myself of my grandparents, of the malaria
and trachoma they had fought, of the marches and the field fires,
of their own encounter with a hostile, foreign, often deadly environ-
ment. The men we trained were not soldiers, and so we didn't
emphasize discipline or drill routines. My job was minor, super-
vising and keeping track, making sure every male had some training, and, when on night duty, reporting emergencies to the central
command or going out to a settlement to calm the people in case
of a false emergency. Involved as I was, I found myself again leading
a kind of double life, and I began to think I somehow needed this
duality. From a clinic in Lachish where I might spend an afternoon
convincing a mother to let the young doctor treat her fevered child,
rather than apply primitive medicine blessed by a "miracle worker,"
I would drive back to the city and spend a long evening in a
restaurant bar with the Spanish consul. After night duty in Abu
Ghosh, where the phone rang to report restlessness in a cowshed
and the stealing of three goats, I was treated to a royal breakfast
at the King David Hotel by a wealthy, caring student friend. A day

that began with a demonstration of the numerous parts of an FN machine gun to a group of bearded, elderly Yemenites continued in a classroom where I listened to a brilliant lecture on totalitarian regimes in the nineteenth century, and, with me still in uniform, ended in a quiet dinner in a small restaurant with my father, or two UN observers, or the son of the Guatemalan ambassador.

I was not condescending with the settlers; I was very obedient with my commander—an adorable major my father's age; and I was not carried to snobbish social heights by the fact that my companions' cars had diplomatic plates. They were an extension of something intangible. As if, where the sign said STOP—BORDER—NO TRESPASSING, there was an unseen continuous road that their cars and houses and language enabled me to follow. There was no sex, or very little of it, and no feeling of conquest. I did not complain about the provinciality of my own country; neither did I blindly admire theirs. I was fun to be with, and their curiosity concerning my father was mixed with the added excitement of dating a girl soldier. I don't remember ever being asked about military affairs, and I was not in possession of any classified material. If my occasional enthusiasm about my work was contagious, it had to do with social or economic achievements of the people under my command. I shared freely and with pleasure information relating to the emergence of people from backward countries into a technologically advanced age.

When my father moved to Jerusalem, I thought we would spend more time together, and was quite disappointed when I discovered how full and busy his life as a student was. He had first place on my own busy calendar, and when he did call or show up, there was nothing and nobody that couldn't be postponed or set aside. My mother's presence in my life was reduced to almost nothing. I went to Zahala on weekends whenever I could, shared with her my Army experience, with which she was very familiar, but there seemed no way of communicating on any other subject. I wasn't grumbling and didn't blame her; it suited me fine and enabled her to avoid confrontations. I was old enough not to interpret her seeming lack of interest as neglect, and I had no illusions as to what she thought of my style of life. As self-centered as I was, I couldn't but notice she was going through a very tough time, fighting to preserve my father's love, if not their very marriage. The fact that we were both in Jerusalem and made guest appearances to enjoy a good meal on Fridays and a Saturday-night outing to the movies put us into the category of parasites, as if all we expected from home was the rendering of occasional services. Both my father and I held Mother in great respect as far as her work was concerned, and admired the initiative and imagination she put into it. I suspect we both were grateful that she was "building something of her own," which gave us license, with different legitimacies, to absent ourselves from her life whenever we wished. She traveled occasionally, and geographic distance allowed her to write letters and express feelings and thoughts she didn't dare put forth in a more direct manner.

In his answer to one of her letters, in the winter of 1958, Father sums up best where he stood and what he wanted. "If we were to get married now, we wouldn't have done it, but this is not the choice we are facing. The question is whether to live together, or apart, and if together, how. When you married me you didn't know me well, and what I am today is totally different from the person you did know. You think my attention is divided between five-thousand-year-old antiques and corrupt young women, that I'm not devoted to the children or to you. If you think that a husband who behaves like that is not tolerable to you, the decision is fully yours. I don't regret anything that happened in the past, nor do I promise or think I can change in the future. The day you ask for a divorce, I'll grant you one, but it's entirely up to you.

"You should have many reasons to be satisfied with your accomplishments at work. These are all the result of your own effort and talent. You are satisfied also with the way you fulfill the role of mother and wife; I'm not sure I agree there. But there our expectations differ. I don't expect you to be more than you are; I don't think we should be a model family living in a model home or that you should be a model mother. I make no pretenses to be a model or an example, as anything to anybody. If you could accept me as I really am and not as you or your friends wish me to be, I don't have any wish to separate. Our life together can be based on mutual respect, common friends, and twenty-two years of marriage, children, and home. I am sure there are couples who share more, who pick anemones every winter until they are 120, who eat the same cake every Saturday, read together the literary supplement, and visit the neighbors regularly, without trying something else or testing other sensations. We are, or at least I am, not made this way. We can base our life on sympathy—and I don't write 'love' so as not to mislead you, though I don't know the difference between 'to like' and 'to love,' and friendship, common ideology, and respect. We have children; they are grown already. I'm not satisfied with Yaël's life at present, and although you are sure I'm to blame, I don't think things are so simple. She is at an age and in a position where she is on her own, and if her friends are not to my liking, there is no way I can prevent her from associating with them. Udi is growing up too, and if our home is not an ideal one, it is still better than no home for the three of them. It should be available to them, when and if they want to use it.

"I'm studying day and night in order to complete my B.A. in less than two years, but I manage to be in Tel Aviv, in addition to the weekend, one night in the middle of the week as well." The letter is signed "Yours with love," and is one of many that followed, as well as conversations, on the subject of compatibility and his inability to adjust and change. Only twelve years later did my mother ask for a divorce, and at the time I wasn't aware of the intricacies of their married life, as my own life had changed. Two things had happened. I moved in with a man I was very fond of, and I began to work on my first book. The man was a journalist who lived in a beautiful house in Jerusalem. His wife had left him shortly before, taking their two children with her, and he was deeply and hopelessly in love with me. For the first time, I encountered a selfless, all-out, giving love, and I tried, in my immature way, to reciprocate. He loved me regardless and in spite of my acts and moods and arrogance. He saw through me, and still loved what was at the bottom of it all, and perhaps helped me to shed a few layers of pretense and falseness and not be horrified at what was beneath. We laughed at me together; we joked about my shortcomings; we seriously examined my ability to write; and we held each other in great respect. He was much older than I was, older than my father, and all the obvious things that could be said and written on the subject were easy to ignore as textbook banalities. I was almost very happy, almost in love, almost faithful, as near to bliss as I could be then, and reassured about my ability to achieve and reach self-expression and some tranquillity in the future. I had a few months left in the Army and was looking forward to full-time writing in the company of a man I looked up to and desperately wished I wouldn't hurt.

One Friday afternoon, a military jeep stopped near the house and I was summoned out. The officer who drove said my father wished to see me—an emergency, he claimed—and off we went. My father wasn't in the Army, and the summons seemed strange and irritated me, first into tears and later into plain fury. The officer drove me from Jerusalem to Tel Aviv, and there to the Security Service HQ. I was shown into a brightly lit room, where behind a large, imposing desk sat a senior intelligence officer. His face had the trained expression of suspicion and mistrust, with an additional wicked glee in his eyes. No, he said, I couldn't call my friend to say I'd be late. No, I couldn't call my father; yes, my father knew I was there and he'd pick me up when they were through.

"Being through" took a few hours of hopeless, trying, unpleasant cross-examination. I didn't lie—I didn't have to—but I was in no way going to be cooperative. They knew everything, it seemed, but they suspected more and there was no "more" and nothing to add. They threw names at me—of students, journalists, diplomats, UN officials, names of friends, names of acquaintances, names of people I hardly or never met. The recurring question was: "Did you sleep with him," and as the answer was, in all but two cases, negative, they tried to squeeze harder. "They" were two officers who joined the senior one, reading from pages which seemed to recount every move I'd made during the last year. I was tired and fed up. "Why should I be obliged to answer you, anyway? What kind of courtroom procedure is this?" The senior officer said I had ignored Army regulations whereby I was not to associate, I or any soldier, with foreigners.

"What do Army regulations have to do with my father? He is a student at Hebrew University and has no authority to have you conduct this 'inquisition.' " The officer was red in the face. "No authority? Moshe Dayan is an authority even if he were a night watchman in a hotel. And he will remain so. I don't believe what you tell us about the ambassador and the UN chief!" "So you don't." I tried to remain calm. "We met for a friendly dinner once or twice. We talked about literature, and art. The ambassador and I share a passion for a little-known book by Paul Valéry. The UN chief is intrigued by surrealism. And I don't care if you believe me or not." He tried another approach and pretended to relax. "We really wanted to warn you, to protect you. After all, you don't believe those illustrious people are genuinely interested in you. What can you offer them that they can't find elsewhere—in art, or literature, or any area other than your father, or military activities . . . and perhaps a bit of sex with a young girl appeals to them."

He looked me over carefully, attempting a piercing, stripping look, and added: "Though I don't quite see the sex appeal either . . ." I must have blushed, and tears of fatigue welled up in my eyes. "I don't know what they can find, or you can't find. I told you there was no sex. No Army topics, no flirting. There is a world out there, General, and it's full of oddities. Like love, and camaraderie, and friendship, and people enjoying each other, and all those peculiar things, *for free*. For fun. For the hell of living and laughing and learning. Not for God, or country, or the service. So go ask them why they met with me. What dark ulterior motives made them have an ice cream with me in a hotel lobby or spaghetti at the Gondola. Maybe Paul Valéry is a code name, and Magritte is a secret agent, and you just discovered an international network of sophisticated spies, and I am its Mata Hari. May I go home now?"

He left the room, apparently to call my father, and I realized how hungry I was. When he returned, he put a hand on my shoulder and mumbled: "You are quite a tough little girl. I should have known, being your father's daughter." I clenched my fists and didn't answer. "The affair with your elderly journalist has to terminate. He's a foreigner, and it's against regulations."

"He's lived in Jerusalem for the last fifteen years," I tried, "and I'll be out of the Army in a couple of months' time." "These are still the regulations," he said. "So why don't you leave him quietly, without a scandal. You don't want to hurt his position, so just find a nice personal excuse." I managed a quiet "Go to hell" and got up to leave.

My father was waiting downstairs in his jeep. He was embarrassed, or at least uncomfortable.

"What was this all about?" I snapped.

"They thought you were trapped, maybe even being blackmailed. It wasn't my own idea."

"Why didn't you talk to me yourself? We meet often enough. You never so much as asked or hinted or displayed the slightest interest."

"I didn't really think it was my business, and felt I had no right to moralize. I figured you'd come to me if you were in trouble. They intended to question you anyway, not on my behalf, and I said I didn't mind."

"Just so. Well, I'm lucky to be as smart and strong as I am. They were stupid, vulgar, and infantile. If I had something to hide, I could easily have done so."

We drove in silence. He had a bad headache, and I was exhausted. When he parked near the house in Zahala, I asked whether Mother was aware of this little drama.

"Not in detail," he said. "Why hurt her?"

He had an extraordinary way of switching subjects and moods. He suddenly smiled, took me by the hand, and exclaimed: "Wait till you see my new acquisition! I've been digging in Givatayim for a month and found nothing, but yesterday afternoon I had my reward!" We walked around the house to the back yard, and he carried me away with him to the year 2000 B.C., holding and touching and admiring a small clay goddess of fertility. He looked at the array of pots in front of us and picked out a small oil lamp. He cleaned it carefully, took a pen out of his pocket, and wrote on the lamp: "To Yaël with love." I thanked him casually and had to give it to him: it was an unconventional way of saying he was sorry.

Back in Jerusalem, I packed and said goodbye, without explaining much. I thought he knew or at least felt that I was not leaving of my own choice. He was gentle enough not to insist, and we were both richer for the time we had together. The outline for my novel was complete, and I somehow managed to pass the end-of-year exams at the university, passing hints or even notes to my father, who conveniently sat next to me for some of the exams. I said goodbye to my commanders and subordinates, and visited the settlements for short, sad farewells. My two-year service was over, and I had no regrets. I liked the uniform; I had met the challenge of giving of myself; I was witnessing the making of a nation and had a chance to contribute my minute share. It didn't lift me to the level of sacrifice and dedication of my grandparents or my parents, but I thought of the service not as a duty, or a waste of two years, but as a right granted me. I was also saying a slow goodbye to the city of Jerusalem. I never felt totally at home in the city, and this lack of familiarity only added to the hold it had on me. I could rub against, touch, or watch, but never own its magic.

N I N E ❧ M Y F A T H E R ,

H I S D A U G H T E R

In my father's autobiography, all 520 pages of it, only seventeen are devoted to the years 1958–67. In the detailed, official biography written by S. Tevet, the years 1960–67 are summed up in eighteen pages. My mother's autobiography mentions in a few paragraphs several episodes that occurred during these years. The proportion is odd, considering Father was in what are considered his prime years. Ten lost years? Stagnation? A repose between military glory and the eminence of a statesman? They were certainly not years of inactivity, but there were fewer highlights, and both my father and his biographer tended to regard his life as a series of peaks, with the personal and national drama intertwined, and the in-between, whatever didn't reach sky-high, was left in a cold, dull, insignificant shadow. Israel was ten years old, and those were its formative years. Foundations were dug and built in the fifties, and in the early sixties the finer shaping and carving took place.

1959 was an election year and marks the entrance of my father actively into the political arena. With a few intervals, he was to serve as a cabinet minister and a member of parliament for the remainder of his life. The Labor Party was in power, headed by Ben-Gurion, and hoped to gain a decisive victory, winning more than fifty percent of the votes. Before it could achieve this, however, the party had to reach a reconciliation within its own ranks. The rift between the "youngsters," represented by my father, Abba Eban, and Shimon Peres, and the "veterans" was growing. It wasn't merely a biological war. The "youngsters," backed by Ben-Gurion, represented a threat to some basic accepted concepts, and took liberties, questioning and attacking sacred cows. In many ways, this first entry into politics resembled my father's early, rebellious methods in warfare. He was blunt, outlandish, pragmatic, and flexible. He attracted large audiences and filled them full of enthusiasm, deriving his power directly from Ben-Gurion, the supreme political authority, and from the people, while bypassing and at times ignoring or opposing the heavy, overpopulated party machine that was the source of power for the "veterans." He was truthful to a fault, and for him what was good for the party was always secondary to Israel's national priorities. It was perhaps typical and significant for his political career that, at the end of some rallies, admirers bore him aloft on their shoulders, crying: "Long live Dayan. Down with Labor."

He was a civilian now, easily recognized by the eye patch, and the fact that he was out of uniform didn't afford him any privacy. Indeed, there were adjustments to be made. A military status had offered hothouse protection which he didn't have now, and the new, unlimited exposure was not to his liking. Verbal expressions, activities, and love affairs which before were censored or covered over were now the stuff of newspaper headlines. Eager, hungry reporters, the barriers of military protection removed, were free to write, gossip, attack, and criticize.

My father was firm in his reaction. He was not going to make any concessions in order to beautify his media image. His private life and morals were nobody's business, and he was not applying for the post of preacher or educator. He did not feel he needed to "set an example" to others, and he didn't feel obliged to apologize for or explain anything he did or said, unless it was in reference to public affairs. His performance as a member of the Knesset or a cabinet minister could be judged by his colleagues, superiors, and finally the voters. Everything else was private domain. He could not prevent or even minimize the exposure, but he was determined not to be affected by it, whatever the price.

He made this clear to my mother, in letters and brief conversations. My brothers, he thought, were too young to be involved, and I was old enough, he believed, to understand. With the same notion of "sharing" that made him take me to the Negev wadis and his archaeological digs, he once invited me to dinner to meet one of his lady friends. To be precise, he invited me to dinner, and the rest was a surprise, which he tried to handle with casual charm. The first encounter in a series took place in his student apartment in Jerusalem. I was just out of uniform and about to go to Europe to complete my first novel. I visited him in the apartment many times, and when I entered on this particular winter evening, hurrying in to take cover from the heavy rain, and up the stairs, I found the door locked. I stood there swearing as he unlocked the door to let me in, quickly saying with a rather shy smile: "There is someone here I'd like you to meet."

We shook hands and she continued to set the table for three, obviously uncomfortable, as I was watching her closely. Father became very talkative, avoiding any embarrassing silences and fussing with the lousy salad and overdone omelette. I didn't sulk and was more or less on my best behavior. The woman was very tall, not particularly attractive, and nervous. She felt at home there, and I could detect occasional intimate exchanges between them, which didn't bother me much. He was having an affair with her. She was not the only one, nor the first, and what bothered me was not her presence there but mine. Why did he ask me over? He couldn't be serious about her. He wasn't a friend introducing me to a prospective bride so I could express an opinion. I never asked him about his women or showed the slightest curiosity: what was the purpose of this burdensome, unamusing, forced evening? I ate in a hurry, said I had a date later, and waited only for the rain to stop. The conversation was indifferent, and the three of us smiled often and out of context. When the rain turned into a drizzle, I put on my wet duffel coat and, with a polite "Pleased to have met you" to her and a kiss to him, walked to the door. He told her he'd be right back and offered to drive me, or at least accompany me to the bus station. We walked in large, decisive steps, hands in pockets, ignoring the rain and the puddles. I didn't ask, but he spoke. "It was her idea, she so much wanted to meet you. She said it was the warmth with which I talked about you that intrigued her . . . A bright woman, interesting." I didn't say anything. I didn't have anything to say.

"It's not serious, between us, I mean," he felt obliged to add. I almost prepared a little speech, which I wouldn't have delivered anyway. A variety of meaningful sentences formed in my head, but as we reached the bus stop, the bus pulled up and I hurried to board it. "Thanks for dinner," I shouted before the door shut and he turned to walk back to his apartment, where his lover waited. I watched him for a brief moment and felt no anger. My father, my mother's husband, a man of forty-five, still young and healthy, bright and famous, courageous and wise, walking alone in a Jerusalem street back to his shabby place to make love to a skinny woman. He read Alterman's poetry to her; she knew how to prepare his favorite salad; and the rest, I supposed, happened in bed. Did I mind? Did I feel for my mother? Was I jealous? I felt irritated and lonely. Here was something I couldn't share with anybody I knew, a secret imposed on me, a trust that made me an accomplice. His infidelity bothered me less than his need for it, and his choice of bed partners was vulgar and in poor taste. The whole thing seemed pathetic and demeaning, lacking in either excitement or dignity.

I walked for a couple of miles in a fog. My mother was in Zahala, forever padding the nest, devoured by love for my father, and daily sacrificing herself, being our—his and mine—absolution. She must know it all, I thought. She loves him and makes love with him and cares for all his needs and she knows it all. The skinny and the plump, the French and the student, the woman officer and the journalist. Was her tolerance genuine—could she really not care, or regard it all as some physical need, a mid-life crisis, an insecurity hiding behind a macho wall? Was she slowly being destroyed by him, desperate and in need? Did she have the strength to cope, or face up to things, or to quit? I had all the questions and didn't want to know the answers. I was self-centered enough to be preoccupied by my own predicament. I wasn't flattered by his choice of me as an ally; I wasn't going to be his alibi or partner. I wasn't jealous, or curious, and when I arrived home, I threw up the salad and the omelette in one violent spurt, and relieved myself of the slight nausea that accompanied the evening's events.

Other meetings followed, and I gave it little thought. Introducing me to Françoise, and Jeannine, Lady Something-or-other, and Gila made him feel better about it and left me indifferent. I didn't show approval; I didn't befriend any of them or treat them with the same wonderment he did; and I didn't feel I was siding with him against my mother. Rahel, who was a more permanent companion than the others at that time, remembers meeting me in her office, though I don't clearly recall the occasion. I graded his taste as very poor, wished he was more selective, and seldom wondered about the implications his affairs would have on his political career.

Many of his affairs passed unnoticed. A few made gossip columns and headlines, and one made a book. A Miss Mor published a thinly disguised novel entitled *Passionate Paths*, recounting in elaborate detail the affair she had with a famous one-armed fighting general. My father tried to ignore it. He dismissed it as "nonsense" and complimented himself for not succumbing to, as he phrased it, "blackmail." "It will soon be forgotten, and so will she," he said to me, but added with childish remorse that he truly regretted the hurt it caused the family. Nothing is unforgivable between parent and child, but at the time it was difficult to face. There, printed and bound, for a few Israeli pounds, one could buy my father's body, his performance in bed, his sweet talk and intimate thoughts. My mother was appalled and helpless, I was shocked at the vulgarity of it all, and Father withdraw further away, taking refuge behind a solid shell of superior indifference. Ben-Gurion was approached by Miss Mor's separated husband, and the old man drew a distinction between a man's intimate life and his public responsibilities. He drew upon the Bible, which offers parallels to everything, and cited the case of David and Bathsheba. My mother also appealed to Ben-Gurion, who understood her anguish, or so he said, but rationalized it in a cold, detached way. Even if he disapproved of Moshe's behavior, he said, he would in no way consider him unfit for a public post because of it. He was destined to be a national leader, and his record in bed was not going to stand in his way. Ben-Gurion was right, of course. The public devoured the gossip, and it added to the multicolor image of my father as a popular hero. Men were jealous, women were intrigued, and admirers forgave and excused. He repeated to me what he said time and time again: "I don't consider it anybody's business, and I am not pretending to be a model husband." He mentioned, with genuine anxiety, that he had given my mother the option of leaving, separating, or divorcing him if she so chose and that he truly hoped she wouldn't. At times he tried to double-check with me regarding her intentions, but I could offer nothing but guesses. "She must know," he said repeatedly, "that most of these things are the product of the imagination of hysterical women."

Passionate Paths or not, Ben-Gurion appointed my father Minister of Agriculture, a post he held for five years in three successive cabinets, from 1959 to 1964. I left for Europe, feeling less of a deserter than ever before. I had the handwritten first hundred pages of a novel in my briefcase, keys to a house in Brittany which was made available to me by the French consul in Jerusalem, and the encouraging interest of George Weidenfeld, the English publisher.

From my mother I received blessings and a small fund, and from Father, confidence in my work and the usual token of love. "You should know it's always there. Whatever, whenever you need—I'm there . . ." The promise of love was like a token, a coin for a phone call—even an overseas collect call. Did he know I would never use it? Did he figure I would be satisfied with the dime alone, with the label rather than the goods? "And don't get married or something without telling me," he added as he saw me off. He should have known that what I saw of his marriage was discouraging enough to put me off the subject for many years, and I definitely ruled him out as a consultant on the matter.

This time I was going away, not running from something, but rather looking forward to a period alone. Two years of military service had made me feel I had paid my dues to the country for a while, and I was as pleased with myself as I could be. The pains of growing up were a dim memory, amazingly free of bitterness or grudges. The security home gave me was a take-it-or-leave-it proposition, and the satisfaction and pleasure I derived from writing made me feel strong and in control. I had come to terms with my own personality, trimming away many false edges. I was not really a romantic; I was never going to be in grave despair or reach, alas, emotional heights beyond control. I was generous and giving, but received with great caution, afraid to owe. The phase of collecting was over, and experiences I missed or bypassed were not catalogued as losses. Life could be fun, not everything had to have a deep result-bearing meaning, and a low-key style was not inimical to happiness. When I finished my first novel *New Face in the Mirror* and it was accepted for publication, I stopped chasing. I also settled for the fact that some things were unreachable and many others not worth striving for, and scope could be measured in depth as well as width. Basically, this was the story of my first novel. My own new face in the mirror was to my liking, irrespective of the blemishes and faults I could plainly see. In any event, reviews and sales were very good, the novel was translated into many languages, interviews and appearances followed, and I swam the pool of fame with long, secure strokes.

I was twenty, and I was fully conscious of the dangers of easy fame and exposure. Israel was much in the news, and there was tremendous curiosity concerning anything it produced—from small arms to literary works. My father's name and image were synonymous with everything heroic and extraordinary that Israel stood for, and the international jet set, thanks greatly to Françoise Sagan's breakthrough, adopted young writers with smothering embraces. I was referred to as the "general's daughter," the "Israeli Sagan," and the "woman–soldier–writer," all irrelevant titles where my writing was concerned, but door openers.

Again, I had to distinguish between what was deservedly mine and the supporting fringes, and the serious good reviews helped me a great deal. Decisions had to be taken. I would wake up in the morning. It's the Hassler or the Plaza or the Browns'. I dress up— it can be Pucci or Gucci or Ricci; I give an interview to *Elle* or *Vogue* or a literary supplement. I have lunch with Juilliard or Weidenfeld or Molden. I rest in the afternoon, I answer fan mail

and phone calls, I go out, dinner or a club, or theater, the Rive
Gauche or the Village or Trastevere or Chelsea, with writers,
artists, publishers, film people, or just rich people who like to be
surrounded by artists, writers . . . And so it went. Life could be a
celebration, yachts in the harbor, private-island parties, festivals,
lecture tours, fast cars, and late nights. The temptation to indulge
in the superficial and the momentary was enormous, but boredom
was my safety valve. I didn't care for the small talk; international
gossip bored me. I didn't drink and hated the noisy atmosphere of
nightclubs. And there is a limit to one's ability to digest caviar
or foie gras, as tasty as they may be.

First priority was writing. I was not going to be a one-novel
novelist, and I had to prove to myself that the commotion, sales,
even the reviews had to do with quality. With a talent I sensed I
had but which was still far from fully consummated. I knew my
first book had charm, honesty, some passages blessed with perception, and a certain flow. It was not much more than "promising,"
and promises, for a writer, always mean the next book. I was, in a
way still am, more confident about my brain, personality, and
integrity than about my ability to master the literary medium, and
somewhere inside I sensed there would always be more to me as a
person than as a writer. My ambition was shaped accordingly. I'm
a storyteller, I'm not an innovator or a creator of masterpieces.
Writing is a craft and a passion, but not a messianic call. I want to
give my readers pleasure, a diversion, an involvement, and share
rather than impose some message. I knew each new book was
bound to be better than the last one; I also knew my limits. Language
was an instrument; profundity should be an occasional result, and
not intentional, and fireworks were not my style. I was never going
to write to dazzle, and flowery, overloaded, pretentious literature
bored me even when I knew it was pure excellence. I wanted to
reach the essential, the bare, elementary, stripped, truthful definition of human relations, predicaments, and sensitivities, while
telling a story. The stories I had in mind were all set in Israel,
against the background of a troubled, striving society, where mere
existence could not be taken for granted.

Yet I wasn't ready to settle down at home and fall into a routine of writing and publishing. Instead of the desire to dig inside and explore the depth of my being and personality, I felt the need to add new layers. Rather than peel, I wanted to grow, as I wasn't hiding anything in the core but was lacking in perspective and dimensions. There was so much to see, and learn, and find out in order to be self-sufficient, and though the process of learning is endless, I was set to embark on it as more than just a collector.

My father was enjoying my success. He obviously realized I wasn't going to be a scientist, agronomy expert, or doctor, and he encouraged me while I was writing, for some good and some less honorable reasons. He wrote me frequently, two-page letters in terrible handwriting, expressing a double hope—that I would write something of quality and make a fortune on it. "I hope you are advancing well with the book. If you started you should invest all efforts in it and produce the best thing you can. I hope you have the patience to concentrate, rewrite, improve and rewrite again. Do you think it could be a best-seller? Or at least a very good seller? It will be great for you, and for us, if you are suddenly a rich lady . . ." He wasn't supporting me then, and I wasn't a burden on his income, and only as this sentence kept repeating in other letters did I think of it as anything but a touch of humor.

"What I really would like to do is come and stay with you, an evening (or two at the most), drink tea, nag, listen to you, get angry a little, and love you a lot. Help you a little and disturb you a lot . . . With much love, Father." Or, still while I was writing: "I envy you, sitting and writing and doing what you truly want to do. I hope you enjoy the work and I expect you to be successful (financially too!) not only because of curious details but for your ability to reach under the skin of feelings and events." "What are your plans? It's obvious you should stay in Europe for publication, but please think of coming home afterward. If you don't, you'll find yourself detached from your roots here and unable to settle in Europe. You should find your place in Israel, regardless of your profession; a writer has to feed on surroundings and sources, and yours are here. I miss you so much . . ."

I waited eagerly for his reaction to the book itself. Not as a literary critic, but because there was so much of myself poured into this first volume, his reaction was the only one I feared. I remembered his violent reaction when he read my diary, and I was shaking with nervousness, until he reassured me. "It is good, honest, readable and moving." He liked the precision and economy of the language, and admitted he himself had been afraid to be disappointed and was extremely happy when he liked it all.

The book critics in Israel hated it. It was written in English, and I was stupid enough to make some haughty irrelevant remarks about the Hebrew language. The language became the central issue, and I was anything from a "traitor" to a "deserter." Writing in English was unpatriotic, anti-Israeli, or at least "fortune hunting." The book itself was dismissed as "kitsch for export," and the last thing I wanted to do was face the music. My father encouraged me to come home, offering me the full width and depth of his support.

"Don't fall into the trap of blaming the Hebrew language. There is nothing wrong in writing in whatever language you choose to, but make it clear it's your choice, or shortcoming or achievement. No theory about Hebrew as unsuitable for expression of modern life will hold, and the animosity you'll encounter here will have nothing to do with the quality of your writing. It is the result of your mistaken declarations about the language, and a great deal of jealousy, which is inevitable. We'll face it together, and the sooner the better. You've been away for so long . . . I'm active, and it bores me to write about it. Mostly I am a target for attacks and gossip. I am not disappointed in what I am trying to do and get done, and although I am not a masochist, I never thought it was always a 'happy state' to be happy. Sometimes I'm happy to be unhappy . . . It's easier to explain face to face, so please come home. If you put aside some money, I'll help you look for a house somewhere . . ."

I did come home, the book was published in Hebrew, and for a while I felt like a leper. I had to cut a path for myself through jealousies and flattery, self-appointed supporters and bitter enemies, and I knew I didn't have the energy and the motivation to fight. There was one thing I wanted to do—go on writing, produce a second novel, let whatever creative talent I had speak for itself and satisfy my urge to expand and learn.

My family was like a rock shelter around me. My mother liked my book but was hurt by some of the passages in it. My father enjoyed being "Yaël Dayan's father" for a while, and eagerly read my fan mail and the American good reviews, and once he realized Israel would always be home and there was no danger of my looking for a substitute, he was carried away by my travel plans, intending to visit me in a variety of exotic places. I unpacked and packed in my room in Zahala, and we had long talks, mostly very early in the morning when everybody else was asleep.

I found Father changed. He plunged into the agriculture scene with the same vigor, imagination, and farsightedness with which he had handled military objectives. He was clear about what he wanted to accomplish, but it wasn't entirely up to him. He thought of agriculture products for export, of modern technology and specialization. He wanted to speed the completion of the National Water Carrier from the Lake of Tiberias to the northern Negev. He had the right concepts, but very few instruments and a limited budget to execute his policies. In addition, the political "machine" in action bored him and made him bitter. He was loyal to his superior, Ben-Gurion; enchanted with the team of professionals he worked with in the ministry, but had no illusions as to the growing rift between himself and his peers—other ministers, party officials, and a variety of powerful veterans who systematically undermined and criticized him. For the first time, he talked about a "hopeless battle." He didn't think he stood a chance, and was not going to compromise. "It's not my game," he said, "and not because I don't know the rules. I can't adjust to the pattern, the hierarchy, the pace, or the style of the so-called powerful members of the party." He thought they were condescending; he thought they were out of touch with the people. He believed they advanced their personal ambitions at the expense of the common objectives, and obstinately dismissed any references to his political prospects in the near future, or ever. "No way," he said. "They aren't going to change, and I'm not going to change, and sooner or later they will have their way and be rid of me. I am a thorn in their thighs, and the party routine is stifling to me."

He was growing bitter without losing his sense of humor, but he made it clear to me that I was never going to be the Prime Minister's daughter. Not that I had expressed a desire to be, but I certainly thought he should get there one day, for the benefit of us all. If I was disappointed, it wasn't from personal ambition. I understood him, and hated to see him give up, not during but on the eve of battle, a battle he was clearly determined not to participate in.

In fact, it wasn't all so simple. I steadfastly refused to accept his lack of ambition, and I was reluctant to admit his failure in the political power plays. For a while, I blamed it entirely on the others. He was above them, he was a pure patriot, he couldn't sink down to their level of little intrigues, he was a national leader while they were small party operators . . . History, I hoped, would bestow on him one day his natural role, up there at the top . . .

But as he grew to accept his predicament and rejected any chances of changing it, I began to wonder: What if it suited him? What if he really didn't want the full responsibility? What if he preferred to be perched halfway, satisfied with his personal fame and happy in his relative freedom?

I was not his "little girl" anymore, and when we sat there in the beautiful garden, eating figs or a watermelon and talking, with long intervals of comfortable silences, we met on equal terms, as two adults. Or so he treated me. Admitting my independence liberated him of any responsibility toward me, and avoiding confrontations, or even debates, was an easy, comfortable way out for him. If I ever so much as mentioned that something bothered me, or hinted at some possible dilemma I faced, he quickly smiled, with all his charm, gave me a kiss, and said: You are a big girl, you'll find the right answers! When I was a small child and cried in pain when hurt, he laughed it off as "psychological" and convinced me that crying would only magnify the pain. Now he felt I was well equipped, partly by him, to handle whatever came my way, and when he said "psychological" he meant imaginary, and in fact my worries were trivial. Still, when at home, I would have liked to have the luxury of support, advice, and guidance, even when I knew I could manage perfectly well without it.

Now that Father was a cabinet minister, he tried to be more discreet about his philandering. The quality of his women and the superficiality of the affairs were the same as ever, and I could not find a physical or psychological justification for his insatiable desires and lack of discernment. Other than occasionally and mostly accidentally, there were no more "planned" meetings between me and his girlfriends, and I was grateful for it. I didn't think too highly of my mother's tolerance, but there was no way I could, or wished to, put myself in her place and seriously consider what her reaction should be. Not until I was myself a married woman did I think of infidelity as detrimental to the preservation of the family.

My parents made love very often, if not nightly, and shared a bed and a bedroom throughout their married life. As a child, a teenager, and an adult woman, it filled me with a sense of warmth and security, as if their physical proximity offered reassurance of the continuity of everything that meant home.

There were two occasions on which we almost had a head-on clash concerning his "affairs." Once, when he courted and probably slept with a girlfriend of mine, and the second time when he almost destroyed a close friendship I had with one of his friends and supporters because he assumed, or took for granted, that we had had an affair.

Among my many friends and acquaintances at the time I could count very few women; in fact, one or two at the most. There was Gila, with whom I served in the Army, enduring the officers' course with her and sharing a bench in the university for a while. She was studying chemistry, was in love with a young interne in a Jerusalem hospital, and our friendship manifested itself in long but infrequent meetings, during which we talked in the utmost confidence and intimacy about our present problems and future prospects. She was bright, quite pretty, and her love of poetry contrasted nicely with her scientific brain, studies, and future endeavors.

On my return home after the publication of my first novel, she was one of the people I called immediately. I had a great deal to share, and little to hold to in Israel, and her personality was an imaginary rock I longed to cling to. She was abrupt and cold on the phone. Excuses followed, and I sensed great discomfort in her voice. I called her doctor friend, who informed me he wasn't seeing her anymore, and I felt I had let her down. She must have joined the chorus of critics without giving me a chance to explain or at least to have it out. In my bitter disappointment, I decided to call on her, uninvited, and standing in front of her house, debating whether to go in or not, I saw them. My father's arm was on her shoulder. Protected, as he thought, by the dark, he embraced and kissed her and walked to his car while she stood for a moment, both of us watching him, my father, her lover.

When I called her next, I merely said: "I know about you and my father; please don't let it stand between us." She choked back a tear and said: "He has ruined my life; please don't call me again, ever." Adult people, I said to myself. They choose and make mistakes and get involved, and destroy themselves and others; but it is not my business. I still felt I was to blame, and never really forgave him for something that I had no logical reason to hold against him. He must have known that I had found out about it, and tried one day casually to ask me: "Do you ever see Gila?" And when I started crying, saying, "Do you?" he sighed, displaying impatience, and walked away, as was his wont whenever an unpleasant topic came up.

It was only natural that some of the people surrounding Father befriended me. As he suggested, I was his favorite. A few tried to channel thoughts, ideas, or criticisms through me, while others shared their anguish at his stubbornness or inaccessibility. One or two grew to like me for myself and to respect my judgment. With them, I could establish a relationship that would soon become independent of my father. My closest friend in the early sixties was Daniel. He was a career diplomat, my father's age, married, with three children, and an expert on modern Middle East history. He was also the least selfish and most honest man I ever came across, and his love for my father was free of personal considerations and bordered on admiration. Without ever admitting it, my father treasured this friendship, and at moments of crisis almost depended on it. There was no reason to hide the fact that we met often, talked on the phone, or wrote each other when one of us was abroad. Of all the intricate relationships I had with men, and women, this was the cleanest and deepest, unmarred by teasing or jealousies, never distorted by pretense or possessiveness. If Daniel gave me the attention, care, and love he gave his own family, it was not because

I felt deprived by my parents; it was a manifest of his own emotional capacity.

One evening I was sitting with Daniel in his car in front of our house in Zahala, deep in conversation. I hadn't even bothered to ask him to come in. My father's cold, rather formal "Good evening" interrupted us, and Daniel's warm greeting to him was left unanswered. He walked away from us, up the stairs, and from the distance we could hear him slam the front door.

When I entered the house shortly after, Father was at the kitchen table, obviously upset. "Does Lina know about you and Daniel?" he asked, referring to Daniel's wife.

I couldn't even pretend not to grasp the meaning of this question. "You must be crazy." I couldn't help myself. "You may suspect me, being your daughter, but how can you for one moment think of Daniel that way?"

"He is only a man," Father said, somehow surprised by my reaction.

"And all men are 'only a man' and sleep with whoever comes their way, and a friendship between a man and a woman without it is beyond your comprehension?"

"Whatever you say, I don't like it—it makes me uncomfortable . . ."

It made him uncomfortable. He switched the garden lights on, and his eye twinkled with satisfaction. "Isn't it the most beautiful garden in the world?"

For once, I didn't fall for it. Damn the garden, I thought. Damn the beauty of stones and pillars and the superficial sense of continuity and security we were supposed to derive from it. So what if Abraham held this piece of pottery and Rachel held this figurine to her bosom? If we didn't inherit their faith and their values, what kind of dead roots was I expected to cherish? I didn't say anything and went to my room. That night I packed, and when the offices opened in the morning, I booked a flight to Athens, one-way.

My mother was in Africa, where, in Lambaréné, she joined Dr. Schweitzer and his team of savior-healers, surrounding herself with human kindness at its deepest expression. She sent us pictures in which she appears with lots of black children. In her letters, she sounded peaceful. She, too, deserved an escape. Athens was not an escape but a home substitute, and Michael was my great unreciprocated love. We met in Cannes, at a film festival, and I found myself attracted to his personality in a strange, uncontrollable way. It was not sex or status. It was an affinity of mind. I had the novel sensation that the meeting of two people can produce something superior to either of them. This quality of "us" became an emotional and creative goal which enriched us both and initiated me into the pleasure of giving, something my mother knew to an exaggerated degree and my father seldom manifested. My need to love was obviously greater than that of being loved, and this slightly off-balance relationship brought out in me total emotional commitment while preserving mobility, and physical and cerebral independence. In Michael I had a home, intellectual stimulation, and integrity, which, coupled with a sense of purpose, made me produce four books. For a time, my parents, my country, Zahala, patriotic demands were all suspended, without guilt or nostalgia.

Greece before the colonels' revolution was a paradise for expatriates and foreigners. Its ancient culture was indescribably nourishing, and the Athenian way of life was unimposing and tolerant. The slow pace accommodated every possible temperament, and what was specifically Mediterranean about it was my home ground anyway. In my imagination I fancied myself a Durrell heroine, Athens easily standing in for Alexandria. Being Jewish held a slight mystic dimension, and being Israeli and my father's daughter generated respect and, often, curious admiration. We had the illusion of a Golden Age. Michael and Dassin were making films. Melina Mercouri, Irene Papas, and Lambetti were acting. Hadzidakis and Theodorakis wrote beautiful music. Elytis and Gatsos held court as leading poets, and the exchange of stimuli was genuine and gratifying. The political and social clouds that gathered above this bluest of seas were easily ignored in a screen of self-satisfaction and internationalism. The real life of the country was very remote from our protective haven.

The close contact I maintained with my family was a very happy one, expressed in weekly letters and occasional visits. My father's letters and visits were both enchanting. In every letter, a few sentences were devoted to the plea: "Do come home, whatever your plans are, please find time to visit, get organized here and eventually stay." In one very touching letter, the tone was more personal: "You must know I miss you terribly. I don't remember ever missing anybody so much. So much so that I am desperately trying to find a way to come and see you . . ." And: ". . . I realize with delight how happy you are. I wish I could sound the same. Ninety percent of what I do bores me, and of the things I want to do, I don't achieve ten percent. If I was good at math I could calculate the balance of my life . . . If you were here the balance would have changed . . ." My mother and Assi came to stay with me, and I infused them with my love for Greece, its landscapes and the intriguing contrast of past grandeur and present simplicity. "My Travels with My Father" could almost merit a separate book. His first visit with me in Athens, which I anticipated with a degree of anxiety, was positively a success. He liked Michael; he enjoyed my friends; and he accommodated to social events, dinners with strangers, and basic sightseeing with the fresh enthusiasm of an excited tourist. For once, I saw him relaxed, in good humor, displaying charm, not at short intervals, but as a result of feeling well. He loved the small fish restaurants in the Piraeus marina, and could spend a long three hours over a leisurely lunch, sipping white wine and watching the fishermen spread their nets, without his habitual nervous need to get up, move, change positions, or even be alone. We hunted for antiquities together, drove to Delphi and the Peloponnesus, returned again and again to the National Museum, and talked. He didn't want to be in charge, and there was nothing I suggested that didn't please him. We were both wise enough to avoid controversial topics. He mentioned my homecoming as his own wishful hope, and not in a national context. He talked about Mother with respect and warmth, imagining they had reached a modus vivendi satisfactory to both of them, and he dismissed any references to his own advancement as a national leader. Not having to face the grave life-or-death military decisions enabled him to widen his horizons and discover the joy of deeper contemplation. He grew more interested in the fate and destiny of the Jewish people, studied the global power games, was aware of the tremendous technological evolution the world was facing, and dressed the bare skeleton of pragmatism with wordly wisdom, tolerance, and knowledge. It was obvious to him that my relationship with Michael would not result in marriage, but he took care to assure me that he would give his blessing to any choice I made. He sensed that my "Greek period" was a passing phase and enriching and was satisfied with my choice of subject for my next novels.

We stayed in my rented apartment. I had a car, and I paid all our bills and I paid for his purchases, which pleased him enormously. "I knew you would support me one day," he said, regarding my Diners credit card as if it were a lottery ticket we'd jointly won. I was sad when he left, and knew he would make an effort to join me wherever I was. I also knew that the chemistry between us worked best when we were isolated from taxing familiar surroundings.

When he returned home, he wrote me immediately: "I don't remember ever feeling so relaxed and happy. It seems that only with a daughter one doesn't have to pretend or playact—what choice do you have but to accept me as I am? I left with a feeling that there were many things I meant to tell you and didn't (mostly good things), but I'm not even sure what they were. Maybe this feeling is the result of a need to explain that we shall soon meet again. There is a good chance that I'll represent the government at the independence celebrations of Nigeria. It is not Athens, but I can't imagine a more pleasant surprise than seeing you on the runway in Lagos . . ."

I arrived an hour before he did, and I was there, on the runway in Lagos, to meet him. The independence celebrations lasted four days. We shared a room in a hotel where nothing functioned properly, and made short excursions to the fruit market, devising a method of peeling pineapples and cracking coconuts in the room. Father was not too patient with his Foreign Office entourage, and very enthusiastic about our massive aid to the budding agriculture of Nigeria and several other African states. We visited farms in cleared jungle areas, met with Israeli experts and local chiefs, had stomach cramps after tasting palm wine, and marveled at the abundance of water and at the lush vegetation. He didn't wish to be alone, and if at moments I found the pace of formal events stifling, he assured me he was as bored. When at home, I was always on guard, choosing my words and tiptoeing around his changing moods, eager to please and compromising my own personal preferences to do so. In Athens, in Lagos, in the capitals of Europe, there was no need. We had the perfect relationship of two adults sharing tastes, interests, and attitudes. A wink, a shrug, the raised eyebrow sufficed as communication. We both got up very early, enjoyed outdoor activities, wanted to learn about flora and fauna, and were bored easily by formality, pomposity, and pretense. He thought we made a handsome pair, and when we walked into a ballroom or a chief's tent, he was happy to be greeted by photographers, posing with a smile, his hand on my shoulder, whispering to me something like "We don't look too bad, for farmers from Nahalal," black tie and all. He was flattered when we were told we resembled each other, and childishly happy with the fact that I didn't use makeup and had no need for a hairdresser. When the ceremonies were over, we went to eastern Nigeria, where a large group of Israelis lived and worked as agriculture experts, and then it was time to part. I was going to take a long train ride to Kano in the Moslem north and fly from there to Accra. He was going home. Before we kissed goodbye, he had a little surprise for me. "I'm sorry about Daniel," he said, not looking me straight in the eye. "He is on the Continent, and I cabled him to meet you in Kano and take care of you. I, too, make mistakes"—he smiled—"very seldom. Give him my warmest regards and my thanks." The train was about to leave and we kissed hurriedly. I was the only white person on this long, monotonous trip through the jungle into the savanna, and the sight of Daniel on the platform in Kano filled my eyes with tears, but the fact that it had been arranged by my father added an unforgettable dimension to it.

With stops in Accra, Conakry, Dakar, and Madrid, I was back in Athens with Michael when my second book, *Envy the Frightened*, was published. The reviews were good, the sales average, and I began to write *Dust*. Though I had graduated from being a one-novel writer to the status of professional, I was still best recognized and often introduced as "Dayan's daughter, who wrote *New Face in the Mirror*." This didn't worry me, as I felt I had secured for myself a small niche in contemporary literature, and it was up to my talent to fill it with better and more meaningful work.

My father stayed on as Minister of Agriculture when Ben-Gurion resigned, swearing to pursue to the end the investigation of the "security mishap." The old man wouldn't rest until the 1954 Lavon affair was clarified, and to exposing "truth and justice" he devoted his political and moral energies. In June 1963, Levi Eshkol became Prime Minister and Minister of Defense. Golda Meir, Sapir, and Aranne, all veteran Labor leaders, crowded the corridors of power, and Father, Peres, and Eban, the "youngsters," were offered cabinet posts, but without Ben-Gurion to support, advance, and lead them, they were bound to make concessions.

My father was clear in his determination and logic. He would help Ben-Gurion, but, as he declared, "If a situation should arise in which Ben-Gurion resigns, and I think that it is in the interests of the state that a Labor government should be formed, and if—God forbid—I'm offered a post in it, I shall join this government." Ben-Gurion was perhaps the only one who fully appreciated Father's resolution. My father identified himself fully and without compromise with Ben-Gurionism as a policy and ideology whereby the state came before all else, even before Ben-Gurion the man. At the risk of being called a traitor and blamed for shrewd personal ambition, he joined the Eshkol government. His readiness to compromise, for which he was attacked, eventually became an asset and was termed "flexibility." He lost support inside the cabinet but gained it outside, among the people.

My father liked Eshkol, and I believe the affection was mutual, but strictly on a personal basis. Eshkol was a good listener, had a marvelous Yiddish-based sense of humor, and was an ardent Zionist in the old-fashioned, emotional, back-to-the-land sense. Whatever qualities my father sought for in a leader, he thought Eshkol lacked them, and when he finally resigned from the government in November 1964, he told him: "There must be mutual trust between a Prime Minister and his ministers. I'm not a minister—or a person —after your own heart, and you are not a Prime Minister after mine."

YAËL DAYAN/*My Father, His Daughter*

With the elections imminent, the minority group that formed around Ben-Gurion had to decide whether or not it would break with Labor and go to the polls as an independent list. My father's views, and thousands of people were awaiting his decision, were contradictory. On one hand, he vigorously criticized the government. He accused Eshkol and Sapir publicly of letting personal political considerations color their decisions on state and economic affairs. On the other hand, he was against a break and announced his decision to stay with the Labor Party, even when his friends, led by Ben-Gurion, split from it and formed Rafi (the Israel Workers list) as an independent political party. I returned home and was soon involved with the new party, preparing for the coming elections. I believed, as many others did, that the old Labor group had grown stagnant and alienated, and Ben-Gurion would lead us to a renewed dialogue with the voters. The country's needs had changed, a new society was forming, and younger leadership seemed called for. All the influence we could muster was exerted on my father. Delegations and individuals called on him, old friends and strangers begged him to join, and yet he hesitated. To my "whys" he simply said he couldn't make up his mind. I believed him when he said it had nothing to do with his own career. He was against splinter parties and was pessimistic about the results of the upcoming elections. He was not highly impressed by the list of Rafi candidates. "On a battlefield," he told me, "a small elite unit can win over a large organized force. In the political arena, the full advantage lies with the powerful establishment. If Rafi could not achieve its aims, what was the use of founding it or joining it?" he asked with self-confessed pessimism, and refused to assume the leadership offered him.

Ultimately, and certainly not wholeheartedly, he joined Rafi, contributing to it little more than his name. Ben-Gurion's isolation and the way he was treated by Labor "veterans" broke through his apathy, and without much enthusiasm, he placed himself seventh on the new list. The fact that I stayed home in Zahala did not seem to cheer him, and he managed to spoil my own political enthusiasm. He talked about Rafi and its members in the second or third person, never using "we," and while we expected to get twenty seats in the Knesset and be an influential factor, his estimate was six or eight. Alas, his pessimistic estimate proved accurate. Rafi won eight seats, and these didn't constitute an important enough factor to be considered in the negotiations to form a new government.

Father's political personality was branded pragmatist, in contrast to "visionary," and by many he was called a follower rather than a leader. I could easily debate the first assumption, since I knew his pragmatism was a tool with which to implement the visionary in him. He was a follower in the true sense as long as Ben-Gurion was his leader, and the proof that he wasn't a leader was in his almost anti-political idea that if people wanted to be led by him, they would elect him for the post. Running on the Rafi list, and the results of the election, confirmed his view. What he had to offer, as superior as it was—and he never underestimated himself—the people didn't choose to have.

From 1965 to May 1967, each of us found a variety of escapes. I worked, mostly in Greece, on my fourth novel, *Death Had Two Sons*, while, in the Knesset, Father became more and more the lone wolf, letting Peres carry the burden of party administration, and not getting involved with the attempt to renovate and change which Rafi promised the voters.

He was restless and impatient. His headaches grew in frequency and intensity, and he devoted more time to archaeology, some writing, and a variety of women, whose common denominator, other than Rahel I suppose, was youth and vulgarity. For a while, we both traveled like maniacs, and often found a moment of pleasure and respite in each other's company in London, Paris, or New York. I was still footing the bills, which always delighted him, and we still made a good-looking couple. He felt he was at the end of his career and developed serious economic worries about "old age," and with a mixture of pride and painful bitterness referred to himself as "Yaël Dayan's father," warning me that my status as the "general's daughter" would soon be forgotten.

My restlessness was channeled in a variety of ways. There was no future for me with him, Michael tried to convince me, and I should not develop dependence. So I let other men enter the labyrinth of my heart, and for a while was satisfied with a turbulent, self-destructive, neurotic relationship with a young American writer. Passion was no substitute for love, as exciting as its manifestations were, and when away from Michael, even when proposed to, made love to, or seriously courted, I felt an emptiness. Udi was married and had his first child, and for the first time, at twenty-five, I thought seriously of marriage and motherhood. It had to happen in Israel, I felt, but I was not yet ready to settle down at home, or anywhere else.

I went to the Far East, to Peru, Mexico, and Brazil, lectured often, fund-raising for the U.J.A., and so did Father. For Diaspora Jews, he was still one of the greatest symbols of "proud and brave Israel," and rather than identified with an impotent small party, his name was synonymous with Israel at large. "My name still holds for fund-raising and for booking a table in an overbooked restaurant," he remarked dryly.

In the spring of 1966, he was invited to visit the Vietnam front and write a series of articles about it. In spite of criticism and objections, he gladly accepted, and soon found refuge in the Nam swamps and jungles. He joined patrols, ate C-rations, and wore fatigues. He was back in his element, befriending GIs and cross-examining generals who sought his advice. When a friend said to him, "I wouldn't go if I were in your place," he replied: "If I were in your place, I wouldn't go either. But I'm going in my place, while you are staying here in yours." I, for one, understood and respected his motives, and if there was in it a touch of escape from frustrations, that was easy to understand, and accept, too. Not for one moment did I worry about his safety and well-being. He was a veteran, and he promised me that, of all deaths, he didn't intend to be shot in a war that wasn't his.

Mother went to Vietnam, too, and spent a romantic, enchanting night with him in Saigon, which charged her batteries for many months. I visited in his footsteps, as a war correspondent, after he left Vietnam, and was proud to find that he had left his brilliant imprint on the minds and actions of the men he met there.

The early spring of 1967 found me back in Athens, polishing my new novel and awaiting Father's visit on his way back from the

United States. We stayed in Michael's flat, as he was away, and in the morning he asked me to get a local newspaper and translate the headlines for him. I walked into an empty street to be stopped by officers in uniform and two tanks. They informed me of a curfew and sent me home, rather rudely. We soon learned of the colonels' takeover, and as sad and upset as we both were at the implications, my father's eye held an excited glint as he considered himself lucky to be where things were happening, even if it was a coincidence.

For a couple of days, he manifested a sense of being involved. We walked to the Israeli legation, and he sent cables home, assessing the political implications, and we visited Mikis Theodorakis and other friends of mine who were under house arrest. The Greek soldiers recognized him, but, out of sheer respect for "generals" at that moment, let us travel freely. The fact that he was totally on the liberal opposition side eluded them. When he left for Israel, we talked in the well-guarded airport about his future. He spoke with disdain about his "aging" without accomplishing much, about being doomed to witness rather than participate, and begged me to come home soon, which I promised to do. Neither of us suspected that we'd both be in uniform when we met next, that it would be so soon, and that he was on the eve of a great comeback, not only as a participant, but as a popularly chosen leader.

TEN ❃ THE
SIX - DAY WAR

On May 20, 1967, my father celebrated his fifty-second birthday. For a few days prior to what for him personally was just another insignificant birthday, a huge Egyptian force, comprising about eighty thousand soldiers and eight hundred tanks, was moving in the Sinai Peninsula toward the Israeli border.

On May 22, Nasser declared a blockade of the Straits of Tiran to all ships bound to or from Israel.

On May 23, I received a cable in Athens, summoning me home. My father was sure we were facing another war, and very soon, and he knew I would rather be home when that happened.

On May 25, my BEA flight landed in Lydda airport, where my mother met me and drove me to my reserve-unit HQ in Tel Aviv, where I reported. I was listed as a lieutenant in the Military Spokesman's unit, and I made it clear that I didn't intend to stay in the Tel Aviv area and brief foreign journalists. It was Friday, and I was told to report the next day. They'd see what they could do, the officers promised. "As long as it is in the south," I pressed. "And where do you think everyone requests to be sent?" On the way home, we listened to Nasser's bragging speech. "Egypt will destroy Israel," he declared. He announced that the armies of Egypt and Syria were now one, and invited Jordan to join. He praised the Soviets, scorned the UN, and his voice held a new self-confidence rather than the familiar Middle East hysteria.

After my rather long absence, the house in Zahala seemed like a safe shore that no war could shatter. Both my brothers were mobilized, and my father was truly glad to see me. "Just in time," he said. "The war may begin tomorrow with dawn, unless it is postponed again, which would not surprise me." He must have been certain enough, though, for he took me out to a "festive" dinner and was quite relaxed during the four-course meal. I couldn't take my eyes off him, and was fascinated by the changing expressions on his face rather than by what he told me. He had been in uniform for a week now, "getting the feel of it" again. Many reservists were mobilized, and the long, nervous wait was demoralizing. His face lit up, as if transformed chemically from inside, when he spoke of the troops, of the commanders he knew; his heartbeat was with them, and all the parental love, all the camaraderie this man could summon glittered in his one eye. When he spoke of the diplomatic efforts to attain American consent and guarantee for free passage in the Gulf of Suez, or the negotiations with the UN and with European heads of state, his face showed dismay, if not contempt. He mentioned Udi and Assi and Zorik's son Uzi and Aviva's son Jonathan with anxiety and pride. They were all good fighters, responsible, reliable, and he said: "I am happy about the fact that they are motivated by love of their country rather than by hate for the enemy."

He was confident of our strength, of our morale, and in all his eagerness for the operation to begin, he did not sound trigger-happy, bent on destruction, or in search of some personal satisfaction. Some of the plans were not perfect, he suggested, but all war rooms and command "pits" were open to him, and his advice at least was heard. It didn't bother him to have no official authority, as long as they let him—"they," meaning Eshkol, who was Prime Minister as well as Minister of Defense—be in on it. And where he asked to be, which was naturally the Southern Command, with an armored brigade. "Make sure you're sent south," he advised me, as if I were a tourist talking to a travel agent. "The best, of course, is Sharon's division, if you can get there!"

The end of May is blessed with warm days and cooler nights, and a reminder of orange blossom is still in the air. We parted, not knowing when and how we would meet again, but sensing a deep harmony. For both of us, for my father in a deep and vast national sense, and for me in a purely personal way, it was a comeback. I came home, and soon I knew it was for good. He was at his best, freed of the frustrations, melancholy, and bitterness of the past few years. His car was waiting, and he drove—it was almost midnight—to the Southern Command in Beersheba, and I drove home to Zahala, to spend one last night, for many days to come, in a comfortable bed.

Twenty-four hours later, there was no orange-blossom scent in the air. The evening breeze scattered the loess dust, powdering my face, my sandaled feet, my writing pad, and the ration biscuits I was eating. I was attached to Arik Sharon's division HQ, "the best post," as my father suggested, for however long the general mobilization lasted. I was to send daily reports to the correspondents' pool, which were to be distributed for publication in Israel and abroad. The definition of my objectives didn't matter. I was in the one and only place I cared to be. The Egyptian threat, less than a mile to the west of where our tents were pitched, was my only reality, and my pulse beat in an impatient unison with the men around me, officers, soldiers, reservists, and innocent, eager conscripts.

The steam that had been bottled up for the last few years had to surface, and an all-out war seemed inevitable. A series of incidents between Syria and Israel and between Jordan and Israel led to the flawed judgments of President Nasser, who believed this was the perfect time to strike and retrieve his supremacy in the Arab world. The Six-Day War, as it was later called, was the third major armed conflict Israel had had to engage in since its birth, and on the last days of May we did not need to analyze or look for a historical perspective. We almost took for granted the fact that we were not accepted as an equal nation by our neighbors, that we were doomed to fight wars for our survival at what seemed to be ten-year intervals. The cycle of hatred, rejection, accumulation of arms, buildup of confidence in their own strength, and internal needs of a military dictatorship offered a seemingly endlessly repeatable pattern, leaving us no options other than tactical ones. Defense, a preemptive attack, the capture of the populated northern Sinai and the Gaza Strip, or a sweeping move toward the canal, one front at a time or all-out war on three fronts, the bombing of civilian targets or the use of the Air Force as an auxiliary to armor and infantry. The preoccupation with these options and others was not limited to government and General Staff meetings. Women in the supermarket as well as farmers in border settlements, schoolchildren, and newspaper editorials, with a varying degree of expertise and anxiety, were hectically assembling the pieces of this political-military jigsaw puzzle. The questions were not "why," as there the answer seemed to be "survival," but were mostly "when" and "how."

Near the Nabatean ruins of ancient Shivta, where Sharon's HQ was camouflaged sloppily, we had all the answers. The "when" was yesterday—at the latest, today—and the "how" was mapped out in the war room tent in large red-and-blue arrows crossing the green border line into the Sinai all the way west. The "how" was also mapped in the experienced, wrinkled faces of reservists, in the shining eyes of tank crews, and in Arik Sharon's diabolically brilliant military brain. Where the question marks were left open and gaping was the corridors of the Foreign Ministry and the Prime Minister's office. It was evident that the political leadership was unable to commit itself to an irreversible course of action and was hesitant to derive the courage and determination to do so from the people and the Army, rather than, as normally expected of leadership, inspire them.

Ceaseless interparty contacts attempted to broaden the framework of Eshkol's government to form a national unity government. Some of the parties, including Begin's Herut, asked Eshkol to hand over the premiership to Ben-Gurion, but the real need was expressed in popular demonstrations, petitions, and tireless exhortations by a stream of individuals. "Dayan for Minister of Defense" was almost a unanimous request. As Shimon Peres was effectively negotiating the proposition, fully backed by Ben-Gurion, his task was made easier by an enormous surge of popular demand. A myth? A craving for what represented military glory and personal courage? Idealists, pragmatists, followers, and political adversaries who joined in a request to have my father named Defense Minister were mostly motivated by a crying need for decision-taking leadership. The emotional horses were pulling the hesitant political cart, and either to steer, speed, or stop it, it needed a superb coachman. The candidate himself, my father, did not cooperate. He would do, he declared, anything he was asked to do, provided it did not keep him from the active front. He was not going to be an "adviser" in a Jerusalem office; he'd rather command a tank battalion. He was not going to interfere with the existing IDF hierarchy or replace someone, thus discrediting him. He rather fancied a position as commander of the southern front, with the current GDC Southern Command as his deputy.

Meanwhile, Peres, Begin, the Religious Front leaders, and others calling on the government to entrust the defense portfolio to Dayan's hands were against compromising. When Golda Meir suggested Allon for Defense, and it was clear that the Defense portfolio was to be separated from the premiership, the pressure mounted, and Allon himself withdrew his candidacy.

On May 30, King Hussein signed an Egyptian–Jordanian defense pact in Cairo, and on June 1 my father inspected the Jerusalem area. His trip was interrupted. At 7 p.m., Eshkol telephoned Father to report that the cabinet had approved the decision to give him the Defense portfolio. As my father said, the following morning: "It took the entry of eighty thousand Egyptian troops into the Sinai to get me back into the government."

The precise series of events, the pressures, the intricate political scheming, are of little consequence now, or even then—once the decision was taken. What was evident then, and later, as before, was the fact that my father's career would never benefit from his own ambition. He would never push or pull to get a position, or even cooperate with those who wished it with his consent and on his behalf. He was content to announce his availability, and his neutrality, meanwhile wasting no time, doing his homework, planning, and applying his mind and talent to what should be done rather than to who would do it. As a result, he did not feel in debt or make an emotional or ideological commitment to the people and movements which placed him where they did. He felt he derived his power, authority, and sense of mission directly from the people, and to them it was owed. Eighty thousand Egyptians motivated three million Israelis to want him there, and the three million's gain was the eighty thousand's loss. There was no time to waste.

That same Thursday, June 1, I was busy brigade-hopping. The frustration was reaching a peak, and an afternoon sandstorm didn't help. Cooks, drivers, privates, and colonels fought apathy and desperately tried to boost morale. Mordechai Zipori, an armored brigade commander, recited Jabotinsky's patriotic verse. Arik Sharon restlessly went over the attack plans for the thousandth time—they were flawless, to begin with—and Kuti, the infantry commander, walked the desert plateau, where I joined him, looking for flintstone arrowheads. He piled them on the sand and sorted them out. The small or broken he said were common; he gave them to children. A few perfect ones he kept; but the best, the largest, and one extraordinarily shiny white one he asked me to bring to my father. "And one for you, to keep you safe," he said, and I put it in my shirt pocket. The night before, Arik issued orders to move our half-tracks to the border. "I want them on the frontier, even if exposed. From border stone to border stone, on the last inch which is Israel." I was watching with Kuti the dusty trails of the approaching vehicles. "An exercise in wishful thinking," Kuti commented. "Lining up for a race does not mean the race will take place." Colonel Kuti Adam looked like a fierce warrior. He was dressed in battle fatigues and a black beret, a pistol and a knife dangling from his belt; a canteen, binoculars, a large map on the hood of his jeep—all contrasting with the extraordinary softness of his voice, and the warm, nostalgic look in his black eyes. He talked of my father, whom he loved and admired, saying simply: "If he leads us, it isn't that we'll go to war, as we should; it is the way we are going to win it which is going to be different." He talked at length, gazing west, as the half-tracks were pulling into a set formation. "Moshe," he said, "is not a mystic mascot. It isn't his military genius either, as he approved of the battle plans and made only a few changes. It is a quality which can't be defined, which represents, and demands, the best in all of us. For me, he is a link between those arrowheads and the half-tracks, and forward in time to, alas, nuclear warheads. At the same time, if we ever have peace, it will be under his leadership, or in his spirit." Kuti felt he talked too much, as he was a gentle, shy person, and to his relief, Colonel Dov Sion arrived to take me to the field hospital and back to Shivta. We had dinner with Arik, in his trailer, and I was too tired to wait for the midnight news, on which my father's appointment was announced.

On Friday morning, the change was noticeable in every face, word, and action. As if we all got a second wind, as if a large brush had painted off the past two weeks and splashed new vivid colors and feeling into the dormant desert, the steel war machines, the spirit of the commanders, all of us. Even the long wait suddenly made sense, and for once I wasn't embarrassed by expressions of affection and pride which were bestowed on me but directed at my father.

At the first cabinet meeting in which my father participated, the die was cast. Eshkol, willingly and with a tremendous sense of relief, asked my father what his proposals were, and without hesitation Father declared: "We should launch a military attack without delay. If the cabinet takes such a decision at its next scheduled meeting, Sunday, June 4, we should strike the next morning. The campaign would last from three to five days." He added his objections to advancing too close to the Suez Canal, and to a suggested transfer of refugees from the Gaza Strip to Egypt. This war should not lay the grounds for a next, harder war. It should eliminate a direct threat and rule out a major armed confrontation.

The long days of avoiding a decision were over. The mood of the entire cabinet was changed, and the Army's self-confidence was restored as if by a magic touch. Those who were in favor of waiting another week, to protect the political flanks, listened to him describe the merits of a preemptive strike. "The first shot would determine which side would suffer the heavier casualties, and if we took the enemy by surprise, their damages would be the equivalent of all additional arms supplies we might receive for the next six months. The course of the campaign should be dictated by us, and the enemy should be forced to fight according to our moves." The next cabinet meeting ended with a vote on my father's proposal that "orders be given to the Army to choose the time, place and appropriate method." All but two ministers voted for the resolution.

Dov, who was Sharon's liaison officer with GHQ and the Southern Command, agreed to drive with me to Zahala and back that Friday evening, on the scant hope that I might get a minute with my father.

The house was full of flowers, boxes of chocolate, baskets of fruit, as if for a wedding. Gifts from people, mostly unknown to us. The comforting aroma of chicken soup filled the kitchen, and my brother Assi, on a three-hour leave from his antiaircraft gunners unit, was the recipient of my first hug and kiss. Father was taking a bath—between meetings. My mother's eyes, though glittering with pride, still had a tear in them when she saw us, both in uniform, aware as she was of what would happen shortly. We were, in fact, prematurely celebrating a victory, but she could not ignore the inevitability of casualties that even the greatest of triumphs incurs.

Father walked out of the bathroom in his underpants and slippers, and without his eye patch. He hardly fit the confidence-inspiring image he represented since the previous day. Yet it was all there. The brightness in his direct look, the youthful stride as if a burden had been shed, the seriousness of a tremendous responsibility, and the bemused half-smile of self-assurance. Most of what we had to say to each other we expressed in a long embrace, and he was as delighted as an infant when he examined Kuti's arrowheads. He spoke admiringly of Arik and his brigade commanders, and promised me I was "in the best of hands." He talked about being for the first time endowed with the highest authority, as Eshkol left all military decisions to him.

In 1956, as Chief of Staff under Ben-Gurion, he carried out orders even when he considered them mistaken. Now the responsibility was his. "For good or for ill, I will be on my own." We all had to leave soon, and wished each other luck. None of us knew when, or how happy, our next encounter would be. Mother packed fruit and nuts and chocolates for me to take to Shivta, and with them her anxiety and love.

Dov called for me, giving me time to get into and out of a hot bath and change, and I hastily introduced him to my mother. I couldn't at that moment share with her the vague but mounting feeling I had for him. I myself referred to it as "nothing personal," just an emotional affinity of two people facing a surge of events.

We did not talk much on the long drive back. Beersheba's main street was dark and dead, and Arik's trailer and the HQ tents in Shivta felt like home. I could not mark it on a calendar, but D-Day tension was in the air, and the precise date didn't matter. We were on our way.

On Sunday afternoon, Dov said to me: "You had better get some equipment." We went to the supply tent, where I exchanged my boots for a better pair, got a new canteen, spare woolen socks, and some ammunition. I handed in my identity discs and received in their place a "prisoner's card" on which were the details I was allowed to give if I was captured. Name, rank, number, blood type. I placed the card in my pocket, next to Kuti's arrowhead, and tried on the helmet, which felt heavy and uncomfortable. Trucks were being loaded, engines warmed, communications systems tested, field kitchens packed, but nobody said D-Day is tomorrow. The most I could get from Dov to my "So that's it" was an enigmatic shrug and a suggestion which seemed wild: "Try to get a few hours' sleep." My father reviewed the final plans that Sunday evening, flew to the Northern Command to get a situation report, and arranged for a field bed to be available to him in the emergency HQ. It was a cool, pleasant night, almost romantic, had it not been for hordes of mosquitoes, and to my amazement, I managed three hours' sleep. I woke up in a dark a.m., with a dramatic feeling. For a brief moment, the last in many days to come, I was an observer. A few soldiers were in prayer next to the war room; two reservists were writing letters; Arik was shaving in his trailer and very carefully applying after-shave lotion, like a youth before his first date; and Dov was packing. A small bag to take along, and the rest of the things to be left behind. I was taking the same stock, mentally and emotionally. Nahalal, my brothers and cousins, my parents, high-school history and geography lessons, oil lamps and arrowheads, were placed close to my skin and would come along, with the reliable boots, the writing pad, and "Don't forget the toilet paper," Dov had said. Athens; Michael, regretfully and affectionately; Rome's cakes and Paris restaurants; London publishers' talk and New York sophisticated dinner parties; Vietnam jungles and Singapore markets—all were neatly compressed and packed, to be left behind. I left on my wrist a gold bracelet given me by that gentlest and most understanding friend, Alain de Rothschild, as a token link between the worlds. He was in Paris, and I knew his heart was with me and the men around me.

When the sun mounted, blessing us with its golden touch, we had already advanced in a compact, mobile HQ formation. Arik's two half-tracks were to move with the force, together with a couple of jeeps equipped with machine guns, and the supply car would trail behind. The brigades were spread out on our flanks, and for the time being the communications system was not activated.

I helped Rachamin, the cook, with breakfast and, when the tea was ready, woke up Arik. On a blanket spread on the hard sand, I got our last "civilized" breakfast of fried eggs, fresh salad, and bread. Next would be C-rations, and who could tell for how long.

My mother prepared an early breakfast in Zahala on June 5. My parents sat at the table at six-thirty, had coffee and toast, and Mother mentioned that she was going to Jerusalem for a meeting later. From Zahala my father left for HQ, made sure the timetable was planned, and took off for a small café around the corner, where he met with Rahel for another coffee and a croissant. He didn't mention to either woman, or as much as indicate, what was to happen within the hour.

At seven-thirty, my father was in the Air Force "pit," and Arik told us to put on helmets and get packed and ready to move. Very few words were spoken. The buildup to this moment was so long, it left no room for last-minute, dramatic excitement. The spring was stretched to capacity and ready to be released, and there was a severe sense of professional awareness in the air.

Between 7:14 and 8:55 a.m., Israeli planes carried out an attack in two waves. In the first wave, 183 aircraft were engaged, rendering six Egyptian airfields inoperable and destroying 205 enemy aircraft, putting sixteen radar stations out of order. The second wave, comprising 164 planes, attacked fourteen bases and destroyed 107 enemy aircraft. The Egyptians lost three-quarters of their air strength. Our casualties were eleven pilots—six killed, two taken prisoner, and three wounded. The air operation was carried out in complete radio silence and at a low altitude, below the radar; and the ground forces did not switch radios on until their own H-Hour, which followed the positive reports of the returning pilots.

Our own generator was activated at 0800, and at 0815, in a strong, confident voice, Arik gave the order: Nua! Nua! (Move! Move!). The vehicles, already in gear, with engines running, headed west, and I could soon see our tanks descending toward the frontier. Arik was standing up, looking through his binoculars, and a few moments later, to the first sound of our own shells, he announced: "Here we go, we are firing!"

On my small transistor radio I heard my father's voice, through the shots and the shells, broadcasting to the advancing troops, to the mothers and wives at home, and, as I felt, speaking to me personally. "Soldiers of Israel," he said, "we have no aims of conquest. Our purpose is to bring to naught the attempts of the Arab armies to conquer our land, and to break the ring of blockade and aggression which threatens us . . . They are more numerous than we are, but we shall overcome them. We are a small nation, but strong. Peace-loving, yet ready to fight for our lives and our country . . . The supreme efforts will be demanded of you, the troops, fighting in the air, on land, and on the sea. Soldiers of the Israel Defense Forces, on this day our hopes and our security rest with you." Dov's eyes met mine, and he understood how I felt. There are peaks in life, national and personal, which one is aware of at the moment they take place. Not in perspective, not as an afterthought or in a final accounting or a historical assessment. We simply knew that what was happening on June 5, between 7:45 and midday, was one of those unique peaks. Everything that was in us, all the accumulated energies and convictions, past tragedies and future hopes, were compressed into the effort of these few hours.

My father was hundreds of miles away from me, finalizing orders to attack Jordanian airfields and prepare the offensive against the outposts around Jerusalem. Jordan and Syria joined the war, Jordan with artillery on the Jewish quarters in Jerusalem, and Syria with its Air Force bombing Tiberias and Megiddo. I was entering the first enemy post that was destroyed. I never felt as close to my father as I did during those hours; in spite of the distance, I could feel his physical presence. His face was with me, his strong, stable gaze, his calm, composed confidence, brain ticking away like a radar searching for options in a circular movement. With the deepest of emotions, I felt privileged. There was my complex, beloved father, living through his greatest hours perhaps, towering above us all in a multidimensional way.

My mother was caught in the first shelling of Jerusalem, in a petrol station near the King David Hotel. She managed to abandon her car, get to a telephone, and reach the Knesset shelter in time for the swearing-in ceremony of the new cabinet. Father showed up, but couldn't wait for Eshkol, who was delayed. They drove back to Tel Aviv, missing the actual ceremony, Mother again witnessing with pride and love the unfolding of events, as Father issued orders and received reports in the car. In the opposite direction, a long line of heavy, dark tanks was silhouetted in the dark night, advancing along the curving road to Jerusalem.

My father returned to the pit as we were preparing for the major breakthrough battle in mid-Sinai. The objective was the Um Katef stronghold, difficult to approach, flanked by mine fields and impassable dunes, and manned by dug-in infantry brigade and heavy artillery. But once the defense line was broken, the central axis to the Suez Canal would be open to race through, since the same operations were in progress in the northern Sinai sector (Tal's force) and the southern sector—all the way to Sharm el-Sheikh and the blockaded Straits of Tiran. Mother refused to join the neighbors in their shelter and felt safe enough in her own bed, listening to the all-night radio reports.

Dov explained the battle plan to me, drawing lines on my writing pad. If we knew we were in love then, there was no room to express it. War does strip one of all fringes, and the bare essentials are so evident that emotional communication is almost telepathic. He was talking of the Russian defense system, of our mobility and their loss of air support. We heard reports of one of our battalions suffering casualties, trapped in a mine field. We listened to reports on the radio, and Dov carried out his own liaison job, consulting occasionally with Arik, and with a matter-of-fact, almost casual, efficiency. I knew very little about him, and had a feeling I would have a lifetime to find out. The bond was there, and there was no call to analyze, examine, or even take joy in it. Just after 2230, the artillery commander, in whose half-track I placed myself that night, was given the order to open fire. The paratroopers landed in helicopters at an assembly point; Kuti's infantry was positioned in the sand dunes near the Um Katef northern trenches, waiting for the artillery softening, and the long, swift fist of Motke's tanks was charging straight for the center of the fifteen-kilometer-wide defense line. Our major battle had begun. Arik's orders were colorful. He used first names for the commanders, announcing: "Let the earth shake." And next to me I could hear the artillery commander answering softly: "Shake it shall," when he ordered a barrage of six thousand shells on Um Katef in the next twenty minutes.

My heart was with the infantry. I carefully isolated Kuti's voice whenever it was heard. They were advancing under heavy fire in the trenches. Casualty reports came in, and I clutched my arrowhead with a primitive faith. The Egyptians in their strongholds were well prepared for the battle, and flanked, they had no escape route. Our timing, coordination, and superior fighting capacity gave us victory, but it took all our flexibility in combat deployment to achieve this.

While we were still in the midst of the battle of Sinai, Mota Gur's parachutes had gone into action in Jerusalem in frontal assaults on the police school compounds and on Ammunition Hill. The parachutists suffered heavy casualties, cutting their way under withering fire to take these two major bastions by dawn of June 6. When I drove in Dov's jeep to the smoke-covered Um Katef battlefield, my father, with Ezer Weizman and Uzi Narkiss, exposed in an open jeep, entered the gates of Mount Scopus. The Old City of Jerusalem was spread out below, and he was under strong government pressure to capture it immediately. The difference between his reactions as Chief of Staff and as Defense Minister was nowhere more evident than in his attitude toward the battle of Jerusalem, and in the south, at the capture of the east bank of the Suez Canal. His restraining attitude called for the Old City to be surrounded first. Entry should be without air or artillery support, causing as little damage as possible to the city and its holy places. When the encirclement was complete, and Jerusalem was cut off from Jordanian reinforcements from the east, we were already on our way on a chase-and-destroy mission into the central Sinai. Our division was lighter and smaller, as Kuti's infantry left for El Arish in the north. "Don't you want to join us for a swim?" he suggested, but Arik promised me a swim in the canal soon, and nothing at that point could tempt me away from Dov's jeep. We were advancing fast, often under an occasional barrage, and I soon became experienced in judging where the rocket would hit and how to avoid it. Holding to a heavy machine gun in the front seat, hearing Arik's voice on the wireless, and finding comfort in Dov's short, well-spaced utterings, I never felt safer. All the years with or alongside my father had obviously contributed to this lack of fear, and I didn't think of it as anything but natural, taken for granted, that there I was, on a dirt road in the Sinai, face covered with a mask of baked mud, and surrounded by tough warriors, fighting my way to the Suez Canal.

On Wednesday, June 7, a helicopter landed with the first newspapers and mail. The headlines declared in big type: "Gaza Strip in Our Hands," "Ramallah Is Ours," "West Bank Cities Are Captured." The small print had greetings from plants and factories, kibbutzim and schools, to "Our workers, sons, or members: we are with you wherever you are." There was an announcement from the American embassy, "advising all American citizens to leave Israel," and in the inside pages, the first terrible sight of names in black borders—the price we were paying. "Captain Yoram Harpaz, killed in action, in the performance of his duty . . ." "Lt. Amiram Manor, killed in action . . ." "Our blessed Chaim . . ." With gray faces, the older reservists among us searched through the lists—their sons were serving on another front—and I couldn't hold back my tears. We were winning on three fronts. We were between Um Katef and Nakhl, and were immersed in our own reality, and suddenly, in the black rules in the paper, war acquired its real horrible meaning of destruction and the loss of lives. A young soldier was looking at the paper over my shoulder, and when I turned to look at him, his eyes were wet. Had he found a familiar name? Or did he imagine his own name edged in black?

We had to move on, and with nightfall, we were advancing very slowly. The wind was blowing. The route climbing up the higher plateau was not fit for a convoy like ours, and soon the reconnaissance patrol ordered us to stop. We hit a mine field and we had to wait until the engineers cleared a path through it. We didn't budge and simply registered the proximity of danger. Arik was listening in on the next frequency when he repeated what he heard. His voice had a dream-like quality as he said: "The Old City of Jerusalem is in our hands." The news was passed from jeep to tank, from the engineers' bulldozers to the supply trucks, from the mobile hospital unit to the artillery, and clusters of huddled men, tired and hungry and weary, started singing softly "Jerusalem of Gold," in hoarse but wistful voices. As if this song was a prayer, answering the prayers of thousands of years. We couldn't move, but we had wings. The night was cold and the wind brushed us with cutting grains of sand, but there was a warmth of surging feelings and an unseen rainbow in the desert sky.

A few hours earlier, my father had walked with Rabin, then Chief of Staff, and Uzi Narkiss, then head of Central Command, through the gates of the Old City, in the footsteps of the paratroopers. They entered the Lions' Gate, turned left, and reached the Temple Mount. The Israeli flag was hoisted on the spire of the Dome of the Rock (and it was typical of my father that he ordered it down, refraining from any national demonstrative acts regarding the holy sites). They turned right through the Mograbi Gate and into the narrow plaza in front of the Wailing Wall. Father, dramatically aware of the historic moment, scribbled on a note: "May peace descend upon the whole house of Israel," and inserted the folded paper into an opening between the ashlars. The place was crowded with soldiers who had been in the battle, some wounded and many weeping, touching the huge stones and praying softly. For most of them, it was the first prayer ever.

On leaving the Western Wall, he was asked to say a few words, and later in the Sinai I heard his voice, as did my brothers in their units, my mother and grandparents, as did every Israeli wherever he was, words spoken with wisdom and thought but expressing a great emotion. He didn't really speak to us, but for us. He said: "We have returned to the holiest of our sites, and will never again be separated from it. To our Arab neighbors, Israel extends the hand of peace, and to the peoples of all faiths we guarantee full freedom of worship and of religious rights. We have come, not to conquer the holy places of others, nor to diminish by the slightest measure their religious rights, but to ensure the unity of the city and to live in it with others in harmony." He ordered to open wide the gates of the Old City wall and authorized full traffic between Jerusalem and the new city. Jordan and Israel had announced their readiness to accept a cease-fire. The West Bank, all the way to the Jordan River, was in our hands, and the fight on the eastern front was over.

Earlier, on June 7, Father had authorized an advance all the way to the canal, and we were heading there, clearing pockets of re-sistance along the way. He was never happy about this decision, and appeared to have made it under pressure. "The Army established facts in the field and I had no choice." Tal's division reached the canal city of Qantara, and when we stopped and established base in Bir Hasana, and later Bir Gofgafa, the entire Sinai Peninsula was in Israeli hands.

My first "visit" to the canal was with my father and Ezer, who picked me up in our HQ as if we were going on a sightseeing trip. We had so much to tell each other, but in fact said very little. He held my arm as we walked along to the helicopter pad, and he smiled when he told me: "Arik thought very highly of you." It was more than easy to return the compliment. We flew, following the road to the canal, looking down at the pathetic sight of the destroyed convoys along it. Ismailia was bathed in red poinciana trees in blossom, and I exclaimed: "Look how beautiful." He answered: "And if it weren't beautiful, it would be just as important." We sat on the small bridge at Qantara, our feet dangling above the waveless water. A large Polish Airlines sign offered trips to Warsaw, and a couple of swollen corpses were floating toward us in the water. "It must be unbearable to be part of a defeated army," he said, looking at the corpses. I felt slightly nauseated, as we were having a K-rations lunch, sitting there. He talked about Jerusalem, Hebron, Jericho, and the Golan Heights. I mentioned how eager I was to go to east Jerusalem soon, and he raised his brow and smiled. "What's the hurry? You'll be able to visit it even with your children . . ." I noticed, although I don't think anyone else did, that I looked at Dov when he said this.

Egypt agreed to a ceasefire on June 9, and allayed whatever earlier fears my father had concerning Russian intervention and Israel's ability to fight fully on all fronts. He ordered the Northern Command to launch a full attack on Syria and destroy the fortified emplacements on the Golan Heights. The cabinet approved the order retroactively later in the day. On Saturday, June 10, Father flew north, and followed closely the bitter assault on the slopes and cliffs along the Golan plateau. The city of Kuneitra was empty as our forces reached it, and Syria asked for a ceasefire. On June 12, visiting the Heights, Father canceled his ban regarding Mount Hermon. Professor Neeman, serving as a reservist, but a noted physicist, convinced him that holding the peak would advance the science of astronomy in Israel.

The Six-Day War was over. It not only removed threats to our existence but also added to the chances of a realistic peace, or so we believed at the time. We were near Damascus, but not down their throats; near Cairo, but clearly had no intent to keep any of the Sinai if there was a chance to negotiate peace; and we had a Jerusalem united, which was the fulfillment of the dream of generations, rather than a subject for negotiation.

I was a happy woman. Falling in love during a war made heart-searching, over-analysis, fancy courting, a need for compliments, and the customary doubts obsolete. Full exposure of good qualities and shortcomings, in a brief and compressed period of time, provided a tremendous shortcut. I knew Dov was the man with whom I wanted to share my life, and in fewer words he expressed the same feeling.

I was back home, in the full sense of the word. Being my father's daughter those past few weeks was not merely a privilege; it was some kind of blessing, and a grace. If I had a worry in the world, it had to do with how long a man's finest hour—or a nation's, at that—can last; and must the attainment of a peak be followed by some kind of downfall.

ELEVEN ❈ BETWEEN

TWO WARS

The aftermath of the Six-Day War was a state of euphoric confusion. About eight hundred families mourned the death in battle of their dear ones, and hundreds of thousands swarmed through the cities and bazaars of the West Bank cities. Dozens of Victory Albums were in print, glamourizing the short war in texts and photographs, and we all felt like supermen. The change from the pre-war depression to the unbelievable new map proved almost indigestible.

If the Arabs were astonished at their humiliating defeat, we were overwhelmed by victory, and my father nearly took advantage of the general confusion to establish facts and patterns with regard to the new situation. He was not shooting from the hip, or working out ad-hoc solutions. It was a lifetime chance to implement ideas and theories concerning our whole future predicament. He believed in "living together." He believed in physical proximity and in dialogue. He truly, and permanently, felt that this was a war to end all wars, if we established close contact with the local population in the occupied territories, without imposing on their autonomy. His new job as cabinet minister in charge of the occupied territories made him in a sense supreme military governor of 69,000 square kilometers and a population of 1,150,000, comprising city dwellers, Jordanian citizens, West Bank farmers, and a multitude of refugees living in cluttered camps. He acted fast. After removing all roadblocks, mines, and barbed wire separating west and east Jerusalem, he proceeded to order all soldiers and guards removed from all control points. He reinstated the High Moslem Council in control over the Temple Mount and its mosques. The curfew which had been imposed for the few days following the end of the war was lifted. Refugees who had left their villages and cities were returning to their places, and he made sure they could repair, with government help in supplies and machinery, their damaged homes. He brushed aside predictions of bloodshed and allowed all Israeli Arabs and West Bank inhabitants to freely attend the Friday prayers in the mosque of Al-Aqsa, and restored within weeks all administrative responsibilities to the municipal authorities.

The income of the West Bank was derived largely from agricultural exports to Jordan and other Arab countries, and with a farmer's intuition paralleling his statesman's foresight, he took a major step, assuring outlets for the summer produce. Visiting a site referred to as the "vegetable market," he watched the "illegal" passage of trucks, carts, and people loaded with agricultural produce, crossing the Jordan at its shallowest point. The crossing was allowed, but only with stringent formalities which he simplified by issuing orders on the spot. In a short while, and before the rainy season, he arranged with the Jordanian authorities to reconstruct two bridges and open them up to traffic of goods from west to east, with a minimum of delay. Jordan gave its assent, accepting reality, but the move was initiated by Father, encountering not insignificant opposition in the cabinet. It was termed "Dayan's open-bridges policy," alluding to an attitude and a political concept far beyond the supply of fresh tomatoes to Kuwait and Iraq. "Normalization" was his key word, and he did indeed feel at home in the houses of the mayors of Hebron and Bethlehem; he understood the prayer for rain of the fellahin in the Jericho valley and with great delight fitted into the bargaining world of the bazaars, searching for new archaeological treasures.

Somewhere, he suffered from confusion too, or perhaps from an optimistic oversimplification. Though he did take into account Arab terrorism, he overestimated the capacity of the local population to disassociate itself from it. His enemy was Jordan, and he was not sensitive enough to the growing gap between the Hashemite king and his Palestinian subordinates. Eshkol, Golda Meir, and other cabinet veterans preferred to remain blind to the complexity of "Palestinian entity," and the Begin group in the government didn't ignore the mounting Palestinian plea for self-determination but dismissed it as invalid and entertained hopes of annexation. Hussein did not dare tackle the peace offers. He didn't rush to the phone or even appreciate the liberal governing of the territories, and on the whole regarded the reinforcement of the Palestinian element in his kingdom as a threat. The open-bridges policy was a success, but it had to be backed by a carrot-and-stick policy in face of the spread of terrorism. Strong measures had to be applied against families and individuals who harbored terrorists. Exile, the blowing up of houses, after evacuating the occupants, proved effective, and the majority of the population took heed and ceased cooperating with the infiltrators. None of the actions Father took immediately after the war was premature, but his hopes for quick, result-bearing negotiations certainly were.

I did not indulge in the post-war euphoria. Two close friends of mine had died in the war, on the Golan Heights, and for a long while their loss overshadowed the ecstasy and joy everybody seemed to be immersed in. The vulgarity that undoubtedly was a form of exorcising bottled-up fears and insecurities was at times frightening. I felt as uncomfortable as I did in Rio's football stadium when the national cup was won and a spontaneous carnival couldn't be controlled. I walked with Dov in the Old City, and I did have a sense of "returning" and "liberating" rather than occupying, but visiting Hebron or Bethlehem, or witnessing the hysterical shopping spree of Israelis in the bazaars—the attitude of "It's all ours now," and a certain megalomania that was evident—repulsed me. On the Golan Heights, looking at the settlements below, now far from artillery range, I felt good again, but my personal, emotional, dramatic decision was overwhelming, and I did anything but concentrate on my surroundings. For it was then that I decided to get married.

I was almost twenty-eight. I had written four books—the last, *Death Had Two Sons*, was about to be published—and I had just undergone an experience that brought me face to face with the elementary, skeletal basics of life and death. If I had always said, as an excuse to myself and others, that when it happens, it just will, and there was no way to predict or maneuver—I found myself facing precisely that. I simply knew that I wished to spend my life with this man. I sensed love and realized friendship and security. I had no doubts or second thoughts, and if I was scared stiff, it was not from some anticipation of a loss of liberty or of limits on my personality but rather the fear of my own ability to accommodate unconditional giving, and receiving. We were not young kids in love, but mature adults who had wandered alone and rather independently through similar corridors of the human experience. We were satisfied, almost blasé, and though there were grounds to explore together like parenthood and the routine of family life, we both had our share of intellect and experience, well molded and formed, to invest into the partnership. Dov was born in Czechoslovakia, in the Carpatho-Russian sector that had changed sovereigns, languages, and nationalities many times. He arrived in Israel as a student on the eve of World War II, and except for a younger brother, his entire family had died in Nazi concentration camps. His education was superior to mine, and long years of Army service, as a combat infantryman in Jerusalem during the War of Independence, as a paratrooper during the Sinai Campaign, and as an instructor in the National War College, had been interspersed with secret missions in diplomatic posts in Europe. He was a colonel when we met, and more than fifteen years my senior. What we had in common didn't come from similarity of background but from convictions and reasoning which were the result of two separate life lines. We had a great respect for each other's individuality and privacy, and I suppose our opposing temperaments complemented each other.

My brother Assi was about to marry his high-school sweetheart. The wedding had been planned before the war, and to the list of guests were now added invitations to West Bank dignitaries, mayors and sheikhs, Army officers and cabinet ministers. Dov and I had a brainstorm. We handed in our marriage application in the rabbinical registration office, and we decided to hitch a ride on Assi and Aharona's wedding. The comparatively minor task of telling my parents made me feel inexplicably faint.

It was a hot July morning. My father was shaving, and the bathroom door was ajar. My mother was making the bed in their bed-room. I felt my knees buckle as I summoned as casual a voice as I could and, leaning on the open door, said: "I think you should be the first to know. I'm getting married, and I thought we could join with Assi in a double wedding, cheaper by two . . ." Only after he kissed and embraced me, shaving cream and all, did it occur to him to ask whom I intended to marry . . . His happiness for me was evident. His trust in my choice, however, touched me enormously. When he did ask me who exactly Dov was, he was only half listening to my vague reply. He had his own ways of finding out, and probably within the hour knew more about Dov than I did. My mother reacted much the same way, only with tears in her eyes and a great concern for the technicalities involved. As happy as they were for me, there was also an element of relief in their joy. I could have married some-one else, out of the country and the faith, out of their context. I could tell my parents, referring to Dov: "You haven't lost a daughter, you've gained a son," and they could easily say to themselves that they had regained their own daughter. We added a few names to the list of guests. Dov's brother and some second cousins were coming from the States, and Maskit dressmakers worked extra hours to prepare my wedding gown in time. Father acted like a bridegroom himself. He pampered me with my favorite fruit, gave me some of his precious antique pieces, worked at night moving stones in the garden to make it look perfect, and daily announced the good reports he had about Dov. The two of them met with me and Mother one evening for an "introductory" dinner. For once, I didn't worry whether or not my father would like someone I cared for. Dov's integrity and wisdom were there for all to see. He never tried to impress, and he dared contradict when he wished to differ. My mother simply liked him, without reservations. The wedding was held on July 22 in the Zahala garden, and was a lavish mixture of the popular and the elegant. It served as a victory ball as well, and Assi and Aharona, who would have had to stand through it alone, were rather grateful to share it with Dov and me. It wasn't intimate, romantic, or personal, but we were all carried away in a whirlpool of festivities. Arik Sharon was Dov's best man, and in general a patron of our love. Ben-Gurion beamed with delight, having known and liked Dov for many years.

And my grandparents, Rachel, Zvi, and Shmuel were grateful to have lived to see the day. Judging by the congratulations, I almost felt like a nearly hopeless case being salvaged by a benevolent, self-sacrificing gentleman.

The chief rabbi of the Army conducted our ceremony, and Assi's followed: he had chosen to be married by a civilian rabbi. When the eating, drinking, and dancing were over, my father simply said: "It's so wonderful to see you really happy." Dov and I drove to his apartment, and the only romantic gesture he offered was to carry me in his arms across the threshold. We were married, we were lovers, but above all we were friends. It wasn't a mere coincidence that the nation's and my father's finest hour, which was also a turning point, produced my own happiest moments and days.

My daily life had a pleasant routine. I worked on a war diary, having a deadline to meet, and read proofs of the new novel. Mother helped me with the settling-down process, though neither Dov nor I had any grand ambitions concerning wallpaper or furnishings. I cooked, laundered, and kept house, and these routines were not new to me. Mostly, I wanted to get pregnant, and quickly. I promised myself, many years before, that I would have my first baby before I was thirty. I visited Zahala daily, and when I didn't, my father summoned me over. The fact that I was married now did not mean separation or detachment as far as he was concerned, though he said he missed our early-morning talks.

His post-war status reached heights which began to affect him. Every magazine in the world had his face on its cover; every second headline had Dayan in it. Every word he spoke and every gesture he made was recorded and eternalized, and even if it added to his ego, he was still careful with his words and selective and responsible in his actions and statements.

For a while, he contributed time and effort to the rehabilitation of the Army, which, victorious as it was, had suffered a loss of equipment and had to look ahead to the new generation of technological developments. Research and development had priority. The Gabriel and Shafrir missiles went into production; missile-carrying craft and the next generation of combat aircraft were budgeted for and rolled into development. For a few months, Father entertained hopes of "peace around the corner," but even when it failed to materialize, and the Arab League's Khartoum decisions meant an all-out burial of our hopes for peace, he invested all he had in the "living together" option. He was encouraged by the fluent dialogue he managed to have with West Bank municipal and even intellectual leadership. He marveled at the leap in the standard of living, and misinterpreted his own popularity as indicative of a general good-neighbor atmosphere. Friction, strikes, clashes, and demonstrations he regarded as local incidents, rather than as representing a large and deeper dissatisfaction, and even when he realized there were no shortcuts, he did not give up. His search for a common approach paid some dividends, and he was realistic enough to understand that "the West Bank Arabs are not going to regard us as anything but an occupying force, but serious face-to-face talks would bring us closer together. We might remain undivided in our views, but at least we would understand each other." While he was preparing the ground for plowing, and perhaps even sowing seeds of understanding, Egypt and Syria plainly declared: "What has been taken by force will be retrieved by force." While rehabilitating their armies with massive Soviet aid, they supported terrorist operations, mostly carried out from Jordan, where King Hussein failed to put a stop to them.

A major reprisal operation was set for March 21, 1968, against the important terrorist base near Karameh in Jordan. My father could not follow the action personally, for he was in the hospital fighting for his life. Having gone over the operational plans for Karameh, Father planned to take a few hours off and go digging in Azur, one of his favorite sites. Aryeh, his young "discoverer" of sites and aide in excavating, had told him of a limestone mound site. Father dug a hole, to discover it led to a narrow cave entrance, and excited at finding early Bronze Age remains, he pushed his body in, when he felt a light showering sand, and seconds later the entire wall of the mound fell over him and knocked him out. The upper part of the cave gave way next, and buried him alive. As he told us later, he had just enough time and consciousness to think: "I can't breathe, can't move, can't get out. This must be the end." Aryeh summoned help and carefully dug around to expose my father's head and later extracted him fully. His own reflection as he gained consciousness was that, "though he felt pretty awful, it wasn't the end." The Tel Hashomer Hospital doctors were not as optimistic.

Ezer, my uncle, always the bearer of good and bad news, the one-man UN of the family, was the one to call me at home and carefully suggest I should go to Tel Hashomer. Dov was already there, and the sight of my father took my breath away. He was black-and-blue from internal hemorrhaging. One of his vocal cords was severed and he couldn't speak. And some of his ribs and vertebrae were injured. I rushed to his bedside with my mother, and she could tell me not to worry. She knew his willpower and physical strength. She had seen him endure pain and injury and she rightly believed, as he did, that his body would heal itself. When they wheeled the X-ray machine to his bed, they suggested I leave the room. "In case you are pregnant." I was one month pregnant, and this was a strange time and place to let my parents know it.

Father must have been near death many a time, and I had learned to think of him as immune. My inability to stop crying in the corridor of Tel Hashomer Hospital had to do with a horrible new sensation. He was out of danger, and there was no question about it, but he was not immortal. One day, sooner or later, I would be sitting in a hospital corridor and he would cease to be. In self-defense we pre-live the experience of other people's death, as well as our own. I thought of my mother dying, my grandparents, my husband, even my unborn children, but managed to suppress the notion with regard to my father. Now it flooded over me, and the pain was unbearable. It seemed a bad omen that the accident had happened while I was carrying my first baby, as if one generation had to make room and be replaced by a new one.

For three weeks he lay there, in traction and in pain. Impossible to be with, and unwilling to be left alone. He was as demanding as a ten-year-old, and Mother cooked and carried, helped wash and soothe him, to collapse each night, fatigued and drained. When my mother left him at night—and often we left together or with Dov—Rahel would show up for a late-night visit. She didn't have to bring his favorite soup or fruit compote or run errands for him, and if this was a turning point for Mother, a blow to her dignity, and humiliating, inconsiderate behavior on his part, I could, for the first time, understand how rotten she must feel. Being married myself, free of jealousies and in love unshadowed by the slightest suspicion, I began to admire the enormity of her love. How long could it go on and why had she endured it all these years were not questions for me to ask or reply to.

Father left the hospital after three weeks, working hard to restore his speech, and depending on painkillers. He was in plaster, shuffling rather than walking, and was unable to sleep without barbiturates. His body and willpower did defy medical predictions, but for some biological reason, unknown to me, the injury initiated a process of deterioration in his health. He would never, from then on, be totally well.

Assi was happily married. Udi had two children, whom my father adored and doted on, but his marriage proved unsatisfactory and had little chance of lasting. Mother had involved herself with the development of crafts in the West Bank territories, promoting Gaza pottery and Bethlehem lace and embroidery. And I was in that serene state of mind in which the whole universe is compressed into the wonderment of a developing embryo. Physically, I was not well, and had literally to stay put for several months, following a cervix stitching. Dov was an angel, considering the fact that he wasn't half as eager as I was to reproduce, and my parents spoiled me as if I were their newborn baby rather than a mother-to-be. Dov was appointed military attaché to the embassy in Paris, and we decided I should stay and have the baby at home and join him as soon as I could. Meanwhile, we were both studying French and marveling at my changing silhouette. Father resumed his duties, and it was in 1968 that his Rafi Party was reunited formally with the Labor alignment. Ben-Gurion opposed the merger and was now, as a member of the Knesset, a party of one. I doubt whether my father, who still regarded Ben-Gurion as his supreme leader and mentor, guessed or suspected that his own political career would follow the same pattern.

My father was torn between hopes for an early settlement resulting from the war and the realization that, for a variety of reasons, this was not going to be a speedy process. Hussein was licking his wounds and intent upon keeping a calm border, but the Soviets were clearly propelling both Nasser and Assad toward an escalation of hostilities. What was termed the War of Attrition began with a few episodes in the spring of 1968. Nasser declared: "We have reached the consolidation stage," and a few months later: "The Egyptian Army has moved to 'active deterrence.' " "Active deterrence" meant raids, artillery and small-arms fire on Israeli forces, and heavy pounding of our positions along the canal. Soviet experts built fortified positions on the west bank of the canal, and our answer was the Bar-Lev line (General Haim Bar-Lev replaced Rabin as Chief of Staff; Rabin had become Israel's ambassador to Washington), a series of strongholds that dominated the waterline, each covered by a small mobile tank squad.

The miniforts were completed, and communication routes to the rear, which crisscrossed the western Sinai. The Air Force had control of the skies, but the number of casualties mounted and the ceasefire lost all meaning.

In October of 1968, Dov reluctantly left for Paris. He had accepted the appointment when everything seemed positive and peaceful, and when he had to leave, we were again in the midst of a frustrating, costly semi-war. Dan, our first child, was born in Tel Hashomer Hospital on November 25, after nine hours of labor and an easy delivery. Within minutes of his birth, Dov called the maternity ward from Paris, by intuition, and actually heard the baby's first cries. He took the first available flight home, and the first and last time I saw him cry was as he gazed at his own son, bundled in white in the hospital cradle. A healthy, handsome baby, third-generation sabra on his mother's side, who would never know his father's parents and might not even be able to grasp the tragedy that befell them. Mother was with me, and my father came over within a short time to be dressed in a sterile gown and hold his grandson. "Lucky for you, he doesn't look like me," he said, which wasn't at all true. He took from his pocket a little "treasure" in a box. It was an Egyptian soft-stone figurine of a she-wolf. Between her front legs, well protected, stands her cub. It was raining outside and I was exhausted, so he sat by my bed and talked for a while, and I must have fallen asleep, as I barely felt him kiss my forehead and tiptoe away. Three days later I was in Zahala, with Dov and Dan, breast-feeding around the clock and doubting that I would ever be happier.

My parents' marriage seemed to be holding, somehow, accommodating the large cracks that continued to threaten it. My father was preoccupied with his work, and, with a new touch of vanity, with himself. He still found time to indulge in amorous adventures. I knew, as did my mother, of his frequent meetings with Rahel, and when my mother asked or reproached him, she later told me, he had an easy, unkind way of dismissing her as: "She is utterly crazy." He assumed the pose of a man chased, nagged, and irritated by women, Rahel included, and claimed the "affairs" would have been over and forgotten were it not for his partners' insistence, at times followed by actual blackmail, emotional—a suicide attempt—or financial. He was not going to change, he repeated. He did not wish to divorce, he loved his home and family, and he saw no reason to be melodramatic about his behavior. The bond that tied us together was a strong bond of love and respect. My brothers had their own lives, and so did I, but Zahala was home more than ever before. We accepted each other's faults and shared political views and visions for the future. There was no competition among us, as we chose different ways to express ourselves, and if our ambitions exceeded our achievement, we were lighthearted about it. Udi, having served a long term of duty in the naval command unit—a fighting arm reserved for the bravest and fittest—was now set to take over the farm in Nahalal, much to my father's delight. Assi succeeded as an actor and saw his future as a film director, actor, producer, and obviously had enough talent to pursue a career in this field. I had gotten excellent reviews on my last novel, and had a happy marriage and, what seemed to me a unique achievement, a hungry, kicking, healthy son. In our own happiness, we failed to notice what Mother was going through. Father was drifting away from her, not because of comforts found in other beds, not because of Elisheva or Rahel or Dalia, but because, as she put it: "He succumbed slowly to being 'a legend.' " I left Zahala with Dan for Paris, without enthusiasm. I loved Paris best of any European city and had looked forward to getting to know it better with Dov. I was also intent on being a full-time mother, and wanted soon to have another baby, so the physical locale didn't make much difference, but I hated to be geographically removed from the uncertainties and mounting negative prospects Israel faced.

Father was very good, and called us a few times a week on the phone. He ignored security restrictions, or rather set his own rules, and whenever something happened, or was about to happen, he made sure I was among the first to know, alerting me when the Soviets introduced, installed, and put into operation the new sophisticated SAM-3 missile batteries; when we shot down in a dogfight five Soviet MIG 21s manned by Soviet pilots; and when, in February 1969, Eshkol died and Golda Meir replaced him as Premier. Father was not jubilant about "beating the Russians." One of his traumatic concerns had to do with an intensive Soviet involvement in the Middle East which might force the Americans to activate troops on our behalf. He feared, and he knew his history well, that Israel would become a global battleground, and whoever the winner might be, we would be destroyed in the process. He was uncertain as to how he would work with Golda, but his doubts vanished after a short time. He found her straightforward and direct, a change from the vague evasiveness of her predecessor, and she gave him full authority within his sphere of work. There was a sad, long talk when his sister Aviva died, of an accidental overdose, but obviously following a no-return route of self-destruction. He had not been close to her in recent years, and perhaps reproached himself for it. Of the Dayan family, only Shmuel and he had survived, and in 1970, another sad long-distance phone call announced the passing of my grandfather. Shmuel had remarried a few years after my grandmother died, and lived in Jerusalem. We saw him as often as we could, and he was a most loving grandfather and great-grandfather. He worshipped my father and treasured every moment my father gave him of his time, and unlike my mother, delighted in being the father of a "legend." On his deathbed, he said he died in peace, having been privileged to see his son lead our people in the Six-Day War. He was buried in Nahalal, next to my grandmother, Aviva, and Zorik. My father, unable to sleep, and taking sleeping pills, which made him drowsy, explained to me at two in the morning, on the phone, that it was now his turn. His parents, brother, and sister were waiting for him in Shimron; so were the worms. But he intended to do a few things still before he departed.

Although the painkillers and other pills he took blurred only his speech, and not his clarity of thinking, I was extremely worried. My mother felt desperate about it, and appealed to doctors he trusted to force him to stop. He was not becoming an addict, but he was developing a dependence, and it was amazing, to the doctors too, that his decision-making capacity, precise thinking, and physical activity during the day were not impaired. I noticed a new streak of deep pessimism in his talks. No loss of heart, no loss of control, no despair; simply a big question mark, following a series of disillusionments.

He came to visit us a couple of times. I joined him twice on a trip to London, and when our U.J.A. fund-raising trips coincided, we met in New York. He took no delight in travel, and if he had, it became less and less evident. He developed a cynical, impatient attitude toward his own fame, the way outsiders regarded it, and switched moods abruptly. On occasion he would patiently pose with fifty couples for a picture with the "General," or stand on a receiving line in black-tie, saying a couple of words to each of the guests, and —this happened more and more often—on other occasions he would trim his schedule to a minimum. "No reception, no cocktails, no photographs, no dinner. I'll come at the end of the meal, give a speech, answer questions for ten minutes, and leave." My U.J.A. friends—Irving Bernstein, the executive director, and Sy Lesser, the head of the speakers' bureau—adapted fast to his moody fluctuations and found a way to accommodate them. He was still the greatest attracter of audiences, a symbol of everything a Diaspora Jew would wish to be proudly identified with, and although his speeches varied from brilliant to weak, a standing ovation and a flow of contributions always followed.

The War of Attrition lasted almost three years. The number of casualties grew monthly, and totaled 740 dead. The general feeling was one of frustration and futility. We were defending the east bank of the canal, away from pre-'67 Israel, maintaining a static formation, without any obvious operational purpose. A war one ate one, would be removed and Egypt would be motivated to seek further agreements. Secretary of State Rogers and Assistant Secretary Sisco were the intermediaries, but Father encountered opposition within the cabinet. Most of the ministers were against the partial-withdrawal concept, unless and until a full peace was assured in return. Even though it was a cardinal issue, and in fact it was a strategy which he consistently advocated, he did not resign when his suggestions were rejected. He did not resign when Golda and her cabinet overruled his choice for new Chief of Staff. He proposed General Gavish, but Bar-Lev was replaced by General Elazar (Dado), and my father reluctantly accepted the decision. Both concessions were major, and indicative of a state of mind, considering the fact that it was clear that sooner or later Israel would be engaged in another major war, at least with Syria and Egypt. Where our western defense line would be, how strong a motivation would Egypt have, and who would command the Army were not minor tactical issues. He was not growing tired of thinking, planning, or searching for solutions, but he was not up to a losing battle for a "principle." "All I can do is propose. It's a democracy and if I am outvoted I have to accept majority decisions. If I had to resign every time the cabinet disagrees with me, I could not last as a Defense Minister one week . . ." And he was comfortable in his post as Minister of Defense. He still concentrated on "normalization" on the West Bank, negotiated good arms deals with the U.S., and regarded his position as "the highest they would let me reach"— they, in this instance, meant the group of people surrounding Golda Meir, her "kitchen cabinet" and entourage. He still felt like an outsider, and although he worked well with Golda and was extremely loyal to her, he remembered how strongly she had opposed his nomination on the eve of the Six-Day War.

Sadat's "year of decision" passed uneventfully. I came home in the summer of 1971, to spend the last month of pregnancy in Zahala. Raheli was born on June 23, in Tel Hashomer Hospital, to Dan's dismay and my great delight. Dov was a trifle worried about having a daughter, and a very pretty one, but my father quickly reassured him: "It's the best thing one can ask for; look at my daughter!" A statement Dov was in no position to contradict. I stayed in Zahala for a month, and we returned to Paris, a family of four, for one more year. When we posed for photographs with my parents in the garden, I hardly suspected that when I next came home, it would be to my father's house with my mother living in her own new home as Ruth Dayan, the ex-wife of General Dayan . . .

Our last year in Paris was a very pleasant one. I was not confined to bed, for a change, and both children were growing nicely. There was time to take in everything that enchanting city had to offer, and Dov's work took us to Belgium and Holland as well. We were surrounded by warm, caring friends like Alain and Marie de Rothschild, Yaakov Agam and family, the Najar family, and others, and Dov's work produced good returns. When my mother visited with us in Paris in the fall of 1971, and mentioned the possibility of a divorce, it didn't quite register. Both Dov and I, and, as I learned later, her parents too, were strongly opposed to it. It wasn't our lives; we didn't know what the limits of her patience and endurance were; but we felt that if she had managed all these years, perhaps with our help and encouragement she could go on. She didn't seek our advice, and didn't share her reasoning with us. I felt there was a realm of her emotional makeup which I could not penetrate. She knew he would never divorce her of his own volition. She had been through the worst of scandals, some recent ones involving tapings of my father done by his lover and her mother, followed by blackmail. She did not stop loving him, but insisted she loved the Moshe he had been and not the person he was becoming. She talked of his hunger for money, of materialism, of loss of ideals, megalomania. She was bitterly exaggerating, and when she left, we doubted whether any of the things we said had an impact, or whether she even heard.

She didn't want me to come home with her, and on a bleak, rainy day, she simply announced to us on the phone, as did my father, that they were divorced. She moved to Herzlia, to her parents' summer house, took a few things she chose to have from Zahala, and accepted whatever settlement my father's lawyer offered her, after thirty-five years of marriage.

Father sounded apologetic. He didn't beg her to reconsider, but it was entirely her decision, and he respected it. I should know, he said to me, that he would always remain a friend of Mother's, that he had no intention of remarrying, and Zahala would always be home for me and my family. He wasn't convincing, and there was something pathetic about his statements. He was testing me for a reaction, and I wasn't cooperating. I felt very close to my mother but couldn't help resenting her decision. My brothers and I were adults, and there was no "children of a broken home" element to cope with. When I wept for hours, it was with love for both my parents, regretting the weaknesses which made it impossible for them to live together.

Dov and I returned to Israel in the summer, to our new apartment on the twelfth floor of a high-rise building just north of Tel Aviv. While waiting for Dov and the furniture to arrive, I stayed with the children in Zahala with my father. This was my way of not taking sides, though my mother naturally misinterpreted it. Her home, wherever she was, was mine, and I could count on it, come what may. My father's house, which I loved and in which I grew up, felt strange and empty. The garden was as beautiful, my small children filled the rooms with laughter and chatter, but the warmth was gone. Father was quite pedantic in his habits. He washed his teacup as soon as it was empty, and his cupboards were quite neat, as were his papers and medications. His books and archaeological pieces were all in place, but the large living room felt like a museum. He was not lonely but seemed grateful enough to have me around for a short while. His real deep anxiety had to do with the missiles along the canal and the imminent, he thought, prospect of war.

I found a changed Israel upon my return in the summer of 1972. The post-war affluence was badly digested. Unskilled Arab manual laborers replaced many Israeli workers, and since Hussein did not take the hand of peace extended to him, people quickly assumed the role of occupants in the territories, dismissing the possibility of ever returning them. The war of attrition over, there was talk of a status quo that "one could live with," and "peace" was no longer a top priority. Father contributed to this by declaring that he'd rather have Sharm el-Sheikh without peace than peace without Sharm el-Sheikh, and he encouraged the settlement of Israelis in the northern Sinai. Jews bought cheap land in the West Bank, and Orthodox religious youth settled where they claimed their roots were, in a land belonging to others but promised their ancestors by God. The Palestinian issue was a time bomb, with a delayed fuse simply because we were too concerned, and for good reason, with our southwestern and northern frontiers.

I realized my father was meeting daily with Rahel, at her place, and was not surprised when he finally suggested that we meet. He was nervous about it, said again that he had no intention of remarrying, added that she didn't want to get married either, and we made a date for afternoon tea in Zahala. Before her arrival, he said, almost pleading, that he hoped I would like her. "She is a fine woman, and I love her. There is nothing in the world that would please me more than that you two get along." I tried to be lighthearted, saying: "Whenever Mother asked you about her, you said she was crazy"—but he didn't think that was funny. The meeting was cool and pleasant enough, and it was obvious that we both made an effort in order to please my father. We were worlds apart— in looks, in manner and temperament, in values, and in priorities. Her love and my love for my father were then and for the next nine years our one strong common denominator. The rest demanded a certain effort. There were times I liked her, and many moments I felt extremely uncomfortable in her presence. She had enough intuition not to stand between me and my father, and I was wise enough to know the limits of my domain. If the competition between mother and daughter is natural, the same when applied to a stepmother is distasteful. My father's health was far from good, and I felt he reached the stage of being a one woman's man not one minute sooner than his body forced him to.

The changes that took place in Zahala, in his life and behavior, and finally in his priorities were not sudden or even immediately noticeable. I was not inclined to attribute them solely to Rahel's influence. Israeli society as a whole underwent a change for the worse, because it lost the strength to resist the chance of an easy life and skin-deep temptations. I supposed the sorry changes in my father's way of life and attitudes resulted from a similar weakness. If Rahel was at all to blame, he wasn't uncooperative, not my father . . .

They were married in June 1973, four months before the miserable, heroic, and traumatic Yom Kippur War. On Saturday, October 6, we were in Ein Hod with the children. It was Yom Kippur, and I preferred to be in our country house, where the imposed silence of this holiest day did not feel like a threat. There was no telegram this time, but an early phone call from my father. He simply said: "War will break out today. I suggest you and the children stay in Ein Hod; it's safer. And Dov should get to HQ as soon as he can." The road was empty when we drove back, all of us, to Ramat Aviv, but for a few Army vehicles headed in both directions. The radio silence, customary on Yom Kippur, was broken, and a general mobilization was announced. Dov went to his office. I prepared a small bag of supplies in case we had to go to the shelter, and tried to keep the children busy. Both my brothers were mobilized, and I talked to their wives. At 2:05 p.m., Syrian aircraft had crossed our air space and Egyptian rafts were crossing the canal while Army bases in the western Sinai and Sharm el-Sheikh were being bombed. A siren sounded, but I couldn't budge. War had started.

Not unexpected, not unprepared for, yet a total surprise.

T W E L V E ⚭

1 9 7 3 – 1 9 7 7

The Yom Kippur War is, by now, so overloaded with "what-if's" that it has become difficult to distinguish between facts and wishful hindsight thinking. Unquestionably, Israel was mistaken in rejecting, or not pursuing to its end, Father's suggestion to pull away from the Suez Canal. He had argued, but had failed to convince the cabinet, that an interim agreement by which we would withdraw ten or twenty miles might remove the immediate incentive for an all-out war. Navigation would then have been resumed in the Suez Canal, the canal-zone cities would have been rehabilitated, and some of the pressure would have been removed. Father was basically a believer in normalization, in the canal zone as much as in the West Bank. Where daily life is possible, where trade and agriculture flourish, where children go to school and shops open in the morning, the cannons and missile batteries are of secondary importance. If peace could not be achieved, in direct talks or by fighting another war, peaceful coexistence would be the best starting point toward it.

But we stayed on the eastern bank of the canal; Russia persistently armed, equipped, and trained the Egyptian and Syrian forces, and in mid-'73 the question was not whether but when.

In May 1973, Father held a meeting of the General Staff and issued orders for the IDF to be prepared to confront an all-out attack by the end of the summer. Extra funds were allocated to speed up the acquisition of tanks and artillery; and detailed plans were worked out for both the Northern and the Southern Commands (dubbed Operation Chalk and Operation Dovecote, respectively), based on the assumption that there would be an advance warning of twenty-four hours, a long enough period in which to reinforce the troops on both fronts with mobilized reservists.

A hot summer went by, and though a few alerts proved false, by September there were ample grounds for mounting anxiety, especially regarding the Syrian front, dense with sophisticated anti-aircraft missiles. In a meeting at the end of September, my father stated his anxieties and was partly satisfied with an increase in the number of tanks along the line. He remained uneasy, however, and when he visited the front on the eve of our New Year, meeting representatives of the settlements, he decided to strengthen the line even more. At the next General Staff meeting, he defined the situation in extreme terms: "On the Jordanian border we have civilian settlements but no enemy. On the Egyptian border we have an enemy but no settlements. On the Syrian border we have both. If the Syrians get to our settlements, it will be calamitous." Golda was out of the country, and as soon as she returned, on October 3, a meeting was arranged. Father reported intelligence data indicating massive reinforcements, and the small gathering—attended by two other ministers, the Chief of Staff, the head of the Air Force Staff, and the acting intelligence commander—accepted the Chief of Staff's recommendation that Israeli armor and artillery remain at peak strength, and buttressed the Air Force to high alert.

The intelligence representative said that, although the Egyptian and Syrian forces were deployed in offensive positions, he did not think they were about to launch an attack. He suggested the Egyptians were preparing for their annual maneuvers. A twenty-four-hour advance warning still seemed a reasonable possibility, and on the basis of all reports, there was no good cause to believe we would be deprived of such a warning. During the night of October 4, however, Soviet passenger planes evacuated Russian families from Syria and Egypt, and on October 5 a C-alert, the highest, was ordered for the Army, and full alert for the Air Force. The High Command post was activated; military leaves were canceled, and preparations were under way for a full public mobilization. Yom Kippur was to begin that evening, with traffic and radio broadcasting coming to a complete halt at sundown.

The evaluation of the Chief of Intelligence, that noon, was that an attack was not likely. General Elazar, the Armed Services Chief of Staff, accepted this assumption, which matched the American evaluation as well. Father disagreed, pointing out that the Egyptians and the Syrians were in a position to start a war within hours. He requested that the Prime Minister be given authority to approve the mobilization of reserves if she should be asked to do so the next day. Next day was Yom Kippur, and convening the cabinet might be impossible on short notice.

Yom Kippur, the Day of Atonement, is the religious day of reckoning. A solemn day of fasting, begging forgiveness, and prayer. My family, my parents and my grandparents, never observed Yom Kippur in the customary way. We didn't attend services, or ever fast, and if we begged forgiveness, we did so privately. God was absent from our lives, as from our education, and the imposed quiet that descends on the land had a disquieting, enervating effect on us all.

When the siren sounded the alarm at 2 p.m. on October 6, I was alone with the children and decided not to go down to the shelter. I looked out of the window at a clear blue sky and felt quite safe. The possibility of the hinterland, the Tel Aviv area, being hurt or touched in case of war seemed preposterous, and the sight of squadrons of fighter-bombers flying north along the coastline added to my sense of security. At that very moment, the Egyptian and Syrian artillery had started shelling Israeli positions. In the south, Egyptian infantry and armor crossed the canal eastward, along its entire length. In the north, using artillery barrage for cover, Syrian tanks moved to attack. Our infantry on both fronts was outnumbered roughly ten to one. A similar disparity existed in armor and artillery. We were numerically inferior in the air, and we faced a sophisticated ground-to-air missile grid which put us at a further disadvantage. The gap in quality was narrowing, as the enemy infantry was highly motivated, deriving extra security from effective anti-tank weapons and the new Soviet shoulder-held antiaircraft missile.

All radio systems were activated now. The streets were bustling with cars and military vehicles and men, still in synagogue attire, hurrying to their units. After eight hours of fighting, the Chief of Staff reported that the situation was under control, considering the circumstances . . .

The Egyptians had hurtled the water obstacle, but the Syrians did not break through our lines in the Golan. The Golan could be reinforced within twenty-four hours, significantly, but the southern front was miles of desert away, and although a sizable armor force was on its way, it could not be fully activated before October 8. The Air Force had to be deployed full-force in the south, to fill in the time gap. For the first time since the War of Independence, in many years of war, we were on the defensive. Our morale, self-esteem, and self-image were traumatized, and it would take courage and self-discipline to face reality and act according to it, rather than ignore and smooth out an unfavorable scenario.

At the end of the first day of fighting, my father found himself isolated in his anxiety, and on a different wavelength, and thus proposed a course of action different from what his colleagues, both in the Army command and in the cabinet, advocated. The Chief of Staff's appraisal satisfied their wishful thinking: the GOC Southern Command estimated that we could drive the Egyptians back to the west bank of the canal very soon and resume control of the Sinai. After evaluating the events of the day, my father predicted that the outcome of the next few days' battles would be different from the more optimistic forecast offered by the Army command. He figured that if a large number of tanks reached the Golan Heights during the following day, the Syrian momentum could be checked. Father remained deeply concerned about the canal zone. He evaluated the enemy as "good troops, using good equipment and fighting with determination." He doubted whether we could interrupt the canal crossing for the next couple of days, and predicted a grim, costly result of the following day's planned battle and the Air Force involvement. He proposed to retire to a second line to fight the enemy from a belt twelve miles east of the canal, and to mass our strength before striking again. He spoke of the heavy blow we had suffered, and the powerful gains the Egyptians had achieved, with relatively little damage and minor casualties.

When he was through, there was silence and discomfort. The cabinet members did not like what they had just heard, and had no means or data with which to bridge the gap between the two contradictory readings. The easiest thing was to attribute his assessment to a softening of the heart, a loss of faith, or his habitual, ingrained pessimism. If ever the term "lone wolf" fitted him, it was on that night. He went to the "pit," the Army war room, which was humming with activity, but he sensed that cool and balanced thinking was lacking there as well. In the Air Force war room, he listened to the next day's operational plans and wasn't satisfied either. He believed the Air Force should concentrate on destruction of armor and on air support to ground forces, rather than attempt an attack, as was planned, on the missile sites and airports. At 2 a.m., twelve hours after the beginning of the war, Father went to his office for a couple of hours' sleep. What upset him most, as he recounted later, was a gap in credibility between the high command of the Army and himself. The Commander in Chief, who had been appointed over his objections, and several other commanders, were, he felt, covering up for themselves, and ignoring his evaluation of developments at all levels. For the first time, Father was not entirely at home with the IDF. He was the political authority, able to give operational advice but not orders, and, contrary to 1967, he was not an integral part of the team, no longer its commander and father figure. He found out, painfully, that the organizational and technical arrangements intended to repel an enemy attack on the canal strongholds had not been carried out, the tank detachments were too far to the rear, and weapons and ammunition were often below the required level. The fighting spirit was supreme, but very heavy casualties were inflicted on us as a result of numerous mishaps.

On the following morning, I reported to Tel Hashomer Hospital and within a few hours was back in uniform, on duty as an officer responsible for volunteers in Israel's Army hospital. I made arrangements for the children to be taken care of, and took short breaks to visit them at home whenever I could. The civilian sick were evacuated, the helipad prepared, and soon we did not need false or true reports from the front, debated on the radio or the TV. We had the sad and depressing firsthand accounts from the men brought in on stretchers.

The eyeless and the burnt, the paraplegic and the bandaged, told of bravery, of self-sacrifice, of unprecedented heroism, but not of victory. The first few days of this war had an aura of loss and futility, and for the first time, the strong supportive link between the front and the civilians was shattered. People didn't know, and what they found out they didn't wish to believe. The official reports were vague, and at times encouraging, and deep, sad anxiety settled in the cracks between reality and rumors. Reports of eyewitnesses arriving in the hospital clashed with comforting official statements, and I myself walked among the infusion bottles and the questioning eyes in a slight daze. I talked to my father once or twice in the first few days, and he had no reason to soothe me or to try to cheer me up. It looked bad; there were obstacles and defeats; and he was tired. He was not broken; he was not hopeless. He estimated we needed a few more days to launch a counter-attack. He even mentioned with confidence the eventual victory, but he was cautious about the way to get there, with fewer casualties, at a lower price. Any attempt earlier and without precaution, he regarded as too costly. He absorbed the first defeat quicker than the others, and was perhaps more confident than others about the end results. He saw no reason for speeding up events at the highest cost, to reach an objective that we could reach with confidence a short while later. My brothers were all right, he assured me. So were my cousins—all in combat units. He summed up his predicament with a degree of sadness rather than with anger. He was not in control; people heard what they wanted to hear . . .

On Monday, October 8, a counter-attack was launched prematurely. It took a while for the Southern Command to realize that just about everything had gone wrong, and the day ended with our line, in some cases, farther back than it had been before. My father had accumulated the anger and frustration I had hoped he would, and was only sorry it didn't happen earlier. He flew to the Sinai after midnight, summed up the day as "wasted, frittered away, leaving in its trail disappointment, casualties and retreat," and demanded to replace the GOC of the Southern Command. His own candidates were Arik Sharon, who commanded a division, and Chaim Bar-Lev, the former Chief of Staff. He told the Chief of Staff he thought a counter-attack should be launched when the Army was ready for it, and suggested that the nation be told the truth. Top priority should be given to the acquisition of arms and ammunition from the United States, and the Golan fighting force should be ordered not to retreat, to fight to the last man and not give an inch. He believed that only then should we concentrate all our forces against Egypt. Father saw Golda early in the morning and got her approval and blessing for the new strategy—the appointment of Bar-Lev and the bombing of military targets in the Damascus area. They agreed that Golda herself should fly to Washington to procure understanding support, and the supply of arms so badly and so urgently needed. But other members of the cabinet still viewed my father as an incurable pessimist, and attributed our problems to some weakness in his character, and not to the objective military situation.

Father was front-hopping everywhere. He did not want to rely on reports, air photographs, or maps, and he kept to his custom of inspecting the battle from the battlefield. The lower the echelon, the more comfortable he felt, inspired by the personal courage of others, and inspiring the local commanders with his own. He felt comfortable with the divisional commanders, who had fought under his command before, and he respected their judgment. He wore Army fatigues without badges of rank, and a windbreaker, a Vietnam rear-echelon crumpled cloth one that served him well, and dust goggles to protect his good right eye. On the fifth day of the war, October 10, he intimated that he had stopped fearing the Arabs might overrun our territory. The President of the United States approved, on that day, most of the electronic equipment Golda had requested, and some additional planes, and agreed, as a matter of policy, to replace and restore whatever matériel we lost in battle. The Soviets carried out a massive airlift, transporting arms to Syria and Egypt on October 9–10, and the U.S. began a military airlift on October 14, which replenished our stocks and clearly boosted our morale. On this October 10, Father visited the southern Sinai and managed a short meeting with Assi, who was serving as a heavy-mortar man with a paratroop unit. He proceeded to Southern Command HQ and made it clear that a counter-attack would be undertaken as soon as the Syrians were dealt a hard blow. He thought about and talked of capturing territory west of the canal. In the north, he clarified the final line that would put Damascus within our artillery range. Always having been considered a pessimist, or at best a pragmatist, my father could not now be accused of imaginary, farfetched, wishful-thinking objectives.

On October 13, a successful counter-attack was launched which brought our lines a few miles closer to Damascus. On October 15, Father flew south to be on hand for the start of the battle for the crossing of the Suez Canal. Arik Sharon, whom my Father judged to be our best field commander, was in command of the attack, and Father was not going to follow this battle from the pit or be satisfied with a report afterward. Arik launched his assault after preparatory aerial bombing and artillery shelling of the crossing area, at Deversoir.

When the armor reached the canal, my father talked to Sharon on the phone, asking for a jeep to come for him and drive him to observe the crossing. His heart was with Danny Matt, the paratroopers' commander, who was preparing to cross on rubber rafts to establish a bridgehead in "Africa." Arik was apologetic. The access road was blocked; the crossing sector was under heavy fire; and all he could do was share with Father the sights he beheld. The advancing tanks silhouetted against a sky lit in red, reflected in the water of the Great Bitter Lake.

The roadblock prevented the mobile bridges from reaching the water during the night, but a decision was made to cross anyway. At 1:20 a.m. on October 16 came the good news: "Danny Matt's force on the water." And soon after: "Paratroopers on the west bank of the canal." It wasn't Jerusalem; it wasn't the materialization of a lifelong dream; but it was more than a turning point. This toughest of wars, against all odds, would end in a tremendous victory. For all the reasons and elements my father had advocated and fostered for decades. Quality, initiative, imagination, and a good measure of caution paid off. Where the price was very high, it was due to commanders deviating from these elements.

By dawn, rafts were ferrying tanks to the west bank, and three major battles were in progress to secure the east-bank crossing sector, to open an alternate route for the bridges' equipment. Bren's division thrust north at the Egyptian Second Army on the access road; south, to prevent the Third Army from sending reinforcements; and west—the Chinese Farm battle—to secure a wider corridor to the bridgehead, linking with Arik Sharon's units. Father stayed in the south. These battles were in the best tradition of the Israeli forces. Commanders and soldiers alike fought with all their might and defeated an enemy that had much at stake and fought well.

The battles lasted the whole day and into the night, extracting a heavy toll, but it was clear that they won us the war. The road was opened, and the heavy bridges reached the canal. By then, a full brigade was establishing itself on the west bank, and my father left with Arik for the crossing point. Rafts and rubber boats were bringing men and equipment from east to west under a heavy barrage, while the engineers were preparing the ground for the projected bridgehead. Reaching the other side, my father preferred to walk rather than ride an armored car. Arik's forehead was bandaged, as he had been hit in the crossing, and the two walked among the weary troops, along the cultivated land and the Sweet Water canals. The war was not over, but it had been won.

For a few days after the initial crossing, the combat continued. The Egyptian forces were deployed for defense, and the initiative had passed into our hands. Negotiations between the Americans and the Russians began feverishly to call for a ceasefire resolution in the Security Council, and we had to act with speed to make sure that the final line suited us strategically and included some vital positions. On October 22, Radio Cairo announced that President Sadat had accepted the ceasefire, and in the early hours of October 23, Syria announced its acceptance. In fact, however, it was on the twenty-fourth that the ceasefire was implemented, and by then several last-minute positions had been captured, including parts of the city of Suez, the port of Abadiah, and Jebel Ataka in the south, giving us an unbroken hold on the Ismailia–Gulf of Suez line, and isolating the Third Army and the city of Suez. In the north, Mount Hermon's Syrian positions were recaptured in the early hours of October 22.

The fronts were quiet, but the battle for life and recovery continued in the wards of Tel Hashomer Hospital, where I worked days and often throughout the sad nights. Hospital life during a war acquires a pace of its own, being the recipient of casualties of battles —lost and won. Surgeons operated around the clock; relatives and volunteers crowded the corridors. The emotional burden was heavier than the medical, and each hospital bed harbored a story of human struggle for survival. There were days when the entire meaning of the war lay in the success of a skin graft, or the failure of an eye-saving operation. Time was measured by infusion bottles and blood transfusions; decisions in the surgical wards weighed tons; and the strain and tension taxed us all. I saw my father several times, and we talked as often as we could. Our lives ran parallel, sharing an agony and a final victory, and there was no need for many words.

If I indulged my readers and myself in somewhat detailed war accounts, I did so because no sooner was the war with the Arabs over than the "Jewish wars" began. The question of "what had happened to us," referring to the outbreak of the war, was on everybody's lips and minds, and accusations, bitterness, and blame crept into most of the answers. To avoid being seen as an apologist, I preferred to give my father's account of the events, from his point of view, as expressed and written by him. In his account there was no apology, and in his own eyes he was not responsible for the desperate, disastrous events of the first days of the war.

Many people—at given times, "the people" themselves—thought differently. The wave of victorious pride that lifted him high in 1967, attributing to him personally achievements which at times he deserved by proxy only, plunged now to a depth of malice and hurt self-pride and turned him into a scapegoat for all the mishaps that befell us. "Dayan lost his nerve"; "Dayan suffered a nervous breakdown" were statements rather than rumors, and when some of the statements bordered on hysteria, there was no way to deny, discuss, or examine them. Bereaved parents wanted an answer, war victims demanded explanations, generals reproached each other, and the appointment of an inquiry commission, chaired by Supreme Court Justice Agranat, did only little to calm the heated spirits.

I watched my father in his pain, and he did not try to hide it. He was not equipped to handle hysteria and avoided blaming others. Again, he stood alone, backed only by Golda, who rejected his offer to resign, and waited patiently for the results of the inquiry commission. He was busy negotiating the disengagement agreements, in which Dov participated as well, and with the surge of protest movements, he was quite concerned about the coming elections. To remain as Minister of Defense was basically his wish, but the decision was not entirely in his hands. The Prime Minister, the party, the electorate, and the outcome of the Agranat Commission, would all help determine his political future.

Golda Meir was reelected to lead the party by a large majority, and she made it clear that she intended to offer my father the Defense portfolio in her next cabinet. The party went along with her decision with mixed feelings. Many of the Labor delegates carried placards saying: "Dayan go home," but they refrained from opposing Golda. The electorate reduced the strength of the Labor Party by five percent, giving it seven fewer seats in the Knesset (49 out of 120).

The elections were over, but the public was not pacified. It demanded a change, a change in policy and in leadership, in concept and in personalities. The Yom Kippur leaders were stigmatized, and if it fell to my father to be the symbol of the mishap and the target for demonstrators, it would soon spread to others. Golda sensed this. She presented a new cabinet, with my father and Peres representing Rafi in it, but could not stand the pressure from within. Her own ministers suggested that the nation had lost its confidence in this "war government," and she subsequently resigned in April 1974. This automatically meant the resignation of the whole government. A new cabinet was sworn in, with Yitzhak Rabin as Prime Minister and Shimon Peres as Minister of Defense. My father was out, with a certain feeling of relief for a while. He did need time off, and made it very clear that he was not retiring from political life. The Agranat investigation had found no fault in the way he had carried out his duties as Defense Minister; most of the blame fell on the military echelons. Four intelligence officers were relieved of their posts, including the Chief of Intelligence. General Shmuel Gonen, who was in charge of the Southern Command, was suspended from active duty, and the commission recommended that the term of office of Lieutenant General Elazar, the Chief of Staff, be "terminated." The full Agranat report was not made public, but my father was satisfied with the partial publication. His integrity was never doubted, but it did help him resume some degree of peace of mind. The emotional damage, the piercing pain he felt when widows and bereaved parents shouted "Murderer" at him, could never be removed; it added a fresh scar to the many his body had received, an undeserved scar that was never to heal.

I stayed in the hospital for a few more weeks, as long as my services were of use. Accusations against my father were reaching me through the back door, in the mail, in staring eyes and occasional remarks, as well as in hostile media attention. The hospital was my escape, and making myself useful was a form of therapy. Dov was away much of the time, in "Africa" with Arik for a while, and in the Egypt–Israeli KM 101 talks, which resulted ultimately in a disengagement agreement. War had brought us together in 1967, and war kept us apart now, and we took for granted that national events and demands always have priority over personal whims and desires.

I did miss him and, even more, needed him, and the fact that words and sentiments that needed to be said and expressed were left in abeyance in his absence only added to my chagrin. The hospital was soon able to accommodate civilians, and among the patients in the internal ward was David Ben-Gurion. On December 1, 1973, he died of a cerebral hemorrhage. My father visited him before the end, but the old man was only partially conscious and could not communicate. Although Father had not been close to Ben-Gurion during the last few years of his life, his death orphaned him in a way. It is difficult to define their relationship as friendship, yet the old man's absence only emphasized my father's aloneness. After seven years in the Defense Ministry, Father was a civilian, contributing occasionally to parliamentary life, and resuming his archaeological pursuits. From center-stage he was tossed to the sidelines, with time on his hands to write, speak, and meditate, things he was capable of doing very well, even though he did not find them totally satisfying.

Did I reproach him in any way, he asked me when we sat together, as we often did, on a sunny winter morning in the garden.

"Not more than you reproach yourself," I said in a low voice. He was hard of hearing and definitely selective in what he took in. There was compassion and love in my eyes, and he knew how deeply I felt for him during and after the war. "I only wish you would get angry more often. Calm and acceptance don't suit you. When you are on edge, you may seem less 'civilized,' but you put up a better fight."

He sighed. He wanted to change the topic. He told me, not for the first time, how he went to Golda twice and offered to resign. How she wouldn't hear of it. He was formalizing something while I was speaking about a missing spark. He spoke of Agranat, I spoke about Moshe Dayan—only it wasn't the same Moshe Dayan. For a while now, there had been a screen between us, thin to transparency, but spreading and thickening like a cataract, protecting and comforting him like a cocoon in the wrongest of time for incubation.

Since he had married Rahel in the summer of 1973, we all played according to new rules. A dimension of bliss had been added to his life, and who can blame a man in love. He adored her with all his heart, marveled at her beauty and charm, boasted about her cultural assets, and was carried on Eros' wings to heights of delicate romance, with gratitude and at times disbelief. He was the frog kissed by a princess, the farm boy dwelling in a palace, the primitive being enlightened.

History often blames women for everything, from taming to castrating men. Samson and Ulysses, King David and Antony, felled, wooed by women's charms. I doubt that any man is altogether an uncooperative "victim." Men don't succumb unless they are ready for it, and willing. The fact was that my father's priorities and life style changed in the last ten years of his life, perhaps reflecting weakness or vulnerability, obsessive materialism, and eventually egocentric self-pity. These were changes by choice, options offered and taken voluntarily. If Rahel was the catalyst, the guideline or prompter, the substance must have been there all along. The timing was most unfortunate, and this may have not been accidental either. The Yom Kippur War caught us all off-guard. Bathing in self-indulgence and carrying the self-image of 1967 supermen to un-toward extremes, we were not ready for the earthquake that struck us. My father's personal state of euphoric contentment didn't con-tribute to the sharpening of his senses, though I doubt that it, in the slightest way, affected his behavior and decisions once we were swept into action. My own feelings were a mixture of love for him, admiration of her uncompromising devotion, occasional nausea at the physical expression his new life took, and many deep regrets when counting the losses inflicted in the process of change.

His good healthy sense of humor disappeared where Rahel was concerned, and I had to remind myself to be on guard. Objectively, it was funny to hear her calling him "darling" in English, see him change to "work" clothes when gluing pottery, in order to protect his new made-to-order outfits. The charm that came with exasperat-ing carelessness, sloppy appearance, lack of tolerance, and devilish mischief was fading away, to be substituted by new mannerisms, tamed behavior, cashmere sweaters, and Dunhill suits.

Rahel, in an interview, did mention the changes and took some credit for them. The fact that I didn't appreciate intimate dinners of delicacies and wine, candlelight and background music, as factors that "humanized and opened him" may be my failing. I didn't regard the reading of a few contemporary best-sellers, the watching of "Armchair Theatre" series, and an occasional concert as "intensive cultural life," and acquiring a wardrobe labeled Céline, Hermès, Gucci, and Cartier did not necessarily mean "exquisite taste." It was skin deep, it made me nervous and sorry for him. And Dov, who could see through it all, insisted it was none of my business. And it wasn't. The luster was real, the self-indulgence was genuine, the woman lived for him to love and be loved, and if he found comfort and delight in lobsters and white wine, admired the gifts she received, and rested on a pink velvet sofa, it was not my concern. His quick and brilliant mind didn't soften; his political courage didn't fail him or us when he applied himself. As for his seemingly new preoccupation with making money, it may have been there, dormant, all along.

I kept my resentments to myself. Zahala ceased to be an open, welcoming home. The new furniture was in great style and cold. I found myself being told to cut a piece of the butter and put it on my bread plate, rather than grate it from the top, and being asked to call before I visited, so "I could have undivided attention."

Rahel was dominant in his life, and I had to learn to live with it, and while I was envious, I wasn't jealous. I couldn't live her life or enjoy her style, acquire her priorities or share her conventionalities. I was envious because his whole being was taken up, and I had to look for loopholes, for myself, the children—an intimate anxiety I wanted to share, a corner of love I wanted to indulge myself with. If I abided by the rules, I could have some of it. Still, the natural, spontaneous father-daughter behavior was gone.

It was only when he died that I realized I hardly knew Rahel. What I saw was a reflection of my father, his aura engulfed them both, and I thought of her only in terms of his personality—good and bad. Our own independent small talk was also related to him one way or another, and it lacked the confidence which could fill the gap between Rahel my father's wife and Rahel the woman she independently was and is now. I never bothered to find out, and I may have been remiss, what was left of the totality that was "they," once he was removed from it by death.

Whether or not Rahel provoked laxity in him on the eve of Yom Kippur, she helped him endure the horrendous personal aftermath of it, and probably prompted him to concentrate on writing his autobiography.

I myself was about to begin work on a new novel when my father called to say he wanted to make me an offer. On the phone, in brief sentences and confident of a positive answer, he suggested I collaborate with him on his book. Only the first few chapters, he said—background, childhood, Nahalal, right up to the War of Independence. He quickly quoted the sum of money he would pay me, and added in good humor: "For you, it's nothing. You know it all, you are a writer, and I'll add my own flavor to your version." I said I had to think about it, mumbling something about authenticity and credibility. I also believed he was an excellent writer himself and had no need . . . I had to think.

He said he would call back soon for an answer. He had diaries and material relating to the rest of the book, but he'd rather I did the first few chapters. The answer was going to be negative when he called again. I didn't think it was a good idea. It wasn't merely "background" but the beginnings of psychological processes which underlined his entire life. It wasn't a story to be told but an evaluation of factors contributing to his making. And besides, I was about to begin work on a novel. After I said all this, he answered very simply. If I was not going to do it, he wouldn't either. Nobody else would. The book would not be written. There was nothing pathetic in his words, just a statement of fact. There was no way I could refuse, and we met the same day to decide on an outline.

My son Dan started school, and little Raheli was in a nursery school in our own building. I had free mornings, and my own writing would have to wait. Father was a slave driver. The first few pages took a long time, but when he declared his satisfaction, I produced more, and faster. He did give it his own touch, made me expand on a few points and do some more research, and was soon happily writing the rest and, in fact, the major part of his thick volume, *Story of My Life*. The obstacle I helped him overcome may have been only technical. As a writer, I know all too well the sheer horror the page numbered 1 inspires. The experience, which meant daily contact and some emotional proximity, may have helped me to begin and end my own novel, *Three Weeks in October*, once my pages of his book were delivered.

My mother was still with Maskit, working hard to keep it from going overly commercial, and concentrating on the artistic, fundamental adaptation of folklore and artisanal wares to the consumers' needs. Since my father had married, and there were now two Mrs. Dayans, she avoided the social scene and managed not to meet with Rahel, seeing my father on rare occasions, on family matters. She held her position with pride and integrity, developing a sense of humor about the many misunderstandings that resulted from this duality of names. Rahel encountered similar incidents and with a smile answered, "No, I am not with Maskit," while Mother explained that she had nothing to do with the PX where Rahel was working. "Thank you," Rahel would say, "but Yaël is my husband's daughter. Ruth is her mother"—whenever she was offered compliments on a speech I made or an article I wrote—mostly abroad, where people were less knowledgeable about the intricacies of the Dayan double setup. I had to react to "I met your mother, she is gorgeous, you don't look at all alike," and understand they meant Rahel, whose own daughters—delightful, intelligent, and very pretty —were often approached about or reproached for something I had done. I, in turn, had the "I understand your sister Orna has remarried" remark, and would explain I had only brothers and a good number of sisters-in-law. And so it went, without aggravations or bickering.

My brother Udi was divorced and remarried, had another child, and worked on the family farm in Nahalal, which was now his. His first wife and children moved to Beersheba, and my father still felt extremely close to them. They needed him, he figured. They were his first grandchildren, and he was going to see to their needs, a few while he was alive (this was principally my mother's task in his eyes) and, as he promised, in his will—a subject which was not discussed other than in this frame of reference. Assi had two children, but his marriage had its ups and downs, and he finally divorced Aharona, which was a sad moment for me, since I had shared a happy wedding with them.

My own life acquired a contented routine. Dov and I cultivated friendship and love, not treading on each other's toes. At least, he accommodated my liberties. I was loyal, easy, and satisfied with my domestic duties, and he let my mind, and too often my mouth, run as free and wild as I chose. I often acted in haste, in contrast to his measured, logical steps. I would come to half-baked conclusions, and I spoiled the children rotten. I treasured my mobility and traveled often—to the United States for the U.J.A., or to Europe on vacation—and when he couldn't join me, or didn't wish to, there was no hurt or annoyance. I cooked well, the house was tidy, I needed no outside help, and his was always available. We visited Zahala together, with the children, at least once a week, bringing a pot of borscht, a tin of crispy cookies, or a tureen of chopped liver, and these visits were warm and cordial. I think my father liked Dov and esteemed him; he was dear to the children and patient with them for the short duration. If Dov was not enthusiastic about Rahel, and I felt on her part the discomfort of being exposed, it was never expressed in words or behavior. "Civilized" was the word, and in their different ways, both embodied that concept.

Shimon Peres was Minister of Defense, and a good one, my father thought. The Army needed rehabilitation from the inside, without political interference, and options were open to a new generation. Peres concentrated on the arms, electronic and air-industries build-up, and gave these technological aspects a tremendous boost. He worked well with the military staff and gave them the adequate freedom to form new doctrines. The Arabs and Israel were licking the deep wounds caused by the last war, and a sense of futility that stemmed from it was perhaps the first element in a search for peace.

Peres met with my father occasionally, kept him informed, and at times sought his approval and advice. When in '76, the Air France plane and passengers were held hostage in Entebbe, my father called me a few hours before the liberating assault took place and hinted with pride, respect, and optimism at what was to happen later that night. Jonathan (Yoni) Netanyahu, the young commander of the operation, was killed in the rescue, and my father's reaction to his death reminded me of his admiration for the war heroes he trained and fought with, and the deep emotion he felt for them. He may have been a civilian, a highly paid lecturer, a collector of ancient pottery (which by now he traded, selling at high prices, with his autograph on the pieces). He was almost fit for the best-dressed-man list, and he could perhaps tell the difference between a Bordeaux and a Burgundy; he was bored in the Knesset; and his social life was aglitter with the wealthy, the diplomats, and high society. But when the commando unit was flying through the silent night to liberate the hostages at Entebbe, when the frontier was threatened by terrorists, and the candle of good old heroic patriotism had to be rekindled, his heart and mind and all his faculties were undivided, putting aside everything else, where they really belonged.

There was no way to think he would sink into obscurity, or not resume a central place in our political scene. He was no longer a wild forest fire, but was reduced to a log in the Zahala fireplace, warm and cozy. He was not the wild prairie horse, but pulled a cart behind him, slowed with the weight of worldly goods—and it was impossible to predict what or who would set the spark aglow again.

In the spring of 1977, the final price of the Yom Kippur War was paid by the Labor Party. It lost the elections, and Menachem Begin, for thirty years the Opposition leader, was forming a government headed by his Likud right-wing party. On Saturday, May 7, 1977, a day after my father celebrated his sixty-second birthday, Begin telephoned Father in Zahala and offered him—a reelected Labor MP—the post of Minister of Foreign Affairs in his cabinet.

THIRTEEN ❊ PEACE

Some knowledge of the Israeli political system is required to understand the shock effect Begin's offer to my father had on all of us. Menachem Begin had led the Opposition Likud Party for thirty years. The gap between his right-wing ideology and Labor's philosophy was such that, at the time, Ben Gurion ruled out the possibility of coalition with him in most vehement terms. Only in 1967, on the eve of an all-out war, was a national unity government formed to share the burden of a possible disaster. The Israeli electoral system of proportional representation has contributed to perpetuating the gap between the two major political groups. We elect a party, the party nominates candidates, and the allegiance of the voter is to ideology, policy, and to some extent the personalities heading the list, but we do not vote for a person, and those elected are not directly responsible to us, the electorate.

If I wanted Rabin or Golda, I had to accept Dayan and Peres and dozens of others who were on the same list. Lines were seldom crossed, and occasionally, a small independent list would make it to the Knesset on the merit of one or two individuals. In 1977, the former Chief of Staff, General Yadin, a renowned archaeologist, presented such a list and captured a large number of votes, mostly the votes of ex-Laborites who were fed up with the thirty-year Labor rule. The Likud emerged as the largest group and was able, for the first time in our history, to form a coalition government with Yadin and the religious parties, placing Labor in the opposition and entirely changing the political map. The 1977 vote was one of protest and punishment. It was a vote of "we've had enough," an expression of anger and disgust and rather naïve hope for a new era removed from the guilts of Yom Kippur and the collapse of a system that had failed to deliver.

My father was on the Labor list—Rafi having merged back into the mother party in the late sixties—and intended to sit in the back benches of the Opposition. If Labor had won, there was little, if any, chance that he would have been offered a cabinet post. He was not popular with the new leadership, and in spite of the Agranat Commission's report, was still stigmatized. It was heartbreaking to drive along a cement wall on the outskirts of Tel Aviv on which, in red paint, I would read: "Dayan, the architect of military cemeteries." Indeed, in making him an offer, Begin ignored all conventions. It was intuition and a touch of political genius that must have prompted him to offer my father a ministerial post in his government. It was certainly against the advice and judgment of both Likud and his Labor supporters.

Father asked Begin for time to reflect. The offer had already been made public, and the popular reaction was violent. The press labeled him an opportunist and a traitor; demonstrators hysterically shouted: "The murderer should not inherit," and even close friends or supporters turned their backs on him with bitter disappointment. My first reaction was similar. I had voted for Yadin, and basically believed a change was welcome. I thought the political system was rotten and hoped for eventual change in the electoral system, but until this change took place, I found the crossing of party lines distasteful. I had no doubt that my father's qualifications for Foreign Minister were better than any other candidate's, but I thought that if he chose to join the coalition, he should return his seat to Labor. I did not think beyond that, and I knew very little of the new postwar overtures which made a peace agreement with Egypt more feasible than ever before. I was upset, and expressed my thoughts in a letter which was delivered to Zahala on Sunday morning. I don't know whether my letter upset Father or, more probably, irritated him, but I felt he should know what I thought. What I do know is that he ignored it, and his two-day shuffling of the pros and cons terminated in his acceptance of Begin's offer.

All the immediate or short-term considerations pointed to a negative answer. The long-term, the future prospects and options which he was wise and courageous enough to consider, determined his ultimately positive answer. He believed we were facing decisions that would determine our final borders; he believed that, four years after the Yom Kippur War, and after thirty years of bloodshed, there was an option for real peace. He thought he had what it took to handle these new options and trusted he would have enough independence and freedom, even in a Likud government, to act without having to make concessions. He felt—and I was the first to admit that he was right and that I was totally wrong—that he could not dismiss such an opportunity out of loyalty to a party. He remained Labor, he declared, even if the party rejected him, but the state's good always had priority over party politics.

On June 20, 1977, I took my children to Jerusalem, to the Knesset, to see my father sworn in. It was an unpleasant, noisy, interrupted session. Fanatic Laborists screamed when he got up to speak, and his first few sentences could not be heard against the shouts of anger and mockery. He stood there like a rock, unbending and brave, and imposed his integrity and superiority over a turbulent House. He was as lonely as he ever would be, and I felt the need to share those moments by being present and offering my humble support. It was my way of admitting I had been wrong in criticizing his decision a few days earlier.

My uncle, Ezer Weizman, was sworn in as Minister of Defense. He was campaign manager for the Likud, and it was not presumptuous on his part to claim full credit for his party's victory. If he, too, had doubts concerning my father's nomination, he was forced, and later privileged, to tolerate the "brother-in-law" image, rather than stand center-stage with Begin alone. Arik Sharon was Minister of Agriculture. Father, who admired Sharon as a military genius, did not have a good word to say about his entrance into the political scene, and this is a discreet understatement. Yadin was nominated Deputy Prime Minister. The party I voted for, which had

generated high inspirations as a new liberal center, eventually failed
to deliver, or even function adequately.

My father, seated across the table from Begin at the cabinet
meetings, was not surrounded by friends or political supporters. He
never treated the political arena as a socializing medium, and being
more experienced than most of the new ministers gave him a sense
of seniority. Begin had complete authority over his own colleagues.
His choice of my father, accompanied as it was with having to
accept Father's preconditions on several major issues, was not a
subject for criticism or dispute. The immediate objective was the
proposed Geneva conference, chaired by the U.S. and the U.S.S.R.,
where, according to Security Council Resolution 338, peace negotiations were to commence between Israel and the Arab countries.
United States President Carter took a personal interest in speeding
up the preliminaries, and my father was busy preparing the policy
papers should such a conference take place in the near future. His
senses, his intuition, his cerebral capacity—for forty years, tuned
to the constraints of warfare, sharpened and molded in the variants
of the battlefield—were now centered on the supreme and coveted
final fight, the battle for peace. As in war, it was a win-all/lose-all
proposition, depending on intricacies of phrase, originality of thinking, and flexibility of policymaking. Embarking on peace negotiations was not a deviation or even a comeback for my father, but a
logical continuation and culmination of everything he had devoted
himself to up to now.

A certain routine was resumed, yet there were differences. The
"office" now meant Jerusalem, but my father preferred to commute
rather than occupy the official Foreign Office residence in the capital.
Zahala was his castle, and the short car ride to Jerusalem didn't
trouble him. The bodyguards, drivers, secretaries had never really
disappeared while he was out of the government, so there wasn't a
sudden reappearance of an entourage to intrude on his privacy.
Yossi, his Ministry of Defense legal adviser and all-around trouble-
shooter, was appointed Director General of the ministry, and Father's
name, which was hardly absent from the newspapers during his
"private years," again captured headlines all over the world. In many
ways, he was the darling of the media. When one thought all was

reported and covered and told, to saturation, he still managed to produce the one unexpected item, the half-phrase, the new key word, or a facial expression that was still "news." Rahel was in her element. Matching accessories and the perfect hairdo, dinner-table conversations with ambassadors and the right remark at cocktail parties, the elegance and charm at home and on their official travels —she was the perfect Foreign Minister's wife and must have made it easier for him to cope with the less exciting or boring aspects of his new position.

The house changed, too. My parents' bedroom was annexed to the kitchen, which was wallpapered and spacious now. My own room became my father's bedroom, smaller for cupboards being put in, and sparsely furnished. My portrait, painted by Boris Chaliapin in livelier-than-life oils, was for a while in the living room and later in Father's bedroom, together with framed photographs of his mother, his sister, and Rahel. My brothers' room, extended to include a walk-in closet, was now Rahel's bedroom, and an additional guest toilet room was added to the house. Later, a "dream bathroom," as my father defined it, was built for Rahel, marble and femininity combined, to Father's delight, and he insisted on showing it to guests, taking pride in his ability to supply his beloved wife with "luxury like in the movies." A well-deserved change from where the family started many years back, when we had to walk to the back-yard lavatory in Nahalal, carying a lantern. New carpets, new vitrines for the collection, new paintings on the walls, some wall-to-wall carpeting, and a few well-chosen pieces of antique furniture. All in good taste, on the cold side, like a well-manicured hand or a fresh hairdo in which no rebellious curl is allowed a mischievous angle.

The garden still had its dream quality, my father's obsession with the height of shrubs and free air passage giving it an added dimension. He was forever climbing ladders, raising branches, and anchoring them up against their natural botanical tendency. Father's own corner, where he glued his pieces together, tested with acid their authenticity, and looked his shabbiest best, remained unchanged. I still had access to that corner, and felt intimate and protected when we had the chance to share a brief hour there.

He welcomed my decision to resume my studies, and I had a now-or-never feeling about it. Raheli, our daughter, began school in the fall of 1977, and Dov was in his second year as Deputy Commissioner of the War College, having served as military spokesman during the two years following the Yom Kippur War. I took courses in the Open University, which enabled me to do most of my studies at home, attending a biweekly afternoon session with a tutor and working at my own pace. My choice of courses was obvious only to me. Biochemistry, biology, genetics, and zoology. A minor compensation for not having studied medicine, and a major effort on my part to keep up with developments in this sphere, which I regarded as an overwhelming breakthrough. Languages, literature, art, history, I felt I could study on my own. The science that fascinated me was a new world. Learning it meant activating a dormant sector of my brain, and I was not satisfied with popular literature on the subject. I listened to lectures with awe, and treated the laboratory like a shrine. Dissecting animals and using an electronic microscope filled me with infantile pleasure, and good results on exams gave me a new sense of pride. I would never be a working scientist (although I would always continue to study seriously), but I felt privileged to be allowed a glimpse into the secrets of creation, rather than remain an ignorant tourist in the palaces of discovery of the elements of which we are composed.

My mother's house assumed its own character. It was crowded with objects, paintings, books, handmade artifacts. It was always spotless but had the warmth of a lived-in house even when it was new. My grandparents' house was an annex to hers, and they spent more and more time there, until they rented out their Jerusalem apartment and started living full-time in Herzlia, north of Tel Aviv. Mother, unwillingly, accepted the fact that I was not about to punish my father (and mostly myself) for having remarried. If I was to remain a part of his life, I had to accept it on his terms. The most important relationship he had was with Rahel, to the exclusion of whatever or whoever didn't find a positive modus vivendi with her. My brothers visited Zahala occasionally, behaving well, though often grumbling afterward. They were never deprived of attention when they wanted it, but they seemed to want it less, finding the new filters in Father's life artificial and not too pleasant.

In October 1977, widows and bereaved parents gathered—the fourth year—in front of the house in Zahala to demonstrate. Those who still held him responsible for the Yom Kippur War dead felt doubly cheated, seeing him tread the corridors of power. Father had good reasons to be less susceptible to the hurt inflicted on him by the silent accusations. We were four years removed from the last war, and he had cause to believe that it would take less time to achieve a peaceful solution to some of the tragic conflicts in the area. Furthermore, in his own estimate, it was the Yom Kippur War that prompted, at least in Sadat, a search for new options at the conference table, rather than risk another defeat in battle. His assessment was based on a series of secret meetings in August and September with the Shah of Iran and King Hussein of Jordan, and, most important, hosted by King Hassan of Morocco, with Dr. Hassan Tuhami as personal representative of President Sadat.

The Morocco meetings were conducted in the best spy tradition. Father, disguised with a mustache, a wig, and dark glasses—a routine which amused him but irritated his good eye—changed cars, exited through back doors into garages, and was driven to remote airports in Europe, to be flown to Rabat by private jet. The very first moments with Dr. Hassan Tuhami were cold. Both men were excited and sent feelers out which served as icebreakers. Both men avoided lengthy, flowery introductions. The subject was peace; compromises had to be made; both countries preferred some form of direct negotiations, followed by American or international sponsorship; and Egypt was reluctant to admit the Russians "through the back door" of a Geneva conference. The central issue was the returning of the Sinai Peninsula to Egyptian sovereignty, and it was clear that the era of interim agreements was over. For the first time, a full and normal peace treaty was discussed in detail. King Hassan helped relax the atmosphere. The hospitality was lavish, in the best Oriental style, from sumptuous meals to carpeted bathrooms with pink towels and a supply of bottled scents.

There were catches. Dr. Tuhami insisted that President Sadat could not meet with Begin before the Sinai was returned. Egypt refused to be the only Arab country involved in negotiations, and it was obvious that the Palestinian claims and the status of Jerusalem would not be treated by Sadat as minor and marginal issues. Father returned to Israel to report and to dispel the rumors concerning his "disappearance." Rahel was in the United States (where they were both headed when he "disappeared" in Brussels on the way to the airport), and he called me from Jerusalem to suggest we meet in Zahala.

The refrigerator was empty, the water heater disconnected, but we managed to produce a cup of tea and some dry cereal. It was too late and he was too tired to worry about physical comforts. He was leaving at dawn for New York, and our meeting was brief and warm. He did not talk much, but what he did say was enough. He did not turn into an optimist overnight, but his intuition was positive. "Something good may come of it all . . ."

My father's reputation as "the only man in Israel who can talk to the Arabs" was not a result of his soft-spoken, easy manner, or of the shrewd, almost frightening image he had acquired as a war hero. His Arabic was basic, and all serious negotiations were conducted in English or with the help of a reliable translator. The Arabs didn't feel too comfortable in his presence, and there was no kissing and hugging, yet it worked. What my father had was what really mattered, authority and credibility. They trusted his word, and he, theirs, and he didn't have to pretend. He did have respect for the Arabs. There was no hatred, and there was a genuine desire to search out the possibilities of living together. He was never condescending; he had a special warm feeling for the Arab farmer and for the wandering Bedouin, and he respected their traditions. In his ruthlessness as a stubborn, tough negotiator, there was always a streak of deeply felt solidarity. He knew when to be flexible, because he realized when their ability to compromise stopped, and in fact he did not turn negotiations into bargaining. His effort was directed at finding a formula that would be beneficial to both sides.

The ball was rolling now, and Sadat's proposal to visit Jerusalem and address the Knesset gave a tremendous boost and momentum to something that was already in the works. This did not detract from the total surprise and sense of disbelief when the actual date of Sadat's visit was announced. On Saturday, November 19, 1977, at eight in the evening, the Egyptian President's Misr 0-1 landed at Ben-Gurion Airport. Like hundreds of thousands of others, we were at home watching the historic event on television, both ecstatic and very nervous. Every minute detail had significance, and we sat close to the screen, as if otherwise we might miss an expression or a word. The national anthems were played; the guard of honor stood proud and erect; the long line of dignitaries, Arabic and Hebrew alike, paraded, their faces mostly set in joyous smiles mixed with an occasional suspicious stare. Were we dreaming? Was it a momentary illusion, a cunning trick, or an act of bravura which would have no follow-up? The excitement was overwhelming, and even Dov, whose pessimism almost matched my father's, allowed himself a moment of hopeful joy.

Sadat himself, at his best, had a hypnotic, engulfing warmth. His gestures were expansive, his frequent smile was like sunshine, and his handshake a wholehearted expression of generosity. An enormous crowd greeted the cavalcade of cars at the entrance to Jerusalem. In one of the cars, my father rode with Butrous Ghali, his Egyptian opposite number. The night was dark, and Father tried to describe the beautiful scenery to Ghali. He talked of the Philistine coastline and the Judean hills, of the ancient trade routes and the fertile valleys, of old Canaan and the city of King David. I doubt that Ghali was able to listen to the description fully, for he kept emphasizing the tremendous risk Sadat was taking. He had embarked on this initiative alone, opposed by all the other Arab countries.

Sadat, in his speech to the Knesset the next day, and during the working session that preceded and followed it, reduced the nation's state of euphoria, and caused it to fluctuate from a wishful high to a dangerous low. It was obvious that we could expect no miracle. Barriers which consist of hatred and gravestones, offensive wars and wars of attrition cannot, and perhaps should not, be removed overnight. Peace, like war, had its price, and negotiating the price and the securities to safeguard it was to be a long process of gains and compromises. Sadat had flown over the barrier, and the psychological impact of his act was enormous. But the patient removal of the barrier's components and the laying down of new foundations for peaceful coexistence had only just begun.

Less than a year later, in September 1978, the Camp David Meeting produced a comprehensive paper titled *A Framework for Peace in the Middle East*. Following Camp David, numerous standstills and deadlocks seemed insurmountable, and only on March 26, 1979, was the final Egyptian–Israeli peace treaty signed by President Sadat and Prime Minister Begin at the White House in Washington, D.C.

These sixteen months of negotiations, varying in intensity, were described in detail by my father in his book *Breakthrough*. A little of what he went through emotionally can be discerned from the fact that he dedicated the book "To the soldiers of the Israeli Army, the living and the dead." What he endured physically, it is difficult to describe, as those were the years when his health began to deteriorate. It was obvious to him that his years were numbered, and in the lifelong dialogue with death he might be a loser sooner than expected. As in other wars, he was short of time, and there were things that had to be achieved at any price, before the ceasefire.

There is irony in the fact that I always thought of my father as a healthy, strong man. Since he lost his eye, I doubt that he had an entirely painless day. The image of health stemmed from his unusual ability to endure, ignore, and dismiss pain, his general ignorance concerning the mechanics of the human body, and a stubborn refusal to give in to physical limitations which would create dependence on medicines, doctors, diet, or a routine other than the one he chose to lead. For the first sixty years of his life, there was nothing frail about my father. His arms were blessed with Herculean muscles; he was of medium height; and in his fifties—though he had a tendency to put on weight—he was still light on his feet, strong in his grip, and seldom complained of pain or discomfort. His body grew used to a meager amount of sleep, and he managed to take a nap, warrior style, between things, in the car or on a short helicopter flight. He learned to live with severe headaches—with or without an occasional analgesic—and joked about his slightly defective hearing. With one eye, and one good ear, there were many things he'd rather not see or hear . . . A renowned neurologist explained to my mother in medical terms his great need for sex as being related to scar tissue formations on his brain, resulting from his head wound. I doubt that my father saw insatiable sexual activity as something "unhealthy."

His general health and his strong torso stood him in good stead when he was buried under the sand while excavating. The doctors were amazed at the speed of his recovery, to which willpower and determination were major contributors. Still, the months in a cast, the traction, the internal bleeding, the damaged spine and ribs, and the severed vocal cord reduced his body resistance, and ten years later, still well despite a most irregular life, Father himself began to notice (and to ignore) signs of far from perfect function of his organs. A stomach ulcer developed; irregular bowel movements, hemorrhoids, the vicious cycle of gastrointestinal troubles—not helped by an uptight nervous system, a series of chronic allergies, and Father's strenuous way of life.

Being scientifically ignorant, he fluctuated from a complete trust in doctors—if you have to cut, cut and get it over with—to a primitive trust in his own sensibilities, which resulted in self-cures and his not confiding in doctors when he thought they were needlessly prying and overanxious. He was not afraid of surgery; he wanted to know the truth; but as he was not motivated by fear of death, his own health was not paramount in his mind.

When he mentioned a difficulty in breathing, having climbed a steep hill in the heat of summer, we would have one of those silly conversations: It seems that my heart is not as strong as it used to be. Did you see a doctor? To which he would say either that they don't know anything or yes, and I'm all right, and anyway I have no time or desire to "take it easy" as they suggest. He did play cat-and-mouse, as when the pains in his chest grew worse and it was obvious to him that his heart was malfunctioning, and he shut himself in the bathroom, leaned against the wall, spread his arms, and waited for the throbbing to ease. He did not want to alarm anybody, and when he told family and doctors, he almost took pride in his success, having managed to keep a major event a secret.

What first irritated and later alarmed him to the point of self-pity and serious depression was a slow loss of eyesight. His right eye, his only eye, became the barometer of his health. As if he knew that it reflected the rest of his body. The less he could see, the more dependent he became. The best eye surgeons in the world tried and failed, and it added to his edginess, fatigue, and fatalism. He was Hercules, he was Samson, and he was Job. His sandglass could not be tilted over and over, and his calendar for two years had had the word PEACE inscribed on it in big letters as his single major objective. It was a desperate race between two delicate wicks, the flutter of the flame for life and the short, easily extinguishable candle of the striving for a stable peace with at least Egypt.

Sadat declared in November '77 that the October '73 war was the last war. In May '78, Sadat said that the October war was not the last war between Israel and the Arabs. In December '77, Father met with Dr. Tuhami in Marrakesh, and in the same month a summit meeting in Ismailia was a disastrous failure. In March '78, President Carter blamed Begin for failing the peace effort, and in July of that year, a meeting between my father, Secretary of State Cyrus Vance, and their Egyptian counterpart was held in Leeds Castle in England. The Leeds Castle conference, free of the mounting tensions between Begin and Sadat, offered a minor breakthrough and in fact paved the way for the Camp David conference.

The obstacles were all too clear and rather repetitive. Egypt insisted on linking the signing of a peace treaty to a solution to the Palestinian problem. Such a solution meant, as far as they were concerned, a total withdrawal from "all occupied territories" and "self-determination" for the Palestinian people. They would not, at that point, sign a separate peace agreement with Israel. The gap between the positions was wide. We insisted that we were not foreigners in these "occupied territories," and we wanted an agreement based on coexistence. Israel proposed autonomy (self-rule) for a period of five years, the question of sovereignty of the areas to be discussed later.

My father was trying to separate issues. Peace with Egypt could be signed and implemented, and the status of the West Bank could be decided later. Details which were in dispute, in Leeds Castle and later in Camp David, he thought, should be handled separately, rather than keep the ball from rolling.

Bilateral letters, appendices, prologues, preambles, and the like could technically solve major emotional issues through the right legal phrasing. Words and synonyms should be instruments for a breakthrough, rather than impede or arrest it. Peace, coexistence, security, normalization had their dynamics, and once they were established, the paperwork concerning the disputed phrases would be forgotten. Leeds Castle broke the impasse, and a date was set for a summit meeting at Camp David—September 1978.

Each country sent a nine-man delegation, and for thirteen days the leaders, ministers, and legal advisers of the three countries were locked and isolated in a concentrated effort. My father wrote that "the summit meeting at Camp David was the decisive, most difficult and least pleasant stage in the negotiations. All three parties had to resolve agonizing psychological and ideological crises in order to reach an agreement. It meant abandoning long-held traditional viewpoints and outlooks and taking up new positions." My father was best equipped to do just that. He was probably the only one able to help Prime Minister Begin abandon his own "long-held traditional viewpoints."

I can only quote others, in saying—as Secretary Vance did—that Father's contribution to the Camp David accord was not only major but indispensable. Many of the experts on these pressured, turbulent thirteen days go as far as to suggest that if it hadn't been for Dayan, there would have been no accord.

Kissinger, who impressed my father "by his wisdom, his broad-ranging knowledge, his prodigious capacity for work and his ability to set things in perspective," said: "War was Dayan's profession, peace was his obsession . . . History will record him as a principal architect of the peace treaty with Egypt . . . A major frame of the Camp David accords."

He was obsessed. Not at the expense of cool, clear thinking, but to the point of enlisting all his faculties, his experience, his aspirations, and his visions. The Fathers and the Kings, the Prophets and the exiles, his own ancestors and his children and grandchildren, were all in the back of his mind. The fertile Jezreel Valley and the Negev Desert, the streets of Old Jerusalem and the cliffs of Judea, the shelled bridgehead in Africa and the vulnerable coastline of Tel Aviv, never left him in the thirteen days of near-disasters, deadlocks, and great triumphs. On September 17, in the East Room of the White House, the Framework Agreement was signed. Late that night, back in his hotel room, my father thought of that evening as "one of the most momentous of my life. I have traveled a long road from the battlefield to the peace table . . . The toughest stretch of that journey had been the years since that fateful Yom Kippur until the White House ceremony I have just attended . . ."

When we met at home he was not at all jubilant. Acceptable principles had been established, a timetable for withdrawal and normalization was set, a proposal for an interim solution to the Palestinian problem was satisfactory to both sides, but a long and difficult journey still lay ahead, and there was more at stake now than ever before. We had yielded a great deal and put our trust in promises and securities, an enormous risk which had to be proved well worth taking.

The next round of negotiations took place in Washington, at Blair House, for a few weeks during the month of October. My father headed the Israeli delegation; Kamal Hassan Ali, the Egyptian; and Secretary Vance, the American. On the agenda was the proposed draft of a comprehensive peace treaty, accepted by both sides as a basis for discussion.

The obstacles were many, and not new. The priority of the Israel–Egypt treaty over Egypt's treaties with Arab states (obliging her to join them if they should go to war with Israel). The linkage of the peace treaty with the Palestinian question and the establishment of diplomatic relations and an exchange of ambassadors between Egypt and Israel—gradual, linked to the pace of withdrawal, at its first phase as we demanded. A few weeks and seven drafts later, the Israeli delegation returned home. The government had to approve or reject the Blair House agreement. Rejection meant that Israel would be blamed for the failure to achieve peace, and Begin threw his full weight into its support, in spite of the good number of objections he had.

On October 26, Begin and Sadat were awarded the Nobel Peace Prize, an award that was very farsighted, as the following four months seemed to lead away from the coveted peace into a maze of legalistic and practical deliberations and a dead end. Cyrus Vance traveled to Israel, demanding more flexibility. What for us were major issues, Carter termed "minor gaps," and the U.S.–Israel rift grew. On Christmas Eve, 1978, a year after Sadat's visit to Jerusalem, my father met with Egyptian Prime Minister Mustapha Khalil in Brussels, where Secretary Vance joined them. The dialogue was candid and open; priorities were reestablished; and Khalil took a clear message home with him. Egypt could not be part of the common front of our adversaries and at the same time maintain peaceful relations with us. If they chose peace, they would have to compromise on their position in the hostile Arab world. In February 1979, I celebrated my fortieth birthday. Mother had been living in Washington, for a year, working as a consultant with the Inter-American Development Bank, and Father was packing again to attend Camp David II. It amused me to think of myself as a woman of forty, as there was a suggestion of middle-age maturity in those words. Father said it was ridiculous, he could never think of me as a "forty-year-old lady," and my grandmother gave me a delicious surprise lunch, attended by friends I loved and was close to. Dov was of the opinion that birthdays were best ignored, and I didn't in particular feel like stock-taking. My children were not babies, but I was still a young mother, and I was healthy and well. I still felt, if it mattered at all, that there was more ahead of than behind me. A thought that was comforting until considered in relation to my father. He was only sixty-four, and there was nothing I knew that could make me think of his life span in terms of years rather than decades. Yet an element of sadness burdened my heart whenever our frequent but short meetings ended. As if time was running short. As if all the unsaid would not have a chance to be said; as if items on the agenda of life might not be tackled, ever. If there was a time when I repressed any feelings, these were the ones. Premonitions, superstitions, vague suspicions were never part of my pattern of thinking. I had no faith in a deity, and neither did he. We treaded a common ground of facts and beliefs, shared a few values, and handled the tangible well. This new sensation I had, whenever I left Zahala, or even at the end of a phone conversation, I had no way of sharing or even admitting to myself. I was no longer anybody's little girl, but I was a mother and a daughter and dismissed thoughts of the three-generation cycle as anything but solid-rock and "forever."

If I reproach myself now for not having succumbed to premonition, for not having grabbed a larger handful of what was left of time and love, I do so because of my loss, not his. He was satisfied with the silences. He was not anxious to pursue a love he took for granted, and was comforted by the fact that the token he had given me was never in fact used and never had to be put to the test.

I was expanding my knowledge and vision and with it my tolerance and patience. He was narrowing his, in everyday matters to the point of exasperating pettiness. The brilliance of analysis, the originality of thinking, and the courage mingled with humor which he displayed on national affairs, historic or current, disappeared in small talk, in melancholy discussions of electricity bills, the cost of living, the wages of maids and gardeners, future financial security. He had treasures, of spirit and mind, and even possessions, and he was counting his pennies, tolerating dull company for free lunches, and saving for a rainy day. He knew as well as we all did that our welfare state took good care of its elected leadership on a rainy day. When he talked, with a deep sigh, about the cost of twenty-four-hour private nurses, whose services he might need one day, he knew very well that these services were all paid for by the state, and yet he was constantly preoccupied with it. Everything he said, or did, or sold or exchanged, had a price tag attached to it during the last years of his life. He charged for interviews, for speeches, for autographed oil lamps, and indirectly for his and Rahel's company. Fortunately, the one sphere that was free, where he didn't spare himself one bit, was his public life.

Camp David II was not a major success, and Egypt's growing extremism was partially backed by an impatient U.S. President. In March 1979, Carter accepted the invitation to visit Cairo and Jerusalem. It was clearly a last effort to end the negotiations on a positive note. The conflict remaining was not over substance and was caused by two technical problems. The participants were tense and tired, and the mood was deflated accordingly. The cabinet repeated its objections and arguments, and Carter sent word of his exasperation. He was packing to leave the next day, empty-handed. Before going to bed, Begin agreed to let my father try another session with Secretary Vance that night, provided he did not commit himself to anything. Only the cabinet could make a final decision.

The result of that night talk was an addendum to the disputed Appendix C of the treaty. The last hurdle was cleared, and Father could take personal credit for the dissolution of another crisis. Sadat, too, succumbed to the last-minute pressure, and Carter would fly back to Washington assured of the success of his mission. It was arranged that the joint signing ceremony would take place in Washington, at the White House, on March 26, 1979, at two in the afternoon.

As it happened, I was lucky. For years, I had come to the United States on the last two weeks of March for U.J.A. fund-raising meetings, and I waited eagerly for my father to suggest I join him in Washington for the ceremony. He did, calling our ambassador to tell him, and it was left to me to decide whether to cancel a meeting in Easton, Pennsylvania, scheduled for that evening. I could do both, I figured. I could attend the ceremony at two and, rather than attend the White House dinner that night, address the Jewish community of Easton. In Washington I was a witness; in Easton the event depended on my appearance, and a glamorous social function should not affect my priorities. I arrived in Washington the evening before —as it happened, from Mexico—and the Israeli actor, Chaim Topol, met me at the airport. We drove to the Hilton Hotel, where I had a room and where everybody else stayed. Ezer and Reumah were there; and my mother, who still resided in Washington; and the Israeli delegation, complete with friends and cousins and well-wishers and whoever was able, with some pull, to secure an invitation to the ceremony or the dinner or had to be satisfied with lobby handshakes.

My father was alone. For some reason, he objected to the wives joining their husbands on this occasion, and set an example (unfollowed) by leaving his at home. We had the happiest reunion. He was still busy with last-minute details. He was not yet celebrating, he said, and there was one official document missing—a letter confirming the arrangement on oil supplies, prepared that night with

Vance. He would have dinner with me, he said, provided it was the best meal in town and he wasn't paying . . .

It was a very good meal indeed, and Topol was paying, and what was best was Father's almost relaxed mood. He was full of charm and humor, letting go after months of accumulated tension. He approved of my decision to go to Easton to speak, and was delighted that I would still be able to attend the ceremony. Back in the hotel, we talked for a while. He made a few calls and had to attend a last meeting before he went to sleep. We talked about Nahalal; he mentioned his parents, his sister, and his brother—all dead—and wondered whether Udi would stay on the farm, and would his children . . . Maybe your son, he suggested, will not have to fight a war, though I doubt it . . . He spoke very warmly of Secretary Vance; he asked about my mother and was satisfied to hear that she would attend the ceremony the next day with her sister. He kissed me good night, and though he looked tired, there was the old flicker in his eye, expressing, almost boasting, a personal achievement. We met for breakfast, joined by a lady friend of Rahel's who had flown down from New York, and we went back to his room, where he had to look at some papers. He took off his shoes and was relaxing when a secretary called him to the phone in another room. I looked for his slippers, and when I found them, I burst into laughter. There were two shoes, each the left slipper of a different pair . . . He gave me his best crooked smile, managed to get his feet into them, and proudly walked the Hilton corridor. What the hell, an architect of a peace treaty doesn't have to be perfect about packing his slippers . . . There was still hope, I figured.

The ceremony itself was laden with emotion. Behind the fence, a group of Palestinians demonstrated against Sadat, and I took my seat, not far from my mother and aunt, looking at the Egyptian ladies sitting a few chairs away and wondering whether they, like me, were thinking about their fathers, husbands, and children.

The speeches included the obvious quotations from the Bible and voiced hopes in prophetic terms. It didn't matter. The substance lay not in the words spoken but in the past tragedies and the future prospects. Carter, Sadat, and Begin signed; the cameras clicked; and many eyes were misty with tears. My father was seated in the front row, and he turned to look for me. I made my way through hand-shakes and hugs and reached him in time to sneak to a side entrance and get into a car and back to the hotel. We had a snack away from other people, and then he was asked to join Begin and the other members of the delegation for a toast, and he left reluctantly. A private plane was waiting for me at the airport, piloted by one of the members of the Easton community, to make sure I'd be there on time, not risking commercial connections.

The next day, I called Father in Washington. He declared the evening gala dinner a bore, said he was exhausted, and reiterated his satisfaction—not thrill—with the final agreement. Take good care and give yourself a rest, I said—needed and well deserved. Neither of us could know that cancerous cells were multiplying wildly in his colon. Malignancy tumors didn't pay heed to his theory that the best way to cure a disease was to ignore it.

FOURTEEN ✖ TWO

YEARS IN MY

FATHER'S DEATH

When he returned from a tour of the Far East, in May, Father had a thorough checkup. The condition of his lungs and spine was unchanged. His heart muscles were weakening and his pulse irregular, but this did not explain his anemia and iron deficiency. In June, after a series of gastrointestinal radiological examinations, the doctors diagnosed a growth in the colon. Only after surgery and pathological tests would doctors define the tumor as malignant, but there wasn't really any doubt about it. My father claimed he had suspected for a while, and rather than use fancy medical terms, he said simply: I have cancer, you mean. When can you operate . . .

The operation was set for three days later, a Sunday, and Rahel called me to come to Zahala. We sat in the garden and she said—there was no other way of putting it: Your father is going to be operated on for a tumor in the colon. When I insisted, and the word "cancer" was uttered, we both had tears in our eyes, and during the conversation which followed, I was in a state of emotional upheaval unknown to me before.

I was knowledgeable enough. I had seen people survive, fight and beat cancer; the word did not have a threatening primitive effect on me; and yet in my father's case it sounded like a death sentence. Not an immediate one, not the following week or anything like that, but rather a sensation of doom. I said to Rahel that I'd tell my brothers, and walked over to the corner of the garden where my father was busy washing some stones. I managed to fight away my tears, but my voice trembled and I couldn't speak. He must have realized the state I was in, and tried to sound lighthearted. "Come on," he said, smiling, "I'll surprise you all. The operation itself is not complicated, and provided it hasn't spread, I'll soon be back to work. Who needs such a long intestine, anyway?"

It didn't work. He showed me the stones he was handling. They had perhaps been used as playthings. He saw in each of them an animal, or found a resemblance to an eye, a nostril, a crack where a mouth should be. They did not seem manmade to me, just a co-incidence of nature. He wasn't sure himself, and there was no way of finding out, but he liked the idea. He was deviating from the precise to the mystic. "What's death anyway, a celebration for the worms. The inevitable, and you know I never feared that moment . . ." "Your feeling is not contagious," I said. "Don't you think of your death in relation to the living? Those who are left behind?" Only when he touched my shoulder did I notice I was crying. "I'm not going to die, not yet, and you're a big girl . . . Here!" He showed me a stone that looked like millions of others. "Doesn't it resemble a lion head?" I nodded and touched its cold surface, wiped my eyes dry, and walked away.

His reconciliation with death was so far-reaching that it stopped just short of becoming a death wish. "Death was not the termination of life, but somehow its peak, a continuation," he wrote, an idea which would satisfy a believer in life after death, which my father was not. I returned home, to my children, and told my family about the operation. I didn't think of it in dramatic terms. There was no reason he shouldn't emerge from it better than before, and indeed, when I entered his hospital room the next day, he had a tranquil expression on his face, and even the smile of a winner. The tumor was local and isolated. There was no doubt—even before the final laboratory results arrived—that it was malignant. It was removed with twenty centimeters of colon, high enough not to inhibit normal functioning of the bowel. There seemed to be no metastases, a con-clusion which was later confirmed by the scans. Father could resume work within three weeks. I visited him in the hospital every single day. At times, he greeted me with a warm, loving smile, and on other occasions, a few, he did not wish to be disturbed but granted me a few impatient moments. He showed my children the scars, explained to them the cardiology monitor he was attached to, and was proudly on his feet very soon, sooner than the doctors expected or wished.

When I visited with my brothers, Father showed us the healing scar, explained to my brothers how well he was, and how lucky, and unexpectedly felt the need to talk about his will. At that time he was talking about a previous will, one which did not deprive us of a fair share, but he chose to remark: "I wrote a will, and I am allocating in it a penthouse I own, to Udi's big children." We must have nodded approval, and as he was well and his prospects were good, there was no reason to pursue, react, or even comment. The three of us found the subject distasteful.

After the signing of the peace treaty with Egypt, Dov was appointed chairman of the Israeli delegation to the Israeli–Egyptian Joint Commission. The treaty had to be implemented, the various phases of withdrawal supervised, the multinational force installed, and the Sinai demilitarized—different sectors in different degrees of demilitarization. His job took him to Egypt often, and he was busy weaving the delicate tissue of coexistence in peace, together with his Egyptian colleagues. The peace agreement became a daily reality. "Cairo on the line"—when the phone rang; Egyptian coins in Dov's wallet; his clean shirts packed in plastic bags from the Mena House Hotel, and boxes of sweets from the Groppi patisserie.

For Dov, a visit to the hospital—other than the maternity ward when I had the children—was an excruciating ordeal. He visited my father with me on several occasions, and was grateful when Father talked business to him, as if they were having a regular office meeting. On July 15, three weeks after the operation, my father attended the weekly meeting of the government and was back in his office. He was still weak and hoarse, his vocal cords bruised anew from the inevitable tubes inserted in his throat. He needed no chemotherapy or radiation.

Why then did I feel this was the beginning of the end?

In retrospect, I can say now that my father lived for sixty-four years and died for two years.

At the time, it was a vague sensation, which I managed with a little effort to quell. Had I pursued this feeling, the last two years we had together would have had a different meaning. But no. I wasn't wise or brave enough, and I let him die for two years, years of pathetic agony. Where I should have screamed, I murmured; where I should have taken a stand, I yielded silently; where I should have made him angry, for often he fed on anger and conviction, I covered things up. The petty, pseudo-sophisticated life he led suffocated him, and what was defined as "protective" was his shroud. My father's constitution was molded in strife and strengthened in battle. He soared on tensions and flew highest in spontaneity, and when he was least protected, most cruelly exposed, and the highest demands imposed on him, he performed best, and in the final account was at peace with himself and as happy as he could ever be. He was a man made for labyrinths, and history supplied him with many, for mazes extracted from his mind the genial sensors to point out the only secure route—not routes of escape, but those that lifted a nation sky-high. For the two years of his death, he was stripped of the fight, padded in endearment, and smothered with comforts. He was loved, obeyed, pampered, and diapered until he withered. A desert plant shrivels with excess watering and lack of scorching sun.

I could spare myself, and declare all these to be afterthoughts. I would be guilty of dishonesty, for I was an active partner in all this. I didn't want to risk a rupture, and I was a junior partner, a dispensable one, in the team that erected a hothouse around him, a hothouse for a plant that needed the variety of changing seasons, the brisk winds of dry khamsins and the chilling frosts of desert nights. In October of that year, 1979, three months after the operation, my father resigned from Begin's cabinet. Begin and his ministers appeared to be willing to enter into negotiations on the proposed autonomy for the Palestinians, but the objective they had in mind, following the five-year interim period, was exercising Israeli sovereignty over the entire territory west of the Jordan River.

Father was opposed to a Palestinian state, but he was against imposing annexation and, in the meantime, against appropriating private Arab land for Israeli settlements. He was prepared to abolish Israeli military administration in the territories and advocated the implementation of autonomy unilaterally if necessary. He believed our armed units should not be deployed in the populated West Bank areas but should serve as a defense element in the Jordan Valley, the Etzion region south of Jerusalem, and on the ridges in Samaria.

Basically, he understood the links of the West Bank population with Jordan to be vital and believed an interim period would create a "functional division," rather than a territorial one, where Israeli sovereignty would not be imposed on Arabs and Jews would not be foreigners in the West Bank, parts of which could subsequently be federated with Jordan on some constitutional basis. He was in a minority in the cabinet on this issue, and the subject was too cardinal for him to compromise.

Begin expressed his regret, but accepted the resignation, praising the Foreign Minister for his service and particularly for his part in securing the treaty with Egypt. Father resumed his seat in the last row of the Knesset, away from the government table. He did not choose to resign from the Knesset, but did say: "This will be my last Knesset . . . I have no wish to form an independent list or join one of the small parties." He defined his feeling upon resigning as "relief tinged with disappointment."

New elections were not due for another eighteen months, and to the obvious question "What will you do now?" he had all the obvious answers. He would write, lecture, meet with the Jewish communities of the Diaspora, and add to his collection of antiquities. As long as he had something to say, he assured me, he was going to make sure his voice was heard, and for this he didn't need a government post, a title, or even a Knesset seat. He now had ample free time, and rather frequently he would summon me to share a morning coffee with him in the garden.

I devoted many hours to my studies, taking a course in cytology, having realized how poor my biochemistry was. I had to work harder than others, and if I didn't give up, it was because I felt I was finally on the verge of grasping the elementary structure of biological existence. Happily, I lost the Alice in Wonderland sensation and was able to treat science, not as a stage where a magician performed miracles, but as an arena where, with trial and error, the human brain in its perseverance and consistent logical pursuit unveiled processes which it then sought to manipulate. Home was center-stage, and it was not with resignation but with a fair amount of pleasure that I ran it, as boring and Sisyphean as the daily chores were. My frustrations did not run deep, and my excitements and aspirations did not soar high. Many external manifestations of status had lost their meaning, and as long as I could travel occasionally, learn, teach, and be left alone, I was quite satisfied. Rather than collecting, I was in the process of disposal. Objects, papers, memorabilia, and people. My address book shrank to the essential minimum, and I was happy to contribute and give, provided I was not obligated by receiving. I was debt-free, other than the self-imposed debt to the immediate family, and I depended less and less on the outside world for stimuli. An occasional letter from a faithful writer or an anxious publisher reminded me that I was a professional writer, but I knew that when I was ready for a next book, it would be written. I never felt missionary about writing, and I was certain that the growth and expansion I was experiencing, together with sharpened selectivity, would produce a fertile sediment.

A year earlier, in 1978, my father published his book *Living with the Bible*, which I think was his most accomplished and beautiful piece of writing. The book was exactly what the title indicated—a perfect juxtaposition of life in biblical Israel and Father's own life as it related to it. A series of episodes, free associations in chronological order as recounted in the Bible. The Patriarchs he associated with the first settlers in Deganya and Nahalal; the Redemption and Exodus call forth in his mind the Sinai wars; the Promised Land, the War of Independence. He was writing of Judges and Kings, of King David's Jerusalem, the Six-Day War, and David Ben-Gurion. Father did not attempt to reinterpret the Scriptures, but he selected the particles, anecdotes, and episodes which for him were the essence of our claim to the land and which gave us the motivation to secure it, to live in it, and to die for it. The sense of continuity which he expressed in his archaeological pursuits gained a deeper meaning when he wrote about it. What was lacking was a whole dimension of Judaism which he failed to relate to. In this book, in life, in the little poem he wrote for us to read after his death.

The Patriarchs, the quest for freedom, the land, a tribal society turning into a nation, and the first Kings. The physical struggle for survival against foes and the elements, men falling in battles—in past and present wars—the pots of clay, the burial vessels, the trophies and the idols. His associations were physical. The cracks in the thirsty soils, the lilies in the Sharon, the caves in the cliffs of Ein Gedi, and gazelles in the Judean wilderness. His heroes were Moses the legislator, Gideon and Barak, Meir Har-Zion of Commando Unit 101 and Yoni Netanyahu of Entebbe, David and Jonathan and Saul, Ben-Gurion and the poet Natan Alterman. Of the three elements—the land, the people, and the book—he took of the Book what related to the land and the people. The vast depths of Jewish morality, the gap in time when the people had the Book without the land and survived on faith alone, the heights of ethics the Prophets demanded of the people, the post-biblical writings, the Talmud and the Mishnah, without which self-preservation would be impossible—he did not relate to. He identified with all his living fibers with the family: "In Wadi Beersheba, two thousand years ago, before the Patriarch Abraham. It knew every wadi and hill. This is its country, its native land . . . I don't even have to close my eyes to relive it, to see the live coals and the woman bent over them with a pot for her family . . . my family . . ." His family was not exterminated in Dachau; it did not worship in secret in medieval Spain or fight in the Warsaw ghetto. His family did not derive strength from the Hasidic tales of an Eastern shtetl or hide in caves in the Atlas Mountains. His family did not joke in Yiddish or read the Bible with a guttural Sephardic accent, and in his poem to us he wrote about the sword and the land to be protected by it.

In his modern dictionary, every milestone and border stone had a meaning. "The future boundaries of Israel is the issue closest to my heart since the foundation of the State of Israel," he wrote on the last page of *Living with the Bible*. The betterment of society, the ideological foundations of egalitarianism and socialism—of which the world of his parents consisted—the spiritual contents of our

revived civilization were not dominant in his priorities. I hesitate to
give him credit for this missing dimension by simply presuming or
taking for granted that he possessed it and had no need to elaborate
on it. I find it difficult to accept that all of us, as a society, are
satisfied with a way of thinking in which this dimension is clearly
absent. Not because we are secular, not because of the absence of
God, but we seem to have failed to substitute for faith in God something more than a golden calf. The tremendous vision Ben-Gurion
had could not be implemented without his spiritual and moral force.
Based on the Prophets rather than the Kings, on Greek philosophy
as well as Talmudic wisdom, and not ever at the expense of clarity
and a deep sense of realism vis-à-vis issues of state. My father had
followed his mentor in vision and farsightedness. What he lacked in
systematic broad education he supplemented with sharp intuition
and discerning perception, but the battle we all go through, between
spiritual monotheism and the golden calf, was not resolved for him,
and in his last two years the clatter of gilded trinkets appeared to be
overpowering.

Not one of these thoughts would I share with my father. His
ill health made him more irritable than ever, and my compassion
for his fragility prevented me from suggesting, repeating, or even
hinting at anything contradictory. If I had reservations—and often
I had—regarding the prudence of my behavior, there was always
Rahel to reassure me, with a ready list of all he should be spared.
With the best of intentions, the deepest concern, and complete
confidence in her judgment, she frisked me, and perhaps others—it
didn't work with Dov or my brothers—upon entry, and cautioned us
against saying anything that might be bad news for him. The gap
between what went on in my mind and what crossed my lips was
growing, and, in direct proportion, so was the distance between my
father and myself. It was suggested to me not to tell the whole truth.
I was afraid of what he knew; I was uncomfortable with the pretense
and was afraid to shatter it, or him. I fell into the trap, which is
excusable between teenagers and parents and is unforgivable among
adults. A vicious circle of pretense in order to accommodate or
please, which results in loss of dignity and confidence.

Thus, we sat near the Corinthian capital in the garden and

watched the birds drink from the stone basin, and talked—in fact, Father talked, about electricity bills, a raise in taxes, and the current inflation rate. The fact that he was miserly had always been a subject for family jokes, but now there was no way to laugh at it. Money became a near-obsession at a time when he needed money least.

And he was not at all well. A hernia operation followed, a diet, and loss of weight, which was welcome at the start but alarming later. He had to take medication to reduce the pressure on his eye socket, which was bad for the heart, as it lowered blood pressure. The heart muscle was weakening, and perhaps his general state did not permit major surgery. What bothered him most was the loss of eyesight, which was evident in his stumbling walk and his inability to read or concentrate. He grew bitter and short-tempered. He did not for one minute lose perspective and scope on public affairs, but privately he walled himself in. A wall which had openings. Often, when Rahel was out, he would call me and ask me to come over. At times, it was to show me a new acquisition or an article he wrote— before sending it to the newspaper. Rarely, to talk about things which he felt uncomfortable discussing in Rahel's presence.

In a strange way, he felt apologetic. Not sufficiently so to change his ways, but enough to want to talk to me about elements in his life which he assumed I would find displeasing.

I sat there bemused as he was; in fact, having dialogues with himself. Wondering about face-lifts, mink coats and diamonds, and cocktail parties. He desperately tried to excuse a superficial, costly self-indulgence as some appreciation of high aesthetics, or attribute it to the intangible but acceptable "feminine mystique." He claimed he was bored with the groupies, with the dinner parties and free lunches, where he couldn't, and didn't much care to, see or hear too well. He did not complain, he made his choice, but he had a bizarre need to make sure I knew what his real priorities were.

He stole moments with me to inquire about Mother, who was still working in Latin America, out of Washington; about her work, her interests, her needs, and her health. He cared a lot for my grand-mother and never failed to ask about her, and of course my brothers, his sons. We talked about Nahalal. Somewhere he was trying to make a point, to say that really he knew the difference between the shallow sophistication of his present life and the basics of the past, and he had a strange childish need to reassure me that the concessions he was making were only skin-deep. Whenever Rahel appeared and interrupted these little reunions, he almost blushed with guilt. She inevitably exclaimed: "Yaël! What a surprise!" and rather than admit that he called and asked me to come over, I almost had to apologize for being there: I happened to be in Zahala . . .

In an odd way, he resented the fact that I traveled with my children on school vacations. Lecturing for the U.J.A. was fine, and he was forever proud to hear of my success, but private travel, at my own expense, he found extravagant. I tried to explain it once and later gave up. We traveled on charters; we stayed with good friends—Mrs. Leonard Cohen and her daughters in Geneva and France; or used an apartment in Paris which belonged to close and dear friends from Chicago. I almost showed him bills, explaining that, rather than have a part-time maid, I saved so as to travel in the summer, but it didn't help. He held it against me as if I were sinning, and I couldn't even share with him the wonderful experience of my first trip to Egypt with the children. I couldn't care less about face-lifting or mink coats, Cartier jewelry or expensive outfits, but when friends of theirs told me they felt they were being used as the Dayans' "credit card," I felt humiliated. My mother was poor and too generous, which fell into the martyr complex I had long resented, but my father was rich and stingy, which was an unattractive combination.

Mother flooded us with gifts from the nothing she had, and my father charged for everything. I went to Paris to celebrate the seventieth birthday of Alain de Rothschild, one of the most sensitive, dearest, and kindest leaders of the Jewish Diaspora, and I paid Father for an oil lamp to bring as a gift. They were selling a Bokhara rug, slightly damaged, and were happy to sell it to me at the "bargain price" the rug merchant had offered them. Another "bargain" didn't materialize when I paid for an Eames armchair and had to return it to Zahala, having found it was an imitation, not leather, and cracked. A visit from my father and Rahel to Assi gained them back a Dali which was on Assi's wall, given to him by my mother a few years earlier; and a Hanukkah lamp in silver which

Mother gave me and the children used was spotted by Father on a visit to my apartment, and I was asked to return it. (Not before making sure it was made of silver, and claiming he wanted it for sentimental reasons, as it was inscribed to him.) Those were petty things perhaps, and as such not worth mentioning, but hurt is very often triggered by the trivial.

Assi divorced; my cousin Uzi—Zorik's son—married; my mother's parents moved permanently to Herzlia in the Tel Aviv area; and Father's book *Breakthrough* was published. Early in the summer of 1981, new elections were to be held, and Father had to make a decision concerning his public life.

When he resigned from the Likud cabinet, he said he would never run again; he was against splinter parties, and his "mother" Labor Party would not forgive him for crossing the lines. What made him ultimately decide to head his own party and present a list to the electorate, I can't really say. His own statement was satisfactory enough: he felt the issues were grave; he couldn't sit on the fence and watch. Writing articles was not enough, and as long as he could be heard from the Knesset floor, he felt it was his obligation to voice his opinions and offer his criticisms and suggestions. He was backed, financially and otherwise, by a good group of followers and announced that he would run. The campaign was a heartbreaking experience. I joined, reluctantly, and for purely personal reasons. His political platform didn't offer anything one couldn't find in the larger parties, and the best of the independent people declined to join. Father's voice was sound and clear on the unilateral autonomy issue and the Palestinian problem, but the internal socioeconomic issues were major and demanding, and Telem, Father's party, had little to offer in the way of renovation or revolution in this area. Father said, when debating whether to join Ben-Gurion's last political adventure, the Rafi Party, that he couldn't see himself waking up every morning concerned solely with the security mishap in Egypt and the old man's demand for truth and justice. His followers now had to wake up in the morning to place on top of their agendas the question of Palestinian autonomy . . .

His presence was sufficient reason for those who loved or admired him in the past to join, regardless of the vague "functional solution" for the West Bank or the obvious "extreme measures and imposed austerity which would lead to productivity" which were his economic platform. Here was Moshe Dayan, a complex national hero, who could hardly see, whose stride was hesitant, whose voice was hoarse, whose cheeks were sunken in, whose head was almost bald. He asked for confidence, he wanted to be heard, and we had to give him the floor with love and respect. We voted for him to remind ourselves of our youthful daring; we voted for him with compassion but without optimism or even enthusiasm for the party he led. It was wrong to deny him the right to strive and at least claim a personal victory. The polls predicted ten to twelve seats, then five or perhaps six, but he was more knowledgeable. For once, his pessimism was accurate. On the morning of the elections—and I had spent the month campaigning with all the ardor and conviction I could muster—we sat in the garden, and he talked about two Knesset seats, which was precisely what Telem got. Everybody but Father was disappointed. The objective of being a "balancing factor," without which a coalition could not be formed, was not attained; and the campaign was costly, deflating to the morale and spirits, and took an enormous toll on Father's health.

My own personal efforts to establish a dialogue between leading Laborites and my father, with the chance in mind of some reconciliation between them, failed. Labor finally lost the elections and lacked the generosity—which perhaps only victors can afford—to offer him a return to where he belonged.

In the twenty years of his political life, there were many times when he could have put up a fight and might have been in the lead. For twenty years he had refused to do so, and waited to be called upon to perform, never as number-one, always loyal to and hence dependent on a higher authority, the Prime Minister. Three months before his death, he took the initiative and faced the people's verdict. He had no illusions, but somehow he owed it to himself. In terms of the courage to admit failure, his whimper was a bang.

Looking at my father, after the elections, there was no way to think he was not being devoured by cancer. His sagging skin had a gray tint; his clothes hung on him; and he was exhausted. I talked to Rahel, I talked to his doctors, I talked to my doctors; I felt everybody knew something I did not, and could not be reassured. The results of a variety of tests were unanimous. His body was clean, as was his blood. There were no tumors, no metastases, and no indication of malignancy. His heart condition did not explain the rapid deterioration in his health, and I was bewildered. If Rahel knew more than I did, she was no less puzzled, and we shared the throbbing pain of helplessness. The more dependent he grew on her physically, the less kind he was to her, at least in my presence, and it was heartbreaking. He cut her short; he wanted full attention and then resented it; he sneered and complained and was unkind. She took it all with great love and understanding, knowing, probably, that he was not fighting her but clinging to life. I have seen it happen with my mother, and I was sure that he regretted, made up, and compensated in private, and she endured with the bravery and determination reserved for a woman in love.

He talked to me about his heart, almost with wonderment. He was amazed at the fact that he could simply not wake up, that the bullet had an address and wouldn't miss, but would hit him without warning. At times he mentioned his will, but there were obviously a great number of them. He told us—Dov was present—that he felt he could entrust to me the archaeological collection, because I would do the right thing with it, not elaborating. On other occasions he mentioned Udi's children with reference to the apartment he owned. He talked in general about being very fair to Rahel, as she had a long life ahead of her, and her well-being was his responsibility. He wasn't concerned with her daughters' future, as much as he cared for them and genuinely liked them, because they had a wealthy and attentive father. I later found out, from a friend who witnessed the will, that he was in fact referring to a previous paper, written and signed after he was married to Rahel, in which he split his earthly belongings three ways—a third to Rahel, a third to Udi's two first-born children, and a third to my brothers and myself. All these words were a monologue. I did not discuss; I did not relate or question or comment upon. He spoke of a future I did not care to admit existed, a future in which he would not be present.

In the summer I was offered a job with a large advertising company, and accepted it willingly. It had become impossible to manage on one salary, and I was studying—rather than writing for income—which exhausted savings I didn't want to touch.

"Don't tell him," Rahel said, "that you are taking a job for the sake of a salary. He would be so upset, thinking of you the way he does—as independent and well off . . ." So I said I found advertising interesting, a whole new field I'd like to study, and left it at that. Although I knew he resented it and misinterpreted it, I did take the children for short summer vacations in Europe. We stayed at the Epsteins' apartment in Paris, drove to the Loire Valley's châteaus, and joined our Geneva friends in a house they rented in the South of France. He did not manage to make me feel guilty about my choice of priorities. I was not in debt; we did not live above our means; and I was not imposing myself on anybody. We were accepting hospitality that was given wholeheartedly, with joy and gratitude.

Driving through Arles and Avignon marveling at the Chagalls and Matisses in Nice, I tried to treat my children to new tastes and sounds, and myself to a holiday, trying to put aside and suppress the pain that came with the knowledge that it was my father's last summer.

We returned at the end of August. I resumed my office job, and Dan began to take lessons for his bar mitzvah, which was to take place three months later. On August 27, my father signed his last will, canceling all previous ones and leaving everything he owned, and whatever was due to him in the way of pension or royalties, to his second wife. He was clear of mind and sane when he did so. He asked to be buried in Nahalal and not have eulogies read or spoken at the graveside. He was in full control of his faculties, and if he did not know his worth, and surely he did not know how independent, well off, or utterly broke his three children were, it was not due to senility or forgetfulness or even—as so many people suggested—to the influence of drugs.

My brothers and I were not aware of any of this, and we shared the concern and the frustration of our helplessness regarding his health. Udi's life was a mess. He wanted a divorce, and it was likely that he would lose the Nahalal farm in the process. "Don't tell your father, it'll break his heart," Rahel suggested, and looking at him, I knew this was not a figure of speech. Assi was wiser and more blunt. He was in debt, and the obvious place to seek backing or a loan was his father. He went to see him, had a showdown, accusing and being accused, airing responsibilities and the meaning of parenthood, felt better for it, and was promised the money he asked for. Father grumbled, was upset and maybe hurt, even shattered, but the confrontation was long due, and Assi was the only one of us to dare cash in—albeit for small change—the token we had all been given.

Summer lingered on with southerly, dry winds and whirlpools of sand. The vines in our Ein Hod garden shed their orange-green leaves, as if stripping would tempt the clouds and the rain. I always found the end of summer, like sunset, sadder than the autumn or night. Jewish New Year, always at the end of summer, adds little to my mood as I go through the festive routine. New Year, like birthdays, calls for stock-taking of the past year, and planning and setting objectives for the year ahead. Two things I wasn't up to. My father agreed—reluctantly, for obvious reasons of ill health— to have all the grandchildren for a New Year gathering, provided it was short and didn't include a meal. Rahel took to her bed with bad flu the day before, and I handled the logistics, except for little packages of sweets, which were nicely gift-wrapped, one for each child.

Father sat on the garden swing, surrounded by his offspring, a tribal patriarch. Udi and his three children and two wives; Assi with his daughter and son; Dov and I with Dan and Raheli. Our cousin Jonathan, Aviva's son, was there with his family, and Rahel's daughters, one with two children. The children were all over the place, climbing into Roman sarcophagi and sitting on Byzantine gravestones and church pillars, dipping apples in honey, as is our New Year custom, and having a good enough time. How could they know that this was the last hour they had with their illustrious grandfather? Assi went to Rahel's bedroom, where she handed him an envelope with the money he needed. The other children, obedient and well-mannered, stood at her bedroom door briefly to wish her a happy New Year, and my father seemed relaxed enough, patting a child here, complimenting another, and mostly talking to us. About rainfall, about his new collection of stones, about a book he intended to write. Through his dimmed sight and bad hearing, the commotion surrounding him may have been a fuzz. Pretty little creatures floating in and out of focus. "All these are yours?" He smiled at us. "Yours too," we said. "Now, now, don't exaggerate . . ."

How I missed my mother then. She loved the ceremonial aspects of family gatherings, be it a birthday, a holiday, or a regular Friday evening meal. In her absence, we had Seder in my house, where the food was good and the traditional Haggada reading absent, at my father's insistence. We celebrated Hanukkah with a party—potato pancakes, candles, and songs—in our apartment, and on Independence Day we held a barbecue in Ein Hod. I did it with pleasure, but my father never seemed comfortable. It was an ordeal to tolerate, not much more. Then he had said he would rather not have had a family, and watching him look at us, I had no doubt that he still felt the same way. It was at that moment that it occurred to me that to accept death, to be reconciled with it and not fear it, was perhaps the greatest expression of selfishness. My own concern with death was similar to his, until I had children. It didn't really matter to me when or how I ceased to be, and I could only hope that it would come with a sudden blow, rather than in small portions of agony and suffering. The only reason to fight death, to avoid danger, to prolong life was not in order to achieve something but rather because of a kind of responsibility. A debt of love to those who may benefit from the fact that I am alive, or suffer at my absence. Father had no such debt or concern. He would rather not have had children. Once we were grown, he owed us nothing, and in his egotistical, self-centered pattern it was not his duty to contribute to our happiness when he was alive or consider our pain and distress when he was gone.

We talked about state affairs, and he foresaw mostly doom. All these lovely children would have to fight to survive, and their children after them. He was not desperate: we'll fight and win, but not for many generations to come, if at all, shall we sit under our vines and fig trees in peace. The epic of Massada, where Jews died by their own hand rather than yield to the Romans, was alien to my father all his life. Now, on the eve of death, he wrote an article in which he set Massada as a spiritual example. Its title was really what he predicted, not wished us: "The Victory of the Vanquished." I looked at the children in the garden, and I could define exactly the distance between Father and myself. I did not wish them to be vanquished victors. I did not see death as a peak of life. I believed in the sanctity of life, and sacrificing one's life was justified only when it contributed to the continuity of other lives. As in no-choice wars. Dan was studying for his bar mitzvah, not because we were Orthodox—he would probably never attend a service after his Saturday-morning ceremony in December—but because his family was not one of the families in the wadi of Beersheba, or among the suicides on the Massada cliff. His family were also people who could survive without the land. We drove home in silence. Even the children noticed how unwell their grandfather was. Raheli fell asleep in the car, her way of fending off thoughts and premonitions she dreaded.

Mother called from somewhere to wish us a happy New Year, and promised to be around for the next New Year celebration. In spite of the enormous difference in style and values, my father's two wives had something in common. Their love for him was uncompromising and total. Mother's expertise was self-deprivation, and Rahel's self-indulgence, and he admired both qualities equally as long as he benefited from the results. Mother rejected the advantages that came with Father's position, but only seemingly and in a righteous way. Rahel claimed them, taking them for granted. Where my mother criticized his shortcomings, Rahel absolved him, and they both shared the comforting notion that he was trapped and seduced by other women rather than attracted to them. In different periods of his life, they both fitted his poor naïve village boy's ideal of a "princess"—only that my mother was a princess whose ideal was to be Cinderella, and Rahel perhaps wanted to be a queen. Had they ever compared notes, they would have discovered there wasn't a Rahel's Moshe, different from Ruth's Moshe. It was he who chose what facet to expose to each and what to deprive them of, according to what suited him at a given time, with the degree of love he was capable of.

I was assured of my mother's unconditional love, time and time again, but I don't know that she really likes me, or feels entirely at ease with me. Rahel tried to like me, and perhaps succeeded occasionally. The worst thing she ever said to me was to quote a friend to whom my mother had said: "I don't envy Rahel for getting Moshe, for she got Yaël as well, as part of the package." It is irrelevant whether the quote was true, but to say it to me, one had to be insensitive, vicious, or plain stupid. The rest were under-currents that lose importance in perspective, as she disappeared from my life and I from hers, leaving no trace of damage or contribution. The vacuum I felt in Zahala on New Year's Eve had to do with some abstract notion I had of "family life," and Rahel could not fill it anyway. Her place in Father's life had nothing to do with family, and could in no way be shared with, or inspire, us.

We went to Ein Hod for a couple of days, and again on Yom Kippur. The pomegranates were exploding in red, and with a prayer for rain I planted winter bulbs. The holiday of Succoth, which lasts for seven days, began on Tuesday and the children had no school. I had to hand in a laboratory report on cell membrane and managed to visit Father once or twice during the week. He talked about the new book he was going to write. It would be about the "heroes of my people." Men and women, his own selection, those he regarded as exemplary. In excellence, in achievement, in values. Heroes of all times. Hanna Senesh, Meir Har-Zion, Yoni Netanyahu, and others. While we were talking, he noticed a bougainvillea branch which had detached itself from the wire that held it high, and he agreed it should be I, rather than he, who would climb the shaking ladder and put it in place. He held the ladder and only said: As high as you can! Don't worry, I'm holding the ladder. I wasn't worried. He was holding the ladder, and I climbed as high as I could.

In the Bible, Succoth, the Feast of Tabernacles, is also called the Harvest Festival, the Feast of Gathering. The words "gathering" and "harvest" in Hebrew stem from one root and are applied to grain and vegetables, grapes and honey, as well as to human life. "Behold, therefore, I will gather thee unto thy fathers, and thou shalt be gathered to thy grave in peace" (II Kings:22).

On the fourth day of the Feast of Gathering, Friday, October 16, 1981, my father passed away.

PART

Five

FIFTEEN ✸ SHIVA

"Three days for weeping and seven for lamenting . . ." And if my weeping was over, my seven days of Shiva were doubled. We did not intend to sit Shiva at all, and I paid for it by "sitting" both in Zahala and in our own apartment. Because it was dignified, I thought then, and because I was ignorant of so many undercurrents. Two houses, two families, two widows, two sets of friends, and too much food.

The custom of Shiva is an old one, though not biblical. Immediately after the funeral, the bereaved family gathers in the house of the deceased. For seven days, people call to pay respects and ease, I suppose, their sense of loss. No chores are done, no manual labor, no business transactions; the days are devoted to lamenting, remembering, sharing. Orthodox Jews pray, wear cloth shoes, sit on the floor, and are forbidden any luxury or indulgence, from the washing of hair to intercourse. It is only after the Shiva that the will is opened and read.

My children didn't want to attract attention, and they returned to school. Dov was busy with an important Egyptian delegation, and my mother held the fort in our house while I went to Zahala every morning, spending most of the day there and returning home in the afternoon.

I was not unwelcome in Zahala, nor was I begged to stay beyond the few hours I did. Some people looked for me there and wouldn't come otherwise, and others just nodded with pity—and felt better for ignoring me.

Rahel's daughters were there all the time, one with the children, the other with the dog, and her close friend from New York was very much there, being so useful and well organized I could have screamed. So, the sentence most frequently repeated was: "Please speak in English, so my friend can understand." I had little to say, in any language, and after three days I almost enjoyed the fact that people were not comfortable in my presence there. Food was brought in, whole catered meals or friends' specialties. Someone did the shopping for the house, and the driver walked around, haunted and wet-eyed, looking for errands to do. I was in tears often, but not hysterical, and I was often smiling. My smiles had to do with little memories; my tears with the certainty of what would not ever be.

Many exchanges stopped when I entered the room, and many phone conversations ended with "I'll call you later, I can't talk now." I was moving with the sensation of being watched all the time, and if someone had asked to search me upon leaving, it wouldn't have surprised me. I was an obstacle, a nuisance, but not of a major sort apparently. I was a thorny reminder of the life my father had which they were not part of. When he was alive, Rahel and those close to her could claim him exclusively, but in his death they had to share, and after all, I did have a unique position. He had two wives he loved in life; he had two boys; he had two mothers-in-law and many grandchildren. He fought side by side with many men and made love to many women, but I was his only daughter, and even if I weren't special, or loved, or wanted, nobody could take this away from me, and nobody did.

My own house managed itself. Three dear friends came every day, saw to the children, and kept the place tidy, dozens of others kept my mother company, and there was no way to feel lonely when I came home, and no need to. Udi was in Nahalal, riding up the hill every day, alone, and accumulating bitterness and frustration, while coping with his collapsing second marriage.

One evening, when we were home with our mother, my father's

will was mentioned. If we didn't discuss it before, it was not out of reverence. We expected Rahel to get a fair half, or more. We also knew he had a great deal, and there was no reason to worry about the fairness of his judgment. I, personally, didn't give it a moment's thought. My mother had to leave before the Shiva was over, back to work—as her widowhood was not an official one, and pay for days of absence was deducted from her salary. She was casual about it. Don't worry, she said. He loved you all, and he was a wise man. He had a lot, and I am sure you'll be well provided for. She even furiously rejected Assi's words about not feeling he deserved anything.

"When I left him," she said proudly, "I took this into account. I left with so little, and I didn't ask for what I was entitled to, because I knew it would be yours one day—much of it, anyhow." After all, she said, "it was my parents who bought us the farm in Nahalal and the house in Zahala, and if he wasn't a generous man in his life"— an understatement we all smiled at—"you'll enjoy his generosity now." End of speech. She was easily overexcited, and she was defending the father of her children.

I was sitting in the garden with the New York friend when she said my father wanted Rahel to be buried next to him in Nahalal. "That's why," she said, "the grave was not dug next to his own parents." "Oh," I said, casually, "my mother will be buried next to my father, too. After all, burial places are to be frequented by the children, and we wouldn't like to do cemetery tours cross-country." "Wouldn't it be better if your mother were buried next to her own parents," she suggested. "Her parents will outlive us all," I remarked, "and my mother's place is in Nahalal, regardless of my father." Weird as this conversation was, it remained with me, as it was on that day that the rift between me and everything that was my father for the last ten years began. That day, some antique merchants walked in the garden, not taking notes, but obviously appraising parts of the collection in detail. Later, a mutual friend sat with Rahel in a remote spot in the garden, and when I walked to the car, he referred to their conversation. "I told her to be generous," he said repeatedly. "Whatever *he* wanted, I advised her to be generous." I smelled problems, and pushed the thought away. I mentioned it to my brothers that evening, and we had a long session of black humor. "I will get the glass eyes," Assi said, Udi thought he might be lucky and get the spades Father excavated with, and I knew I'd be getting my own oil portrait. Mother had left already, and the Shiva was to end the next day. We were to go to Nahalal, lay flowers, and say Kaddish, a family affair, private and intimate. A larger public ceremony was to take place later, on the Sheloshim, thirty days after the burial, when a tombstone would be placed on the site—the final, heavy gesture.

The Shiva was to end, and life had to resume its normal course, only without him, and the last seven days were totally, intensively his. The Zohar, the book of Cabalistic mystical wisdom, suggests that during the Shiva the soul goes to and fro between the house and the grave, mourning for the body. After the seventh day, the soul departs as well. I doubt that my father's soul bothered mourning his body, and to this day his soul certainly never left any of us. In life, and in death, he never sought peace of mind, nor wished to inspire it in others.

The lawyer called me in the morning to set up an appointment. Despite all the jokes of the previous night, and the suspicions we had voiced, I didn't notice the peculiar tone he used. Then he fumbled for words. "You do know more or less what the will says," he said, hesitating. "More or less," I answered, short of words on my part. Then he followed with one long, unpunctuated sentence: "You know then that the house and its contents, the collection, and all the moneys and the pension and the royalties all go to Rahel. However, he left you a piece of land he owned, and Udi's older children get half an apartment that was his—so, is tomorrow afternoon suitable for you and your brothers?" "What for? Can't you put the good news in the mail?" I snapped. He apologized for troubling us, but this was the way it had to be done; and he had suggested to Rahel to have two separate sessions—with her, who of course was familiar with the contents, and with us. But she preferred us to be there together, and he was not too happy about having to implement . . . He was talking too much, and we left it at that.

Very calmly, I called my brothers with the news. Whatever they expected, and I didn't know what they did or what they felt they didn't deserve, they were wordless. I had a strong feeling they mostly felt upset for me. They knew I didn't expect much, but they thought I deserved more. Our poor naïve darling mother was thousands of miles away, so she didn't have to face us with a sense of guilt and shame.

The boys' first reaction was to avoid the graveside ceremony. I begged them to come, not for our father, not for the press, just for me, as I couldn't face it alone. Dov was with the Egyptian Minister of Defense, and I wanted us three to stand there, proud and belonging, as if he had bequeathed us the world. I didn't take into account the security of tears. I didn't think these glands and ducts could pour out more liquid, ever, but there I stood, shaking and crying as if Father had died a second ago. Assi said Kaddish quietly. It was short and sad and tired, as if the past week, with the coming and going of the soul, had exhausted us completely.

Udi had removed the dry wreaths of flowers during the week, and fresh ones were laid now. When the tombstone was placed, we should plant some shrubs, I thought: my father didn't like cut flowers. I watched Rahel, across the mound of earth under which her husband rested, the way I had watched her across his deathbed. My mother had said before leaving, or rather implied, that there was no need to keep up a relationship. She had said it before when my father married Rahel, and there was no way I could satisfy her then. Now there stood a blond woman in her mid-fifties, beautiful, and feminine, well dressed, well combed, composed and elegant, but what we had in common was dead and the distance between us seemed unbridgeable, or at least I felt no need or desire to cross it.

When the short ceremony was over and we were walking to the cars, I asked her whether I could come that afternoon and collect a few things I kept in the safe in Zahala. I must have said it in a harsh tone, suggesting I was off on a journey, breaking away, never to return. She nodded, and referred to it later as the peak of bad taste, which I suppose it was. Severing, unlike the intricate weaving of ties, could and I thought should be swift. She must have known I knew what was to come that afternoon, and if I showed bad taste, there was more than a touch of nervousness in her reaction.

The lawyer's office was on a high floor in a modern Tel Aviv building, and the fluorescent light in the elevator bothered me as we were going up—Udi and Assi and myself. We talked to our own attorney, or rather a friend who was a brilliant young lawyer and a political associate of our father, and arranged to come to see him with the will later.

The building was deserted, as it was after working hours, and we encountered nobody, going up or, half an hour later, down. My father's close friend and lifelong legal adviser, Yossi, was away (he lived in New York), and Mr. Nahir, the local lawyer, showed us in, fidgety and pale, wishing it were over already.

The small boardroom had a large table with chairs, and we sat there facing Rahel. Nahir sat at the head of the table, and said he didn't mind leaving the room if we wished it; actually, he said, he'd rather leave the room. He gave us each two typed pages and rose to go. Udi, or was it Assi, ordered him in a flat tone to sit down. We came to your office, and if there is any embarrassment, you are a party to it.

We quickly read the document. It plainly said what I knew already. Rahel was to get everything that had belonged to him, everything that was coming to him, exclusively and totally. We were given the quarter of an acre of land he owned; and Udi's children, half an apartment. He also asked to be buried in Nahalal, not to have obituaries or speeches at the graveside, no gun salute at the funeral, and not to name anything in his memory. Yossi was appointed executor of the will, and a special request was added—not to take the will to court in case of a dispute over it.

Paragraph 3 said that if Rahel and he died at the same time, all properties, moneys, and income were to be distributed in equal parts among his three children. The will was dated August 1981, six weeks prior to his death.

It took us two minutes to read, and the silence that followed was deadly. Rahel asked to say a few words, and in a trembling voice, looking none of us in the eye, delivered a small speech. She realized we were hurt and she could understand it. This was his will, his last will, and she intended to see that it was respected. However, she thought she should compensate us to a degree, and was offering to give the other half of the apartment—Udi's children had one half—

in Eshkol Street for our children, his grandchildren. Each grandchild would get a fifth of a half of the apartment, after taxes . . . provided we did not do anything to hurt his name or hers or show disrespect to his memory, as unhappy as we might be at that moment. We looked at her bewildered. Could it be that she felt it was genuinely a generous offer? The lawyer tried again to get up and leave, and Udi ordered him to sit down. I said, suggesting I wasn't a spokesman for the three of us, that I was not willing to make any deals right there and then. Whatever she felt she wanted to offer should be directed to us, and not our children, as I didn't feel we should be punished or be made to feel guilty by being bypassed. Udi quickly added that he wasn't about to be pressured into any promise of silence, and he felt free to express his feelings about his father any way he chose. If this was silence money, he didn't care to discuss it. Nahir gave us two more pages, a duplicate copy of a letter our father had written to us, and a copy of a poem he had written a couple of years earlier, both to be given to us after his death.

He very quickly added that the will was legally sound, had no flaws whatsoever, and he suggested that we not even try to dispute it. Rahel's offer was the most she could do, and the strings attached concerned a desire to prevent any damage to his memory. I asked the obvious question, to which the reply was as obvious. What happens after Rahel's long life, or, using the legal term, after her hundred-and-twenty? After all, he did not mean to totally disinherit us, or take revenge, or he wouldn't have mentioned the possibility of both of them dying at the same time . . . No provisions, he said, were made in his will for his estate after her lifetime. This is up to Rahel when the time came. Was it possible to receive some personal things, mementos, not valuables? Like what? she asked suspiciously. Udi mentioned a painting of his eldest daughter that hung on the wall in Zahala. She would give it to the girl herself, she said. I asked about a Hanukkah lamp which my mother had given me and which my father had asked to have back many years later. No, she said. But I could have my grandmother's photograph, and my own portrait, of course . . .

We skimmed over the poem, but this was not a fit time for poetry reading, and we read the letter attached. Desperately I hoped, though it was dated almost two years earlier, that a beacon of light would flicker between the lines, an expression of great love for her or great hate for us. I wanted with all my being to find a way to justify this unbelievable blow.

The letter was handwritten on Knesset stationery. It was one page, dated February 1980. There were many wills written and rewritten, and this same letter was attached to them all, indicating they contained similar messages.

Dear Yula, Udi and Assi,

I thought it proper to add a few clarifying words to the will.

The apartment in Eshkol St. I left to Gal and Saar because I think that they, more than the others, will need material support in their adult life. The pieces of land, in Shefayim and the one in Tivon (if I get it), are yours.

All these things are detailed in the will, and this letter I decided to write concerning one point. It isn't a secret that my heart is damaged. All the treatments and medications haven't been effective and it may suddenly cease to beat (maybe during my sleep)—what is referred to as a "heart attack."

If this happens soon, Rahel will continue, I hope, to live for scores of years. She is healthy and ten years younger than I am. This is why I decided to leave her the money we have jointly. I am afraid that life in Israel will be hard and expensive, and in order to maintain the standard of living we all enjoy now—a small car, house and garden—one would need a reasonable (net) income. Because of economic difficulties, taxation (freeze of capital, foreign currency, etc.), taking all these into account and knowing that Rahel has no profession, and other than me she has nobody to take care of her, I thought it proper to leave to her, in addition to the house and its contents, whatever money we have accumulated since our marriage. As to you, one generation younger than Rahel and myself, I believe that each of you will be able to take care of himself and his family.

Yours,
Father

The text in front of me was incredible. My strong, beloved father, a fighter and a poet, a man of precision and foresight, writes his children a prosaic, banal, flat, one-page statement. Years of complex ups and downs, trust and love and disputes and arguments, all summed up in terms of net income and currency control, as if he were some accountant explaining a paragraph in a textbook on economics. He shrank to a size I refused to accept. He could tell us we were rotten bastards; he could write about his infatuation, love, and gratitude to Rahel; he could add a few words of apology, or blame, or something spiritual and enlightening, but no, he left us a salesman's letter, and in my disappointment I started crying.

Very coldly, Rahel added that he didn't really want to leave us the piece of land (a quarter of an acre, heavily taxed and about to be confiscated by the state, categorized as agricultural land), but she convinced him to do so.

I took out of my purse a few envelopes. In each was a copy of a letter I had written that afternoon, before reading the will, but when I knew, vaguely, what was in it. I passed the envelopes around—to Rahel and my brothers, and one to Nahir to send to Yossi. A few days later I heard from mutual friends that Rahel found it shocking and insulting, the more so because I had distributed it, and had it not been for this letter, she might have considered a greater generosity. It obviously had the impact I wanted it to have, though it didn't bear the results I thought it would.

The letter was handwritten, several pages long, and it was obvious that I didn't mean them to sit and read it in the lawyer's office. Each in his own privacy and time, they read:

Rahel,
Everyone is busy "preserving the dignity of the dead," tiptoeing
and whispering in corners, while "honoring," smoothing and
cementing, and beautifying "In honor of" . . . I'd like to share a
thought about the honor and dignity of the living. The
dignity of my mother, who for decades—the rough ones, the
ones lacking in glory and wealth and means, years paved with
battles and dangers—stood beside him. Mother's dignity,
in years of love, of raising children, of anxiety, of building homes

*and a farm, caring for his wounds, and contributing a human
dimension to his world, which often lacked it—poet that he was.
And her less dignified years—when, unbearably, she lost
dignity and carried on "for the children's sake," until she could
do so no longer and broke her own path, having nothing and
leaving you both with it all—all but the responsibility for
taking care of the children and grandchildren, which remained
hers. Mother's dignity, who left the home—against our advice—
in which we grew, into which both my children were born, the
home I left only when I got married, a home her father
purchased, the way he did the farm in Nahalal, she left the
Zahala home, supported Udi and Assi, who needed help, and
believed—so she told us then—that she was not jeopardizing us,
because our father loved us, and was fair and wise.*

*The dignity of my brothers. The living, the young, who are—
despite their errors and tempers—his sons. The good and the
bad in them are his, very "Dayan" they are. Udi's adventures,
Assi's talents, Udi's courage and restlessness, infidelity and
gloom—Udi is, as Father was, an artist, while Assi has all the
Dayan charisma, and I wish our father had some of his
sensitivities. Don't think of them as if "they happen to be his
sons" because in the last few years they have grown estranged and
distant. Fatherhood, or "to be the son of," isn't measured in torn
segments of time. There were years when Assi was Father's
favorite, his baby, Udi was his source of pride, and I was
trouble.*

*The dignity of Udi and Assi, who will be—they and their
sons—"Dayans" forever. Expected to continue in his path, they
will often fail, but then, sometimes Father failed us, too.*

*My own dignity. I who never asked for anything, never
appealed for help or burdened him with my worries, so as not to
spoil the luxury and comfort of the image of "a daughter who
is independent and takes care of herself," even when I needed
him and had nobody else to turn to. When I had, I shared with
him; and when it was tough, I didn't bother him.*

His dignity, when alive, was dearest to me; his pain and

*sadness he shared with me when we were alone, without barriers,
never holding back.*

*We did have a special relationship. Father–daughter, friends
at times, teacher–pupil; and often I did things I wasn't totally
happy about, because I believed he knew better.*

*How a wise man like Father, who managed his life so well,
didn't think all the way—a generation ahead, when he came to
settle his after-death affairs—I'll never understand.*

What are we to tell our children?

*The children I'm supposed to bring up in the light of his
memory, to be like him—patriots, brave, wise, proud of him—
what do I tell them about morality and justice, of parents taking
care of children? What do I tell them about generosity?*

*What to tell Udi, who may have to sell the family farm to
afford a divorce; Assi, who lives in a rented flat; my mother, who
believed the burden would be off her shoulders one day. As
tragedies go, Dov's parents were killed in the Holocaust. My own
children had only one grandfather, special and wonderful, a
source of pride and affection. Now they'll have photographs,
his books, some letters and they will look from the outside in on
everything that was his that will now belong to your own
grandchildren. What do I tell them?*

*My love for my father remains untouched; not so my respect.
I never expected, I don't think he "owed" me, and if there were
nothing, it would have been easier.*

*When there is so much, it takes an enormous lack of generosity
to "divide" it the way I am told he did.*

*The law accepts situations that are unacceptable to reason
or heart. Father's will does not "honor" him and doesn't add to
your "dignity" either. The archaeological collection should be
made available to the public; the house—at least after your
lifetime—should remain in the family, for our children and
grandchildren, and even then, it would have left more than
ample for you, the way Father wanted it.*

*So what he didn't do when alive, maybe we'll do after his death,
letting justice and fairness win. I want you to know that this*

letter, in fact, isn't just between us. It's meant for Mother and my
brothers, and whoever cares to judge the dignity of the living
and the dead.

All your years with Father, I respected his love for you.
Without effort or bitterness or blame. If there were moments of
misunderstanding, they were not unnatural or many. I didn't have
to playact. It was a Dayan-like pragmatism, mixed with a degree
of affection, and recently compassion for the hard months, the
impossible daily suffering, the helplessness you went through
at his ailing side, a feeling I shared—though my contribution
was not often wanted.

The real addressee of these pages is, of course, my father, and
so toward him only is directed any feeling of hurt, bitterness,
or disappointment that may emerge between the lines.

Yaël

We took the elevator down, and this was the last time I saw Rahel of my own volition. Earlier that afternoon, I collected my belongings from the safe in Zahala, and did not return there until a year later, when it already belonged to the lawyer who had purchased it. The street was empty, and we drove together to see our lawyer, knowing there was little he could do.

SIXTEEN ⚔ LAST

KADDISH

With Udi and Assi, typed pages in hand, I entered our lawyer's apartment as if he were a magician or a miracle worker. Time was not wasted on preliminaries, and he sat us down in the living room, quickly reading through the legal phrases, which were his territory and our misfortune. Well controlled and dry as he was, he could not repress a bewildered anger. He threw the papers on the coffee table and sighed. Reason, he said, doesn't tolerate a document like this one. Had he come to me, as a lawyer, he said, I wouldn't have let him sign a paper like this. No way. He paused, and resumed his cool legalistic tone. As much as I admired him. Because I admired him.

He read it again, between the lines too, I suppose, and with a defeated expression laid it on the table. Now he addressed us.

I doubt it can be taken to court. There are two ways to dispute a a will. We could claim he was not in his right mind, under drugs or whatever, which I, and you, know he wasn't. I wouldn't do it anyway, I quickly volunteered, not for anything. True, he continued, he was sick, and this paper was signed only a few weeks before he died, but his mind was clear and sharp. The other way, it is proved that the will was written under the influence, accumulative or momentary, of the benefactor. That's a hell of a thing to prove, and I don't know of any evidence we can use to show that. He looked at us with a degree of pity. Unbelievable! he exclaimed.

We told him of Rahel's offer. Good, he said, relaxing. Obviously, there is a crack there, and we should try to negotiate. Her offer is unacceptable, but I believe she will realize that, for his sake, she can do better. I suggest meeting with her, to see what I can do.

He figured the will would be made public in a few days; there was no way to prevent the courtroom reporters from getting it. One hell of an embarrassment. For everybody. Embarrassed and rich is still better than embarrassed and poor, one of us said.

I'll let you know when I meet with her, our friend concluded, seeing us to the elevator. This was one case he was going to lose, but then, this was not a case, or one he had chosen to take.

As I drove home, my head cleared somewhat. Normally, under circumstances which called for common sense, for objective and cool thinking, I'd go to my father. In his absence I had to apply these faculties myself. I hoped they were in me. I realized that, as in a war, when one is defeated and an extra effort might prove heroic but suicidal, this was a time not to fight. All my life I have resented obsessions and kept away from fanatics. Preoccupation with the will and fighting for a settlement, in or out of court, could become an obsession. A full-time, unsettling, one-track experience. Even if it were to produce results, they would be measured in terms of dollars and cents and would come at the expense of respect, self-respect, peace of mind, and productivity. There was the golden calf again, winking and tempting, and a poor shiny substitute for some promised land of a normal, stable life. What was lost could not be returned, and to add to it the anguish and frustration of a futile fight would be destructive and pointless. I was not going to indulge in it, and when I opened my apartment door, my mind was made up. What I inherited nobody else did, and this could never be taken from me; and what I didn't was not worth the disintegration of values and standards. I was not going to destroy my love for my father, or let anyone doubt or damage the memory of the love he had for me. I was not going to harm any chances my brothers had, or any hopes they entertained. Let the mediators talk to Rahel, and whatever the result was, I would not pursue the matter further.

Dov read the document with a look of disgust on his face. He was against minor negotiations. Either you leave it and let go, and let her have the piece of land as well, or you contest the whole thing, which he basically thought could or should be done. He had his own thoughts regarding the circumstances and influences that brought about this will, and he chose the easy and evasive way of leaving it up to me to decide what to do. Close friends reacted strongly. An all-out fight, they suggested, not with compassion for me as much as with hurt and hatred for "that woman." It would be very easy to be trapped into a battle where we would all be losers, and I was determined. Let the lawyers discuss, and let me accept whatever resulted. I started feeling a deep sense of embarrassment whenever the subject was brought up, as if the relationship of a lifetime had to be measured and weighed according to a figure on a check.

A few meetings followed, each less pleasant than the previous one. Rahel was surrounded by friends and lawyers who advised her to be firm and stubborn. That's the way he wanted it and they don't deserve better, they suggested—advice she found easy to accept.

The first meeting with a mutual, objective friend was disastrous. Her nerves gave way, and she cried angry tears. The "civilized" façade was gone, and she said Assi was a worthless playboy, Udi a corrupt, lazy no-good, and I was a cunning, dominating bitch. A second meeting with lawyers produced a paper suggesting we would get half of Zahala. This was extracted under pressure, she suggested a few days later, and she wouldn't sign it. Half of the house in Zahala was too much, Yossi suggested, and she should and could settle for less.

The press had a ball. The will was published in an evening paper. Lawyers offered free advice; gossip columnists and reporters offered interpretations and theories. My mailbox was filled with letters of solidarity and encouragement, as if I were fighting a battle on behalf of all the children of the world. Only I wasn't fighting, and both the battle and its results had a stale, irrelevant taste.

The thirty days of the Shloshim mourning period were nearing their end. The deep pain turned into a scar, never to be fully healed, but not an open wound either; and the first rain wet the soil in the graveyard when the tombstone was placed. A heavy marble rectangle bearing in metal letters my father's name and the dates of birth and death. A larger rectangle made of rough stones framed the flat marble, the space between them filled with earth and the few shrubs planted in it softened with an aura of green the austere, sad site. It would look sad and austere were it not for the valley below, which was a continuous burst of life, a patch of fertility, a weave of all the wonders that compose life, as far as the eye could see.

The thirty-day period, the length of a full month, was considered by some psychiatrist in Talmudic, ancient times as the proper time for intense mourning. Afterward, life resumed. Visits to the bereaved family then became less and less frequent; men shaved their beards, and business affairs were conducted once more. On the thirtieth day, ads announced a gathering at the graveside, and buses were available to the public.

No government officials came this time. There were very few men in uniform, although there were a couple of hundred people who came by bus.

Rahel, dressed in shades of brown and in a cardigan, flanked by her daughters and her mother, stood next to the rabbi. If she had tears, they were concealed by dark glasses, and we exchanged nods, no more. Compared to the funeral, the small number of people was evident, and Rahel seemed alarmed by it. She asked the rabbi to postpone the ceremony, expecting a few more creeps to show up.

We stood there in a circle, waiting.

I walked across the small cemetery to visit other graves. The uniform line of war casualties was drenched with flowers. These were the beloved sons of the village, and caring mothers and widows visited daily, tending to them as if fresh flowers prolonged these young lives, perpetuated their memory in a colorful, growing manner. My father's brother, Zorik, was buried there. I could see his face, his clear eyes, square jaw, and the short, fair hair as he smilingly lifted me up in the air, higher and higher, accompanied by my giggles. I was a small child when he died in the War of Independence. Aviva's grave, a naturally shaped black basalt stone, like a rock, part of the eroded hill. The letters of her name were barely visible, and there were no flowers. My father's beautiful sister died young, and her small grandchildren played in the circular road of Nahalal, a living memory.

My grandparents' tombs looked deserted. Very seldom visited by my father or any of the grandchildren. Were we ruthless to the dead, or merely realistic and devoid of ritual habits? How often would we visit our father's grave? Did it really signify anything?

A soft wind was blowing from the west when I joined the circle and let go of accumulated tears. The rabbi read a prayer, and I realized I was crying for myself, out of frustration and self-pity, as much as for him. I loved him too much to blame, but not enough to sanctify.

Most evident was Udi's absence. Assi read a fast, dry-eyed Kaddish; the cantor sang "El Maleh Rachamaim"; and a young woman read an Alterman poem my father loved.

Udi had shut himself away from us all, being or pretending to be sick, huddled in bed under blankets, and the wind didn't carry the prayer all the way to his farmhouse. He vowed never to say Kaddish again for his father—rejection for rejection. Hidden in his drawer and heavy on his heart was a written accusation, composed between the Shiva and the Shloshim, to be published later. "People will perhaps say that it's a shame for a father to be eulogized by his son that way. I will reply it was a shame to have had a father like you . . ." Udi wrote about our father's greed, his lust for third-rate women, exposed his weaknesses, his craving for fame and publicity, his translating ideals into hard cash, and his immorality. Most of the piece read like an index of the scandal articles published through the years; some of it was written from deep hurt and with a morbid humor. "Those who blame me for desecrating the honor of the dead should know the dead, in his last will, also buried his dignity . . ." The words were in the second person present. "You might remember that I, your firstborn, Ruth's son, came to visit you to talk about Pen and Sword, and instead you showed me the bathroom you had built for Rahel. Did you not know that interior design was not one of the talents I admired in you? . . . From the day you brought this woman to your home, your hair was being cut and your power gone. From one day to the next, 'Moshe Dayan' shrank and you became more and more Rahel's husband; this is my private diagnosis of your fall . . ."

And so it went on. Harsh accusations, the settling of accounts with the living and the dead. Udi didn't spare himself, but certainly didn't spare others, and this "Letter to a Dead Father" was to become his sign of Cain. We hoped he had the strength and conviction to bear the burden without collapsing. His real support, in spite of it all, in case he fell, was buried up on Shimron.

The ceremony in the cemetery was over, and people dispersed. I sat there, leaning against a tree trunk, still crying, when someone helped me up. I was the last to leave, and it was growing late.

Before driving to Tel Aviv, I stopped to see Udi. The house was locked and dark. I knew where the key was and let myself in. Udi had said earlier he wasn't coming to the ceremony, not ever saying Kaddish again. He also mentioned the publication of his "real feelings," and said he'd written it all and was waiting for the agreement to be final between Rahel and us. Self-destruction is not unfamiliar among the Dayans, but a good share of it fell to Udi, and all my adult life I have had a sense of anxiety concerning him. His whereabouts were unpredictable; he was inconsistent and insecure; and in spite of a façade of carelessness and humor, he was often melancholy, lonely, and unreachable. His artistic gifts were not sufficient to bridge the gap between reality and his dreams. I tiptoed in and noticed the spare bedroom door open. He was lying in bed, covered to his ears with a blanket, half asleep or pretending to be. He wasn't feeling well; no, he did not want to see a doctor. He would be all right, not to worry, shalom, over. I was not an intruder, but neither was I welcome, and I left. Udi shared doubts and questions when it was too late, as if he had a need to err alone, to take all the blame. He realized he was mistaken only when things were hopelessly beyond recovery. Rather than confront me with his written pages—and there was no way I could justify or find them tolerable—he withdrew, extracted all the bitterness and pain accumulated over the years, and spat it out as a fact in print for us to digest and face. This was his act of independent expression, unsolicited and not totally courageous, for cowardice and bravery are mixed in most self-destructive acts.

The next day I recorded a half-hour TV interview, in tribute to my father. Prime time on Wednesdays is usually devoted to the controversy of the week; a panel of journalists fly at a cabinet minister or some other top personality. This week was to be different, and where my father "faced the nation" on many happy and sad, but always dramatic, occasions, I sat, facing one interviewer, trying to reach the essence of what he was and what he meant to us all.

My voice may have quivered, my hands trembled slightly, but I was sure of what I had to say and selected my words carefully. The evening paper on the following day remarked: "The daughter does not evade or apologize. This was not an advocate speech but a firm statement of love, comprising an eloquent defense of the right of the man to be different, original, strong, proud and even alone."

Toward the end, I read the poem he wrote which had been attached to the will. Translation certainly doesn't do justice to whatever poetic merits it has, but the contents, curious as they are, weren't harmed. It was written in Tel Hashomer Hospital, shortly after the surgery to remove the cancerous tumor from his colon, fifteen months before his death.

At the End of the Day

Come, my three children and Rahel, and let us sit together
around the stone in the garden.
I find myself at my nightfall, the wind is blowing from
the sea.
My days were not devoted to you. I was never the perfect father,
I followed my own path, never exposing my grief and joy.
I lived my own life.
Only two things I could do:
Sow, plow and reap the wheat
and
Fight back the guns threatening our homes.
Let each of you cultivate our ancestors' land, and have the
sword within reach above your bed. And at the end of your

days, bring it down and give it to your children.
And now, let each of you take his bundle and walking stick
to cross his Jordan in his own way.
My blessings be with you, do not let the hardships of
life paralyze you.

[*Written at Tel Hashomer Hospital, July 29, 1980*]

The camera didn't notice the tear through which I managed to read the text. I put the paper down and shared my feelings about the poem. It amazed me. There was something primeval about it. Coarse and frightening. The land and the sword—these are the necessities of survival. Not the Bible he admired, not Alterman, not the written word or the expression of morality, not the wisdom of generations or the mystique of a people for generations swordless and landless . . . It was a biblical command, clannish and almost primitive, no faith or spiritual command. It had the feeling of Adam's exile from Paradise, rather a curse than a gift. We were doomed to till and fight, and this is what we were to bequeath our children. We were each to cross our own Jordan, equipped with the spade and the spear. Did he write it in a melancholy moment of poetic mood, or did he mean it verbatim? I'll never know, as I'll never find out many other answers, and I don't dare suggest them in his stead.

The weekend papers carried the last tributes to my father, marking the end of the thirty-day mourning period. Among the many printed pages was a long—the first—interview with Rahel, titled "The Other Moshe Dayan." The article is a hymn to a great overwhelming love, in which everything is "for the first time" and "nobody would have thought he could" . . . Bring flowers, a box of strawberries, drive in the moonlight to a romantic site, share inner feelings or a meal consisting of rare and expensive delicacies . . . "The Other Dayan" was able to fight wars and write books thanks to the inspiration of his wife; he drank wine with his meals and had no patience for fools. The journalist, after this interview, "was not at all surprised to learn the contents of Dayan's will." In her presence, the other Dayan was "warm, sensitive and generous." The article ends with a description of his last hours. A strange one, to say the least. Friday afternoon, she left to go home and freshen up. "But around five she felt uneasy and hurried to the hospital. Dayan was conscious but his body frightfully cold. He asked the doctors and nurses to leave the room; she wiped the cold sweat from his forehead. 'I am tired,' he mumbled. Rahel lifted him up, and then all of a sudden he slipped from her arms and sank into bed. Rahel cried out, noticing his open eye, lifeless. She knew that Moshe Dayan was dead; he had died in her arms . . . For the last time, she took his rough hand, with its thick, bony fingers. This hand now, as if shrunk, was very thin—and lifeless . . ."

Weren't we there too? Was it all a figment of wild imagination? Did we not enter his room at six? Did I not wait with her outside his room when attempts were being made to save his life? Did she not entertain a slim hope with us when we held on to the counter on the intensive-care unit, watching on the screen his failing heartbeats? Did I not hold his other hand across the bed from her? Did it really matter?

A source of light produces rays; sound reaches us in waves. What we see and what we hear are a reflection or an echo deflected or returned by the objects the rays and the waves break against or pass through. Their full spectrum never reaches our senses in the ordinary manner. Nature has equipped us to absorb only a given fraction of these sensations, thus safeguarding us from overwhelming, dangerous, harmful light and sound.

My father's personality varied, we all do, according to the receiving end of his beacons and sound waves. We each had our own "other Dayan," loud and clear or a distant murmur, bright and colorful or sultry gray, blinding or deafening. The exposure varies; so does our ability to contain it. Now that the source of his specific light and sound waves is gone, what remains is a projected picture, reflections and echoes which we can refer to as selected, probably slightly distorted, memories. Evoking those, through the strainers of my cornea and eardrums and brain cells, is the purpose of this book, without a sense of mission, but definitely with a sense of responsibility stemming from the grammatical structure of the phrase: He was my father, I am his daughter.

E P I L O G U E

My father's archaeological collection was bought from his widow, through the most generous contribution of an American philanthropist, by the Israel Museum in Jerusalem.

The house in Zahala, its extraordinary garden and many of the less valuable antiques scattered throughout it, was put up for sale by Rahel, soon after my father's death. A wealthy lawyer purchased it and lives there with his family and fearsome dogs. The small building in the garden was turned into a study, and on the shelves where ancient vessels were exhibited, there is an impressive collection of dolls, each wearing a different national costume, still encased in plastic.

After lengthy and unpleasant negotiations, Rahel's lawyers offered Udi, Assi, and me a "settlement." I would not embarrass her by quoting the sum, or its size in proportion to the wealth that was my father's. The spirit in which it was given induced me to donate a fair portion of it to charities and a few individuals who deserved and were not beneficiaries of my father's financial attention while he was alive.

On the first memorial day, a large crowd gathered at my father's graveside, and Assi said Kaddish.

The second and third year, a smaller faithful group heard Dov's Kaddish. My brothers chose not to attend the official ceremony. We all visit the Hill of Shimron when our mood or need takes us there. Respecting our mother's wish, we have made sure that the lot next to Father's grave is kept vacant for her, may she live to a hundred and twenty.

Telem, my father's political party, ceased to exist. I joined the Labor Party, which I believed to be, in spite of bitter sentiments, the closest in ideology to my father's political heritage. I campaigned in the 1984 elections, which resulted in the formation of a unity government, with Shimon Peres, the Labor leader, as Prime Minister. My place on the Labor list was low enough to preclude any possibility of my becoming a member of the Knesset, but I could at least make sure that since the foundation of the state there would always be a Dayan on some list.

It is impossible to keep updating the turbulent chronicle of my family. Udi divorced his second wife. Assi remarried after the 1982 war in Lebanon and had a baby boy, Lior, who will know his father's father only from photographs. Dan celebrated his bar mitzvah, in synagogue and in the intimacy of our home, shortly after the period of mourning for my father was over. Rahel sent him a tallith and a gold watch which had belonged to but were never worn by my father, gifts he must have received from admirers.

My mother left Washington and returned to live in Israel. She continues to work as a consultant in Latin America and Africa, but it is her house which is home for all of us now.

My father was born in the spring and died in the fall. This is the cycle of fruit-bearing trees. Against the basic laws of nature, while the tree itself is gone, its roots are not dead, and it continues to bear fruit.